T0272659

Praise for *DISPLACEMENT CITY*

"*Displacement City* is a timely and unique exploration of how the COVID-19 pandemic has exacerbated urban homelessness in Canada. It centres the voices of practitioners on the ground and those with lived experience of homelessness. This forward-looking book offers powerful insights into the central role played by frontline workers in advancing the fundamental human rights of access to health care and housing."
– Idil Atak, Associate Professor in the Department of Criminology and the Faculty of Law, Toronto Metropolitan University

"*Displacement City* tells the story of Toronto's pandemic health and homelessness crisis, tracing the structural roots and disastrous impacts of organized state abandonment. It exposes the brutal failure of the settler-colonial capitalist state to provide housing and care, while documenting inspiring stories of collective struggles for survival, life, and human rights. Essential reading for all who share their vision."
– Martine August, Associate Professor in the School of Planning, University of Waterloo

"Our collective failure on housing as a human right has very real human and health costs. *Displacement City* is exactly what we need to better understand why the status quo on homelessness has been so cruel. The authors illuminate what is ultimately the strength and resilience of communities fighting for a more just city. We must dedicate ourselves to these learnings to truly honour all of the lives lost."
– Dr. Andrew Baback Boozary, Primary Care Physician and Founding Executive Director of the Gattuso Centre for Social Medicine at the University Health Network

"At first glance, this is a story of suffering, pain, and trauma. But far more, this book brims with resistance, hopefulness, and solidarity. The authors labour in the shadow of every duplicitous 'we are all in this together' platitude and emerge with a powerful vision of care, health, and love. I urge you to read it – you will not regret the effort, and it will leave you with a powerfully different story of what community health can look like."
– Matt Hern, Co-director of Solid State Community Industries and Author of *What a City Is For: Remaking the Politics of Displacement*

"This is a timely and necessary book, and one I wish didn't have to be written. It paints a stark picture of the pandemic and the City of Toronto's housing crisis – and what many recognize as a complete disregard of people's human right to housing. Bringing forward the voices of those most affected by the crisis, the book shows readers a way forward and what needs to happen to create a city that makes room for everyone."
– Elizabeth McIsaac, President of Maytree

"This thoughtful and powerful book explores the devastation of the pandemic on Toronto's homeless. *Displacement City* relates our long, disgraceful history of dispossessing the vulnerable. It also shows how we managed to briefly do better with significant housing programs in the '70s – and could easily do so again, if only the pampered elite could be forced to recognize that the unhoused are people too."
– Linda McQuaig, Journalist and Author of *The Sport and Prey of Capitalists: How the Rich Are Stealing Canada's Public Wealth*

"From the beginning of the book with its historical timeline and list of the deceased, we are in a very special publication that is both gripping and compelling. It reminds us how the ravages of COVID-19 have worsened the risk of those who are homeless. This is a clarion call for action, based in transdisciplinary analysis and learning through action, to address the social crisis of homelessness."
– Ken Moffatt, Jack Layton Chair, Faculty of Arts and Faculty of Community Services, Toronto Metropolitan University, and Author of *Postmodern Social Work: Reflective Practice and Education*

"*Displacement City* is an urgent call to recognize and oppose the willful abandonment of and deadly violence against community members who are the targets of colonization, racial capitalism, and hetero-patriarchal and ableist institutions and policies. The truth-telling, insight, grief, and rage expressed in these pages *must* move us to demand radically different responses to housing and health crises from all levels of government and society, grounded in the lived experience and expertise of unhoused people."
– Anna Willats, Coordinator/Faculty with the Assaulted Women's and Children's Counsellor/Advocate Program, Social and Community Services, George Brown College

DISPLACEMENT CITY

Fighting for Health and Homes in a Pandemic

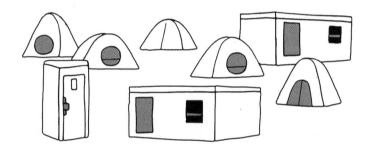

EDITED BY **GREG COOK** AND **CATHY CROWE**

Foreword by Robyn Maynard
Afterword by Shawn Micallef

ÆVO UTP

Aevo UTP
An imprint of University of Toronto Press
Toronto Buffalo London
utorontopress.com

© Greg Cook and Cathy Crowe 2022

ISBN 978-1-4875-4649-6 (paper)   ISBN 978-1-4875-4650-2 (EPUB)
                                     ISBN 978-1-4875-4651-9 (PDF)

Library and Archives Canada Cataloguing in Publication

Title: Displacement city : fighting for health and homes in a pandemic / edited by Greg Cook and Cathy Crowe.
Names: Cook, Greg (Outreach worker), editor. | Crowe, Cathy, 1952–, editor.
Description: Includes bibliographical references.
Identifiers: Canadiana (print) 20220269084 | Canadiana (ebook) 20220269300 |
    ISBN 9781487546496 (paper) | ISBN 9781487546502 (EPUB) | ISBN 9781487546519 (PDF)
Subjects: LCSH: Homelessness – Ontario – Toronto. | LCSH: Homeless persons – Services for – Ontario – Toronto. | LCSH: Shelters for the homeless – Ontario –Toronto. | LCSH: Housing – Ontario – Toronto. | LCSH: COVID-19 Pandemic, 2020– Social aspects – Ontario – Toronto.
Classification: LCC HV4510.T6 D57 2022 | DDC 362.5/9209713541 – dc23

Printed in Canada.

Cover and interior illustrations by Michael DeForge.

We wish to acknowledge the land on which the University of Toronto Press operates. This land is the traditional territory of the Wendat, the Anishinaabe, the Haudenosaunee, the Métis, and the Mississaugas of the Credit First Nation.

University of Toronto Press acknowledges the financial support of the Government of Canada, the Canada Council for the Arts, and the Ontario Arts Council, an agency of the Government of Ontario, for its publishing activities.

Canada Council   Conseil des Arts
for the Arts   du Canada

ONTARIO ARTS COUNCIL
CONSEIL DES ARTS DE L'ONTARIO
an Ontario government agency
un organisme du gouvernement de l'Ontario

Funded by the   Financé par le
Government   gouvernement
of Canada   du Canada

Canadä

MIX
Paper from
responsible sources
FSC   FSC® C016245
www.fsc.org

We would like to dedicate this book to each person who died without housing in Toronto during the COVID-19 pandemic. These deaths were preventable, they were unjust. We want to honour and remember each of their lives. We mourn, we grieve, we keep fighting for a city where each person has a home.

Snickerz (Snicke's) had signed a contract to write a chapter for this book. She died on 10 September 2021, at the age of thirty-six. May she rest in peace.
Credit: Greg Cook

Contents

Pandemic Timeline

2020

January 14: The one-thousandth name is added to Toronto's Homeless Memorial. Shelter and Housing Justice Network (SHJN) leads a march to City Hall and holds a rally and die-in at Mayor Tory's office.

February: Canada's first isolation site for people experiencing homelessness opens at Family Residence shelter in Scarborough run by the Shelter Support and Housing Administration (SSHA), Inner City Health Associates (ICHA) doctors, and Inner City Family Health Team (ICFHT) nurses.

March 10: Toronto Public Health (TPH) releases interim guidance for the housing and homelessness sector, including shelters, respites, and drop-ins.

March 11: World Health Organization (WHO) declares COVID-19 a pandemic.

March 12: Toronto's Emergency Operation Centre opens in Don Mills led by Toronto Fire Chief Matthew Pegg.

March 13: City's shutdown begins. Libraries, pools, recreation centres are closed. Many drop-ins closed.

March 15: The volunteer-based Out of the Cold Program announces closure.

March 17: Ontario's Premier Ford declares a state of emergency. This closes all bars, restaurants, indoor recreation programs, public libraries, private schools, licensed childcare centres, theatres, cinemas, and concert venues. Service shutdowns hit homeless population, including refugee families, particularly hard.

Toronto closes Metro Hall, City Hall, all civic centres.

Advocates immediately begin calling for more access to water, washrooms, showers.

There is a drastic reduction in services for people experiencing homelessness.

March 19: SSHA opens up five new physical distancing facilities. All are congregate shelter settings, largely housed in shuttered community centres. By the end of March, eight sites open with a total capacity of 350 spaces.

March 20: A homeless person staying in a Sprung structure congregate setting tests positive for COVID-19.

March 23: Mayor Tory declares a state of emergency.

Ontario Coalition Against Poverty (OCAP) and SHJN hold a news conference to demand the following: (1) An increase in shelter spaces to allow for physical distancing, (2) an increase in social assistance rates, and (3) expanded access to safe supply and other harm-reduction services.

March 24: A second homeless person is diagnosed with COVID-19.

March 25: SHJN members Cathy Crowe and Yogi Acharya take Toronto Board of Health chair Joe Cressy and Medical Officer of Health's senior staff Chris Phibbs on a "disaster walking tour" to highlight the COVID-19 risks for people who are homeless.

Front-line workers continue desperate appeals for washrooms.

March 26: Cathy Crowe, Greg Cook, Zoë Dodd, and several other front-line health workers have a conference call with Toronto Medical Officer of Health Dr. de Villa and Councillor Cressy to present concerns about shelter crowding, physical distancing, and other issues. There are no commitments made on the call.

March 27: A legal coalition is formed to explore legal remedies to protect homeless people.

Four homeless people are diagnosed with COVID-19.

Seven sites for portable toilets were green lit days ago, but toilets have not appeared.

The *Toronto Star* reports on modelling that suggests on average there could be 800–1,200 homeless people with COVID-19 at any given time.

March 29: Canadian Civil Liberties Association (CCLA) writes Mayor Tory asking for the implementation of extraordinary measures, including reduced shelter crowding and physical distancing standards.

March 31: Health workers hold a media conference by Zoom. A Toronto Anglican bishop is one of the speakers. They call for numerous measures to protect homeless people.

April 2: The City tightens restrictions on people's use of parks.

April 3: Cathy Crowe makes a complaint to the Toronto Ombudsman that the City is not directing shelters to physically distance beds 2 metres apart.

April 4: The City begins to acquire hotels for use as shelter-hotels for physical distancing: twelve hotels with 1,200 rooms. On a

City–community call, Cathy Crowe asks for the City to call in the
Red Cross.

April 6: A broad community call happens to express concerns that
ICHA's proposed COVID Alert Risk Evaluation system is problematic. It could have included homeless people wearing bracelets to
identify their risk status. People argued this was triggering and could
lead to stigma.

The first unhoused person, "Rocco," a resident of St. Simon's, dies in
hospital and is found to have COVID-19 at the time of his death.

April 7: The City opens a COVID recovery and isolation site at the
Four Points Sheraton Hotel, initially as a site for people awaiting
COVID-19 test results, then later as a designated recovery site for
homeless people with COVID-19.

SSHA distributes emergency funding of between $2,500 and $15,000
per drop-in provider to purchase personal protection equipment
(PPE) and related supplies.

April 8: SHJN and OCAP hold a physically distanced media conference
outside City Hall and call for stronger actions, including more hotels
or apartments for physical distancing, screening, and testing, and a
safe drug supply. Dr. de Villa states at a media conference there is
"no merit or need for an order to be given" (for physically distancing
shelter beds). She cites a preference for voluntary action by shelters.

April 10 (beginning of long weekend): The province adds homeless
shelters to priority list for testing; however, the roll-out of testing is
cumbersome and not transparent.

A shelter outbreak begins at Willowdale Welcome Centre. It ultimately results in 185 infections and three hospitalizations. Many
children from this site are infected in the first wave.

April 14: Four Points Sheraton Hotel is now a specific COVID Recovery program with up to 173 rooms for people who are homeless and

24/7 health care. It is coordinated by a partnership between the City of Toronto's SSHA and The Neighbourhood Group (TNG). They are later joined by Parkdale Queen West Community Health Centre and the University Health Network.

April 15: OCAP holds a media conference at City Hall with over twenty health workers. Speakers include Noa Mendelsohn Aviv from CCLA.

Seven shelters are in outbreak.

April 20: A legal coalition that has formed writes the City to notify them that if they do not take action, the coalition will initiate legal action.

April 22: A plan to operate a COVID Recovery program for up to 400 people at the Better Living Centre with input from Doctors Without Borders is now cancelled.

April 24: The legal coalition issues a Charter Application in Superior Court alleging the City's failure to ensure physical distancing was contrary to the constitutional rights of homeless people.

April 29: Washrooms and showers open at Harrison Baths and Regent Park Community Centre.

Mayor Tory announces the building of 250 modular units and the leasing of two apartment buildings and 117 Toronto Community Housing units that people from encampments can move into temporarily. Sanctuary and Streets to Homes involved in move-ins. Sanctuary alone has over thirty-two community members move into temporary housing.

April 30: *A National Protocol for Homeless Encampments in Canada,* authored by Leilani Farha, the UN Special Rapporteur on the right to adequate housing, and Kaitlin Schwan of The Shift, is released.

Refugee determination hearings shutdown affecting tens of thousands of families.

City Parks Ambassadors post eviction notices on people's tents in George Hislop Park.

May 8: Joseph Chibala from the Republic of Congo dies of COVID-19. He was staying at the School House shelter. Chibala is widely reported as the first casualty in the shelter system due to COVID-19.

May 9: The first female shelter resident, residing at Warden Woods' 24-hour respite, dies as a result of COVID-19.

May 11: Another homeless man in his seventies dies of COVID-19. He was staying at Seaton House.

May 14: The legal coalition reaches an agreement with the City on 2-metre physical distancing of beds and discontinuation of use of bunk beds.

May 15: The City evicts people near Lakeshore from Bay St. to Spadina Ave. Chief Pegg cites fire risk. Front-line workers intervene to stop most of the evictions.

May 15–18: The Bond Place Hotel opens as a 297-room isolation site for people who are homeless.

May 19: Two more encampments are evicted on Power Street and Lakeshore. Most of the encampment residents are moved to the Broadway apartments.

May 30: Ten encampment sites are identified as priorities for eviction, likely due to the number of 311 complaint calls.

May 31: Seniors protest the opening of a respite on the Esplanade. Similar protests occur at some shelter-hotel sites as they open.

May–June: The Encampment Support Network (ESN) forms and begins providing support to major encampments.

June 2: Fifteen shelter-hotels now have 1,300 people in them.

June 9: Four names of homeless people who died of COVID-19 are added to the Toronto Homeless Memorial.

June 18: Activists hold a media conference at Moss Park encampment calling for water taps to be turned on, for more washrooms, and for the City to not evict.

June 19: The City delivers seventy cases of water to Moss Park encampment.

June 24: Front-line workers report having to turn women away at a full shelter and no spaces are available via Central Intake.

July: Anti-poverty activists, including encampment residents, file a suit against the City to fight encampment evictions.

July 23: Lamport encampment threatened with eviction.

Early August: The Bond Place Hotel, opened as a COVID recovery site for people experiencing homelessness, is consolidated with the program at the Four Points Sheraton Hotel, resulting in a loss of 250 recovery beds. The Bond Place Hotel is converted into a shelter-hotel, primarily for residents of encampments.

August 10: The City announces it will purchase a hotel to develop into social housing.

August 12: The City's mask by-law does not apply to shelter residents, however shelter staff must wear masks.

August 19: There are now seventeen shelter-hotels with 1,960 residents.

September: Khaleel Seivwright, a carpenter, starts building tiny shelters for distribution.

September 4: City officials announce they will phase in mask use for clients and provide masks.

September 15: SSHA releases the *Interim Shelter Recovery Strategy* in conjunction with the United Way. The stated goals of the strategy are to minimize the spread of COVID-19 over a six-month period, and lay the groundwork for SSHA's five-year plan.

September 23: ESN and the encampment at Moss Park hold a "Meal and March" for housing; hundreds of people march down Queen Street East.

October 6: SSHA releases its *Winter Plan for People Experiencing Homelessness*. The plan does not include strategies for bringing bathroom and running water facilities online or the distribution of fire-safe camping equipment for encampment residents. It also does not include any improvement in strategies for extreme cold weather alerts.

October 21: The encampment injunction is lost.

November 23: Groups hold a National Housing Day media conference at 214–230 Sherbourne, an empty lot that groups want the City to expropriate for social housing.

November 25: There are now over fifty encampments with 400 tents, according to statements by City officials.

December 7: SHJN coordinates dozens of deputations to the City's Economic and Community Development Committee to demand a moratorium on encampment evictions.

December 29: A fire at the shelter-hotel Hotel Victoria leaves a trans woman hospitalized. She later dies.

2021

January 14: The Four Points Sheraton Hotel recovery and isolation site is running out of capacity; intake is no longer "first come, first serve."

February 10: Toronto Drop-In Network's (TDIN) Diana Chan McNally authors *Demands for Immediate Action to Address COVID-Related Risks and Harms for People Experiencing Homelessness*, which argues for action from all levels of government to commit to housing and health supports for unhoused people, as well as support for front-line workers.

February 12: The City of Toronto files an injunction application against Khaleel Seivwright to stop him from placing shelters on city-owned land.

February 28: ESN holds an action outside of Mayor Tory's condo in response to the injunction against Khaleel Seivwright.

March 11: On the one-year anniversary of WHO's declaration of a pandemic, TDIN holds a media conference with faith leaders, medical doctors, executive directors, front-line workers, and unhoused people to demand that all levels of government address the calls outlined in *Demands for Immediate Action to Address COVID-Related Risks and Harms for People Experiencing Homelessness.*

March 16: The City announces the Pathways Inside Project focusing on four encampment sites and indicating they will offer shelter-hotel program rooms.

March 26: The COVID Recovery Hotel program at Four Points is reported full.

May 5: Ten homeless men and women have now died of COVID-19.

May 12: The City evicts encampments at Barbara Hall Park, George Hislop Park, the University Avenue median, St. James Park, and Lamport Stadium. People were threatened with $10,000 fines if they did not leave.

May 18: TDIN hosts a multi-agency media conference titled "An Urgent Call from Encampment Residents, Human Rights Lawyers, Health Providers and Community Service Leaders: Stop the Evictions of People Staying in Encampments."

May 30: A total of 128 shelters have had outbreaks with 1,657 people infected.

June 4: Multiple organizations sign a joint TDIN statement entitled *COVID-19 Response Update: Protecting People Experiencing Homelessness and Ensuring the Safety of the Shelter System.*

June 22: The City evicts Trinity Bellwoods encampment in a heavily militarized effort.

July 9: A total of 207 organizations and civic leaders sign TDIN's *A Path Forward*, demanding that Mayor Tory and the City end the forcible removal of encampments and the use of force by police against unhoused people and commit to a human rights approach to housing.

July 20: Alexandra Park encampment is evicted.

July 21: Lamport Stadium encampment is evicted.

July 26: SHJN and Health Providers Against Poverty (HPAP) host a rally and media conference at City Hall to demand Mayor Tory stop violent encampment evictions by Toronto Police, and that the City of Toronto defund the police and fund a *true* human rights approach to housing.

The June–July evictions are reported as costing $2 million for personnel, including private security and policing.

August 11: The City of Toronto launches a pilot project in Dufferin Grove Park, which adopts some of the recommendations of *A Path Forward*. This pilot is time-limited and does not extend across the city; it also does not entail feedback from advocates or residents to strengthen the approach.

August 27: The City of Toronto reaches an agreement with Khaleel Seivwright. The City withdraws their court application, and Seivwright agrees to not install any new shelters on City land.

October 9: A second pilot is launched in Councillor Mike Layton's ward to provide outreach to encampments in Bellevue Park. This pilot is a relationship between the City and TNG. While promising, it does not end the eviction of encampments, the arrest of encampment residents, or the removal of encampment infrastructure.

October 12: SHJN releases *Emergency Winter and Shelter Support and Infrastructure Plan* with numerous recommendations for the City, including the addition of 2,250 non-congregate shelter beds. The report is dismissed by the City.

October 15: The City announces shelter vaccination statistics among residents: 69 per cent have a first dose, 57 per cent have a second dose.

November 1: The City announces the purchase of 660 HEPA filters for sixty-five shelter sites. The Ontario government announces $2 million for shelters for improvements to ventilation.

December 14: A record thirty-four names of people who died homeless were added to the monthly homeless memorial outside of the Church of the Holy Trinity in downtown Toronto.

By year's end, 132 homeless people had died in city shelters.

Late December: The City is not providing K/N95 masks for shelter residents or people using drop-ins. The Rotary Club of Toronto steps in to provide 30,000 K95 masks with the assistance of the Toronto Drop-In Network and the Church of the Holy Trinity. By January the City reverses its decision.

2022

January 7: SHJN issues a media statement that Toronto's shelter system has collapsed, citing crowding, poor standards, an escalation of COVID-19 cases, and low vaccination rates.

January 17: There are fifty-one shelters in outbreak with 416 people infected.

January 20: Shelters directed to isolate infected people "in situ."

January 31: SHJN and Maggie's Toronto Sex Workers Action Project issue a request for humanitarian aid to the United Nations, Doctors Without Borders, and the Ontario Red Cross.

February 11: The Bellevue Park encampment pilot, extended to Randy Padmore Park and Sonya Parkette, is further extended to Grange Park.

End of February: There have been over 225 outbreaks in Toronto shelters with 2,500 people infected.

March: The City of Toronto announces its plan to gradually decommission its shelter-hotels and emergency shelters, including the Better Living Centre and the Days Inn. Advocates point out this will create absolute homelessness for hundreds.

Ontario's COVID-specific funding for forty-three nurses providing health care for homeless people ends and they are terminated by ICHA.

May: The City allocates $1 million for private security to provide encampment surveillance in parks.

June: The City continues encampment evictions, notably at Clarence Square and by Power Street.

July 6: Dr. Kieran Moore, Ontario's Chief Medical Officer of Health, confirms that Ontario is in its seventh COVID-19 wave.

July 14: The Toronto Ombudsman releases an interim report with recommendations to improve the fairness of the City's encampment response.

We Will Remember

These are the people who have died without housing since the beginning of COVID-19 in Toronto.

March 2020

Zac

April 2020

Al Honen
John Doe
John Doe
Rick Weerts
Samson Kahgee
Unknown

Unknown
Unknown
Unknown
Unknown
Unknown

May 2020

Adam Robinson
Cory McKintyre
Darryl Monast
Flex

Jane Doe
John Doe
John Doe
Joseph Chibala
Quincy Williams
Unknown
Unknown
Unknown
Unknown
Unknown
Unknown
Unknown
Wayne (Hollywood)

June 2020

Jane Doe
Jane Doe
John Doe
John Doe
Unknown
Unknown
Unknown

July 2020

Doreen Upson
Jane Doe
Jane Doe

Jane Doe
Jane Doe
Jenny Penny
John Doe
John Doe
John Doe
John Doe
John Doe
Kurtis Hamilton
Michael Paul O'Hare
Seth Durrell MacLean

August 2020

Andrew D.
Craig Ogle
John Doe
John Doe
John Doe
John Doe
Tara Morton

September 2020

Jane Doe
John Doe
Rampreet (Peter) Singh
Sebastian Martin

October 2020

Derek Ramdhannie
Donnie Hill
Everette Sheldon Ritch
Jane Doe
Larry Donald Jones
Michael
Michael Kent

November 2020

Billy Malloy
Brandon Kelly
Jane Doe
Jane Doe
Jeffrey Dagg
Jesse (Sketchy) Iker
Jessica Lawrence Konopka
Sheldon Chisholm
"Tattoo" Dave

December 2020

Douglas Blake
Jane Doe
Jane Doe
Jason Mitchell
John Doe

John Doe
John Doe
John Doe
John Doe
Shaun Carlson
Steven Mills

Month Unknown, 2021

Unknown
Unknown

January 2021

Aurele (A.J.) Durelle
Caroline Kurowski
David Smith
Diane
Jane Doe
Jane Doe
John Doe
John Doe
John Doe
John Doe
Joseph Beauprez
Sasha Gray
Unknown
Unknown
Unknown

Unknown

Unknown

Unknown

Unknown

Wasse Abino Kwe (Lenore
   Jackson)

February 2021

Gordon

Jean-Michel Corriveau

Jeremy Dubuque

Joanne (Jojo) Elsie Rhodenizer

John Doe

John Doe

Johnny (Longhair) Findlay

Oliver (Slim) Smith

Phillip Michael Sweet

Sean Boyd

Unknown

Unknown

Unknown

Unknown

March 2021

Andrew

Jane Doe

Jane Doe

Jane Doe

John Doe

John Doe

John Doe

John Doe

Melanie Elizabeth Lemieux

Mike Akiwenzie

Robert Thompson

Unknown

Unknown

Unknown

Unknown

April 2021

Aileen (Ali) Lee

Christopher King

Cowboy (L.T.)

John Condos

John Doe

John Doe

Rocco (Rocky) Romeo

Rosie

Unknown

Unknown

Unknown

May 2021

Audrey Singh

Bridgett Garcia

Gordon Cronkhite

Harold (Cuz) Dunham

Holly
Jamie Parnell
Jane Doe
Jane Doe
John Doe
John Doe
John Doe
John Doe
John Doe
Kaleb
Natalie Smith
Roxie Foxx
Unknown
Unknown
Unknown
Unknown
Unknown
Unknown
Unknown

June 2021

Andrea (Rain) Fischer
Dan
Holly
J. Doe
Jamie Barber
John Doe
John Doe
Shayla Azure
Tasha Tenn
Unknown

July 2021

J. Doe
Jane Doe
Jane Doe
Jane Doe
Jeff
Jerry Arevoredo Creador
John Doe
John Doe
John Doe
John Doe
Scott Sutherland

August 2021

Christopher
Danny Echeverri
J. Doe
John Doe
John Doe
John Doe
John Doe
John Doe
John Doe
John Doe
John Doe
John Doe
John Doe
John Doe
Jon (Jonny) Abotossaway
Michael (Mikey) Thiele

Randy Collier
Shelley (Turtle) Marie Isaac
Steven Smith

September 2021

Damian Michale Newberry
  Addie
Dennis
Jane Doe
Jane Doe
John Doe
John Doe
John Doe
John Doe
John Doe
Lena Wiens
Matthew Vito Iozzo
Tania (Snickerz) Pelletier
Thomas Lloyd
Trevor Comden

October 2021

Billy Ray Manitopyes
Francesco (Frankie) Macri
Jane Doe
Jane Doe
Jane Doe
John Doe
John Doe

John Doe
John Doe
John Doe
John Doe
John Doe
John Doe
John Doe
John Doe
John Doe
John Doe
John Doe
Jonathan Steven Stavrou
Nicholas

November 2021

Alexis (Debby) Matos
Antonio (Turtle) DeSousa
Brenda Christine Connor
Daisy Sarah-Anne Warriner
Derek Lefrancois
Domenico Saxida
J. Doe
John Doe
John Doe
John Doe
John Doe
Josephine Scott
Marcus Catrie
Mike Yankowski
Nuno Moniz
Raymond Anthony McGregor

Steph
Steven (Littles) Tibbs

December 2021

Branko Topolovec
Gord Guitard
Heather Green
J.J. Stephens
Joel
Johnny
Jolene
Justin Cormier
Rachel Stinis
Shirley
Terry Herman
Zack Humby

January 2022

Alex Robinson
Arlington (Wild Bill) Pawis
Billy
Davin Barsch
Jane Doe
Jane Doe
John Doe
John Doe
John Doe
John Doe
John Doe

John Doe
Marci Reisborough
Reynold (R.J.) Mixemong
Stephanie Williams
Tracey Smallgeese
Trevor Parkinson
Tyrell Fuller
Unknown

February 2022

Danielle Buffalo
Eddie
Jackson Lyons
John Doe
John Doe
John Doe
John Doe
John Doe
Marci
Sanel "Bosnia" Cehaja
Yen Sze

March 2022

Anika Ashley Copegog
Handsome Pihiri
Jane Doe
Jason Hughes
John Doe
Unknown

April 2022

Andrew Johnston
Gary Richards
John Doe
John Doe
John Doe
John Doe
John Doe
John Doe
John Doe
John Doe
John Doe
John Doe

May 2022

Arthur "A.J." Ballard
Jane Doe
Jay
John Doe

John Doe
John Doe
John Doe
John Doe
John Doe
John Doe
Justin Nezezon
Myles "Nanook" Kakegemic

June 2022

Graeme Dring
James (Trice) Tylee
Jane Doe
Jane Doe
Jane Doe
John Doe
John Doe
John Doe
Wendy

Note: This list of names is from the Toronto Homeless Memorial, online at homelessmemorials.com. The terms *John/Jane/J. Doe* or *Unknown* are used due to reporting and identification challenges.

Foreword

Robyn Maynard

Early one July evening during the summer of 2021, my cell phone began exploding with texts from dear ones: the Toronto police had just undertaken what had euphemistically been described as the "clearing" of the Lamport Stadium encampment.[1] A number of comrades had just been arrested, some quite violently. Many more had been pepper sprayed, some injured more seriously. All of this had taken place as part of the City's forcible eviction of the homeless residents who had been camped in tents there; they had undertaken, too, a mass arrest of those who had been there to stand in solidarity with their neighbours' right to stay in the park. As the sun was going down, I joined the several dozen people who had gathered to regroup at Christie Pits. All around me, I could see and hear evidence of the brutality showed by police in the preceding hours: swollen eyes, the confirmations circulating through the conversations that one community member was still in the hospital, and that many more were still in police custody (there had been forty people arrested or detained in total for events that day, it was later confirmed).[2] These were not, though, the only types of stories that emerged from the events of the day. I also heard about encampment residents supporting one another as the police approached and began tearing down their homes. I spoke with a Black woman who had courageously put her body between the police and several younger Black women as the police approached them with nightsticks. Over several hours and into the night, I was made aware of a multitude of displays of courage in the face of the merciless brutality that had been organized by the City and enacted by hired private security and the Toronto Police Service. Next to the fire being tended by Indigenous Elders, I saw mutual aid in action: alongside short speeches about the day's events, community members strategized against future raids, shared food and beverages, rinsed pepper spray out of one another's eyes. These people were recovering from the violence of the day's events, while still planning how to support the remaining encampments.

It is clear to me now that what I witnessed that evening was the tail end of a broader struggle over the city, a struggle over whose lives are valued in the city in the context of a pandemic and a housing crisis. A struggle, too, against forces of state abandonment and violence and the liberation-oriented visions of those on the frontlines, working to build something *else*. It is this struggle that appears throughout the pages of *Displacement City*. Cogently articulated with insurgent love and rage, this anthology is at once a diagnostic and condemnation of the failures of the City's COVID-19 response, and a movement snapshot that captures those who insisted, instead, on other possible, more liveable futures.

The pandemic was not experienced evenly, not a "great equalizer," but it quickly became apparent that "we are [not] in this together," to use the words of Lorraine Lam from this volume. In the *Toronto Star*, Dionne Brand described the pandemic as an "x-ray" that made all the more clear the sedimented racially and economically uneven inequalities of our city, and of Canadian society more broadly.[3] And indeed, long before 2020, it had been apparent that *we* were not in this together. The pushing out of Black, Indigenous, low-income, and other marginalized city residents from their homes to make space for empty high rises and upper-middle-class families has been underway for decades, the result of generations of purposeful political choices. Shelter overcrowding, lack of decent affordable housing, homelessness, a poisoned drug supply, these were already a public health crisis disproportionately impacting Black and Indigenous communities, people living with mental health issues or disabilities, working-class and poor folks of all ages, races, and genders. Yet as this book carefully documents, these inequalities were massively exacerbated as shelters, prisons, jails, and detention centres became hotbeds of COVID-19 outbreaks, and the places most abandoned by the public-health response. These abandonments are infused with *history*: in the words of Sandra Campbell and Leigh Kern's contribution to *Displacement City*, "dispossession is part of the continuing legacy of the colonial project in Canada ... The COVID-19 pandemic provided a window into this continuum and what has been inflicted on our communities." In a country with a history of slavery, Indigenous genocide, the mass incarceration and then wholesale abandonment of people with mental health issues, rampant ableism, and a generations-long criminalization of drug users, it is alarming, but not surprising, that many of these same populations would be left, far too often, under-protected in shelters and carceral sites wreaked with outbreaks in the context of an unprecedented health crisis.

Displacement City meticulously archives the brutality of City policies that forced its disenfranchised residents to fend for themselves during a global pandemic. But this book is not only a story of abandonment and negligence. It is also an archive of a living struggle, one that took place in the public realm, if often outside the public eye. While baking bread became one of the official narratives of how the pandemic was being weathered by more affluent North Americans, others turned not only towards their hobbies and their families, but towards one another, and their neighbours – forwarding a demand, and a lived practice, that *all* city residents' lives should be protected. The year 2020 is widely remembered as a year of massive protests against policing and in support of Black lives, but the historic struggle for liveable futures for Black and all communities did not take place only on the streets. In addition to the historic protests for racial justice, there are many locations where struggles for more liberatory futures were waged in and across the plague times: behind bars in Canadian carceral sites, in city parks and reappropriated hotels, alternative ways to fashion life in a crisis were being born.

The city has always been a site of struggle. These pages tell the story of mutual, collective support, of refashioning public space to truly meet public need. In this book, readers can bear witness to accounts of encampment residents, Indigenous Elders, street nurses, shelter workers, harm-reduction workers, and many more, whose words come together to weave a tapestry, and a broader constellation, of what it truly means to work to fight for one's life and one's neighbours in the throes of catastrophe. Khaleel Seivwright, Derrick Black, and Nikki Sutherland, among others whose voices are highlighted here, came up against and refused a politic of what Ruth Wilson Gilmore has called "*organized abandonment*"[4] and, instead, forwarded visions for a liveable city for all. The authors tell stories that attest not only to death and loss but to *life*, and to those who worked to protect life: reversing overdoses, supplying water, providing legal support, distributing harm-reduction supplies and PPE, defending themselves and their fellow neighbours, building homes – even when they faced the threat of arrest and injunction for doing so.

The words in the following pages are an important intervention that asks us to be attuned to all of the ways that life was protected, fought for, and mutually supported by those at the front lines of the crisis: an accounting by and of those who insisted, and most importantly *showed us*, that there are more human and emancipatory ways to address a housing crisis, a drug-poisoning crisis, a pandemic.

"What is to be done?" These are not words meant to foster hand-wringing and inertia, but can and must be, instead, a point of departure from which to take action. After spending time with this anthology, readers will have a kaleidoscopic array of examples of what it means to join a freedom-oriented struggle: neighbourhood mutual-aid projects, the push for a safe drug supply, the movements for affordable/free and decent housing, to name only a few examples. Indeed, what *Displacement City* makes clear is that there is not *one* way to take action, but multitudes, an abundance of ways to reject systematized cruelty and to build care-based alternatives. The contributors show us the many ways forward, the many possibilities for organizing urban life, and we would all do well to listen.

ROBYN MAYNARD is an assistant professor of Black feminisms in Canada in the Historical and Cultural Studies Department at the University of Toronto Scarborough. She is the author of *Policing Black Lives: State Violence in Canada from Slavery to the Present* (Fernwood, 2017) and the co-author of *Rehearsals for Living* (Knopf/Haymarket, 2022).

Introduction

Cathy Crowe and Greg Cook

In my memoir *A Knapsack Full of Dreams*,[1] I recount my three decades of street nursing through what I call "the plagues" – the disastrous consequences of intentional government policies that repeatedly ignore basic human rights: housing, income, food security, safety, inclusion, and freedom from racism.

The outcomes include mass homelessness, tortuous deprivation of the human spirit, and real physical consequences that include serious chronic health conditions, malnutrition and hunger, actual plagues such as tuberculosis, Norwalk virus, and Strep A outbreaks, and an epidemic of deaths. Even when the physical outcomes were blatantly obvious, officials buried their heads in the sand. I remember the day a public health manager called me to explain why they had kept news of the early 2000s tuberculosis outbreak in the Seaton House shelter "quiet." They had decided they didn't want homeless people to be afraid to enter the shelter.

In the early 2000s, community groups were expected to prepare pandemic plans. Literally.

Toronto's experience of SARS in 2003–4 exposed how totally useless our community agency pandemic plans, in the middle of a homelessness disaster, would be. Congregate style shelters were even more crowded. There were no isolation locations, no PPE (personal protective equipment), not even a guaranteed supply of soap in washrooms in drop-ins or shelters.

I finished writing *Knapsack* before the COVID-19 pandemic. What has happened next became what I would coin "A Knapsack Full of Nightmares."

I remember in March 2020, when it became evident that we were facing a global pandemic, I printed the most colourful image of the coronavirus that I could find and made a sign with it that read War Room and slapped it on my home-office door. Why the militaristic language? Well, quite frankly, I knew we would have to fight for every single measure that would be needed to protect people who were without a home from the virus, and I knew there would be casualties.

The fight became a fight for portable toilets and safe drinking water for encampments, a fight (that ended up in court) for 2 metres of physical distancing of beds in shelters, a fight for a moratorium on evictions in both housing and encampments (that also ended up in court), a fight for testing and PPE in shelters, a fight for shelter-hotels to protect people, a fight for harm-reduction supports, for vaccination priority for people who were homeless, and I could go on and on.

Quite frankly, the fight was with all levels of government.

The authors in this book, including my co-editor Greg Cook, are all from the front line. They provide extraordinary witness to existing inequities and demonstrate a scalpel-sharp critical analysis of the political landscape that continues to deny protection for people in a global pandemic.

Many would call these political decisions that deny the basics social murder. I do too.

It speaks volumes that during a pandemic these authors agreed to create space in the chaos to tell their stories.

Our fight continues to this day and the fight is for homes.

Housing for all.

Cathy Crowe

✷ ✷ ✷

As I write, the Omicron variant of COVID-19 is ripping through the Toronto shelter system. Last night, the temperature dropped to −26 degrees Celsius with the windchill, and hundreds were stuck outside without housing or even a shelter bed. Many slept in doubled-up sleeping bags near City Hall or on exhaust vents in the shadow of downtown corporate offices. The shelter system in Toronto has essentially collapsed. This is not the image of the city that the mayor or Bay Street want people to see. "The truth is, cities are increasingly being built for the rich to invest in rather than for regular people to live in. This dynamic is accelerating ..."[2] Our governments' priorities are to design Toronto for the benefit of the tourist gaze and investment portfolios. To do this successfully, it is necessary that the inhumane and unjust consequences of this agenda are covered over. The amount of bureaucratic energy and money spent to make people without housing invisible is staggering.

I decided to co-edit this book with Cathy because I am compelled to share unhoused people's experiences, their profound analysis of the situation, and their creative response to aggressive displacement and erasure. These stories, photographs, and poems offer rich and nuanced counternarratives to the one City Hall wants us to believe. The work of connecting with over twenty authors has been a profound responsibility and honour. My own understanding of my job as an outreach worker has been enriched and challenged. Acquaintances have grown into friendships, and conversations about grammar and chapter titles have often dovetailed into the unfolding of these stories: the joy of hearing about a friend who has acquired housing, or a space for the shared grief of another death. One of the authors, Snickerz, who was signed up to write a chapter, died of an overdose before she had a chance to write for this book. I know the rushing river of crisis and death that surrounds so many of those who have contributed has been difficult, and I want to thank each writer for sharing a piece of yourself with us.

In this book, you will encounter the story of a Mohawk Auntie who collaborates with colleagues to connect the history of Residential Schools with the ongoing dispossession of Indigenous people in this city. The story of a refugee family who shares their experience of creating connections and meaning while in a shelter in a new land. The story of a middle-aged man who speaks out about the terror of living in a congregate shelter and then being sick with COVID-19. The story of a woman in a wheelchair who describes her fight to acquire accessible housing while fighting for basic accommodations and dignity in the shelter system for herself and her friends.

You'll also find the story of a musician and a photographer who explain how hundreds of people came together to support strangers living in tents. These people nurtured deep friendships while pushing the City to hold off clearing prominent encampments for over a year. You will read the words of a community director at a downtown church who pens some poems to offer to their congregants as the city goes into its first lockdown. You'll also read the story of two doctors who describe what it is like to offer dignified care for people who are dying without housing amid the pandemic. Here, too, a harm-reduction worker writes a letter to a friend about the ways communities are responding to the horrific number of people dying from a poisoned drug supply.

These are just some of the stories of work, hope, resistance, grief, strategy, and imagination that this book contains. As an editor, I have been moved by the creative vision and compassionate urgency for justice that I've been privileged to gather in these pages. These narratives offer a detailed picture of the care people have collectively offered each other and the fight to build communities of solidarity, the fight to make sure people get water, food, and housing in spite of the overwhelming forces of racial capitalism and ongoing colonial governance. Importantly, this is not just a story of resistance but also of practical steps for people who want to build something different. These are visions of a city where there is space for safety, care, and home.

Greg Cook

CATHY CROWE is a recipient of the Order of Canada and a pioneer of street nursing. She is currently a public affiliate in the Department of Politics and Public Administration at Toronto Metropolitan University. She has fostered numerous coalitions and advocacy initiatives that have achieved significant public policy victories, including the 1998 Disaster Declaration. She is the author of *A Knapsack Full of Dreams* and *Dying for a Home* and producer of the Home Safe documentary series. Her work is the subject of the documentary *Street Nurse*, by filmmaker Shelley Saywell.

GREG COOK is a white settler who has been a drop-in and outreach worker in downtown Toronto for over twelve years, and at Sanctuary since 2009. Greg partners with community groups and agencies to agitate for a more just and equitable society. He is on the steering committee of the Shelter and Housing Justice Network, and he volunteers for the Toronto Homeless Memorial. He has worked on two documentaries: *Bursting at the Seams*, about the shelter crisis, and *What World Do You Live In?*, about police brutality.

PART I

WE ARE [NOT] IN THIS TOGETHER

 **CHAPTER 1**

Displaced Again and Again and Again

Nikki Sutherland

Hello there, my name is Nikki Sutherland. I am an Indigenous Cree woman from Constance Lake First Nation. I am forty, but feel much older because of many stressful and challenging situations I have experienced during the past couple of years around the time COVID-19 made its appearance. I am part of the Sixties Scoop. My brother and I were taken by the Children's Aid Society (CAS) from our Reserve and placed into foster care. He was three and I was one. After being moved around from several different foster families, we were eventually adopted by a white family and relocated permanently to North Bay. Our childhood was far from what many people would deem normal. I try not to dwell on it. I went to a French school growing up and graduated from a French Catholic high school. I am completely bilingual. I learned from and thrived in certain sports like cross-country running and cross-country skiing as well as basketball. I completed my Grade 8 Royal Conservatory piano exams with a 93 per cent. My white parents kicked my brother out when he was sixteen years old. I was shocked, in disbelief, and most of all devastated without my big brother. When I turned sixteen, I went with my luggage and whatever I could bring of my belongings to the North Bay Crisis Centre. This was my first and certainly not my last taste of homelessness.

I have five beautiful children between the ages of five and twenty-one. I wasn't able to be there for them in the way I wanted and would have loved to be. Now I am blessed to have them back in my life and am enjoying every single second I get to spend with them. I think that now is also the time that I am actually truly living.

COVID-19 affects everyone in many different ways and at many different levels. I was staying in a shelter with Romeo who was my partner at the time the pandemic surfaced. All of a sudden, everywhere you looked there were more and more people wearing masks. Something I had only seen in movies and never thought I would experience. My mind raced even more, thinking about my little ones and their well-being and safety. Feeling helpless, not being able to shield and protect them the way I wanted to. It was a mess at the shelter. There was talk of making sure to social distance, and I was always afraid of being infected. I didn't feel very safe there. I was exposed to many different people who have been who knows where and with who knows whom?

Romeo got restricted from the shelter because, apparently, he had tested positive for COVID-19, which isn't true. The staff wanted to put me in quarantine since I was in direct contact with him. Instead, I decided to stay with him in a tent in a park not too far from the shelter. I didn't want to leave Romeo's side, and the shelter was very disorganized. It didn't take long for the City to get complaints about our being there, as there were also two other tents that had been pitched since our arrival. A week or so later, we were told to pack up and leave. Fortunately, the staff at Sanctuary Toronto told us to pitch our tent alongside their church's wall where the City could not chase us away, treating us like we were just a burden to society. We are human too, but we felt like we were not being treated humanely. Although we were safe for the time being in our tent amongst many others, it was still stressful. I don't think I had one full night's sleep. Our future seemed uncertain and weighed on my mind constantly. All public washrooms were inaccessible, which was another stress factor. Porta potties were set up but were quickly made "unusable" by inconsiderate people who would leave a mess of urine, feces, and syringes.

Eventually, we were moved to a temporary two-bedroom apartment for a few months in a building that was meant to be torn down. Then we were shipped to different hotels for a while. I was grateful to be indoors during the cold winter months. Many organizations were also helpful with providing masks, hand sanitizer, and other COVID-19 kits. In October 2020, I ended up being hospitalized for liver failure. Drinking more during COVID-19 eased some of my anxiety. But years of drinking took a toll on my liver. I was terrified that I would not walk out of the hospital. COVID-19 prevented friends and family from visiting me during this dire time. My doctor said I was lucky to be alive and I was discharged back into a different world. A sober world. I was worried about contracting COVID-19 during my stay at the hospital so I went to get tested to make sure I would not be a risk to others and to reassure myself. Being homeless makes you more susceptible to getting sick, and I got my nose swabbed at least ten times to make sure I was safe. Some organizations offered us $20 as an incentive to get tested. That was a great idea.

A few months after my health scare, I was finally told that I would have my own place ... a place to call home. I'd have my own kitchen to cook whatever and whenever I wanted, and also a clean bathroom and shower, a bed to sleep on, a couch to relax on, and a roof over my head. And a feeling of relief.

Some people take things for granted. They look down on the homeless and wish they wouldn't be bothered by them when walking by with looks of disgust and disapproval. They have no idea what their lives are like and what might've led them to "polluting" THEIR streets. Being homeless is no joke and is not fun and it is not by choice. If only more people didn't lack the sense of sympathy and were more understanding and less selfish … maybe we could live in a world with less judgment and instead find the time to help each other thrive.

Nikki Sutherland at Harold Town Park, where she and Romeo pitched a tent after leaving a respite in April of 2020. Nikki and Romeo were threatened with arrest for living in this park and moved their tent next to Sanctuary, a drop-in and health clinic located in Toronto.
Credit: Chris Young

NIKKI SUTHERLAND is a Sixties Scoop Survivor and has been housed since April 2021 after years of confronting homelessness. She hopes to thrive being off the streets and to successfully manage her way through several difficult transitions, including sobriety.

 **CHAPTER 2**

The Housing Crisis and the Indian Residential School Legacy

Blue Sky, Leaders from the Houseless Community, Sandra Campbell, and Leigh Kern

Content Warning: *This chapter contains a description of the violence of Indian Residential Schools and ongoing colonial harm towards Indigenous peoples. Trauma-sensitive counselling can be accessed through the Indian Residential School Survivors and Family crisis line at 1-866-925-4419 or the First Nations and Inuit Hope for Wellness Help Line at 1-855-242-3310.*

＊ ＊ ＊

On 17 March 2020, the City of Toronto fell silent. When the first COVID-19 stay-at-home orders were put into effect, Yonge Street emptied, and one could almost see Lake Simcoe when looking north from Dundas Square. People living on the land emerged from their corners of near-invisibility and began taking up space for themselves and helping each other survive in a shuttered city. Encampments grew across the

Encampment at the Church of the Holy Trinity, next to the offices of the Toronto Urban Native Ministry and the Eaton Centre.
Credit: Zachary Grant

city, as houseless and internally displaced peoples began to build stable shelters in places where they felt safe and were able to congregate. They protected their shelters through the strength of their communities from threats and intrusions by those who police public space. The stay-at-home order interrupted the constant game of cat and mouse between houseless people and those who confiscate their equipment and push them from place to place. The pandemic paused this reality long enough for houseless people to come together and organize in meaningful ways for their well-being and survival. In March 2020, an encampment formed around our offices at the Toronto Urban Native Ministry and the Church of the Holy Trinity.

This community was led by Indigenous Elders of the encampment, who worked diligently to reverse hundreds of overdoses, respond to health crises, and gather and distribute supplies so people could have access to the things they needed, day or night. They would work to resolve disputes, offer support in times of mourning, distress, or anxiety, and would smudge the encampment as the sun rose each day. During this crisis, the Toronto Urban Native Ministry worked alongside these leaders to support the needs of houseless communities. Together, we worked to support their right to choose to live on the land as well as to advocate for the need for permanent subsidized housing that prioritizes their autonomy, self-determination, and inherent rights as Indigenous people.

Demonstrated during the onset of COVID-19 was both the will and resiliency of people to live on the land in collective ways, as well as facing the ongoing threat to their ability to exist on the land. Dispossession is part of the continuing legacy of the colonial project in Canada. Indigenous peoples' lifeways and community formation have been degraded to assert the primacy of the settler state. The COVID-19 pandemic provided a window into this continuum and what has been inflicted on our communities.

Genocide and the Crisis of Houselessness

While the Canadian Constitution recognizes the Treaty Rights of First Nations, Métis, and Inuit, settler policies undermine the effectiveness of these treaties, enacting continued colonial policies of forced displacement and genocide. For instance, the Canadian Observatory on Homelessness recognizes the traumatic effects experienced by the houseless population imposed through the entrenched structural systems of discrimination. Dominant understandings of property and poverty do not take into consideration traditional Indigenous lifeways and understanding of home. This narrow definition of homelessness – limited to the widely accepted four major categories of unsheltered, emergency sheltered, temporary sheltered, and at-risk for homelessness – is at odds with the Indigenous world view and re-enacts the legacies of genocidal practices that aim to implement institutional systems of assimilation. The Canadian Observatory on Homelessness states:

> The Indigenous definition of homelessness considers the traumas imposed on Indigenous People through colonialism. According to the Definition of Indigenous Homelessness in Canada, it is "a human condition that describes First Nations, Métis and Inuit individuals, families or communities lacking stable, permanent, appropriate housing, or the immediate prospect, means or ability to acquire such housing … Indigenous homelessness is not defined as lacking a structure of habitation; rather, it is more fully described and understood through a composite lens of Indigenous worldviews."[1]

Indigenous ideas of home are rooted in relationships to family and community, and related to interchangeable links to land, animals, and plant life; it is not a permanent building. Home is the web of relationships and families beyond blood. Thus, policies intended to alleviate homelessness instead pressure Indigenous people into mainstream social services and the settler housing system. And, in doing so, they criminalize traditional lifeways and houselessness, and force assimilation by separating Indigenous peoples from sovereignty and self-determination in their homelands.

The current housing crisis, commodification of land, and aggressive policing of houseless people are nothing other than a continuation of the colonization and seizure of Indigenous lands and an assault on the inherent rights of Indigenous peoples. Toronto, situated on the northern shores of Chi'Niibish/Lake Ontario/Niigaani-gichigami, is the home of the Michi Saagiig Nishnaabeg. The Nishnaabeg since time immemorial have lived in their homeland, moving seasonally, and living off the land.[2] The Michi Saagiig Nishnaabeg made treaties with the Wendat and

Haudenosaunee that allowed them to farm the land between the water-ways that the Nishnaabeg followed and camped along. The Michi Saa-giig showed hospitality to European farmer settlers in the first Toronto treaties, but the settlers had a very different understanding about land and home. Instead of recognizing the entire homeland and waterways as the sovereign home of the Michi Saagiig Nishnaabeg, the settlers used violence to chase Nishnaabeg off what settlers understood to be their sole private property. Present-day authorities continue to crimi-nalize Indigenous peoples for camping on their own territory. Settler society codifies whole ways of living in relationship with creation as ille-gal: people without access to private property and who live on the land are disempowered from traditional lifeways, self-sufficiency, and self-determination in building their own housing, and labelled "homeless." A leader from the houseless community comments on this dynamic:

> When we camp on the land, we share and are respectful. We take care of each other, we're a family. Security guards always come and kick us out, they say, "You've overstayed your welcome." I say back, "This is our land; this is Native land." And they reply, "This is the Queen's Land," and then call the cops on us and escort us off the premises.

From the first, Canadian society has funded itself through extrac-tive resource projects that have pushed Indigenous people into internal displacement on their own homelands. Deforestation, environmental destruction, ongoing occupation, and pollution have turned homelands into hostile, inhospitable, and policed zones. Canadian government pol-icy and seizure of Indigenous homelands has forced Indigenous people into confinement on small parcels of land known as Reserves, without adequate housing and without clean drinking water. The lack of hous-ing leads to mass crowding along with the increased risk of spreading disease and increased social disharmony. Such conditions have pushed many Indigenous individuals and families to migrate to urban centres with hopes of increased opportunities for and accessibility to education, employment, health, and housing. But those who leave harmful conditions on Reserves find similar conditions within cities: a housing shortage, mass crowding in shelters, a lack of safe self-determined housing, a lack of safe housing for the elderly and Survivors of confinement institutions, a lack of running water, and infestations and mould in public housing.

For many community members, houselessness began when they were kidnapped as a child from their families and home communities. Canadian policies and the Indian Act disempowered Indigenous governance by separating children from families, clan systems, and intergenerational ways of knowing and self-understanding. The RCMP kidnapped many of our community members when they were just children, placed them in church-run group homes, Indian Residential Schools, mental asylums, or foster care outside their communities. If a child spoke their own language, they experienced severe abuse as punishment. At the Indian Residential Schools, many children contracted illnesses because of intentional systemic spreading of disease. From there, they were often sent to Indian Hospitals where many children suffered medical, sexual, physical, and psychological torture. Indigenous children were often detained for years in Indian Hospitals until they were sent back to Indian Residential Schools or aged out of the system and were sent to the streets. Survivors of assimilationist policies continue to be directly impacted and affected by the ongoing legacy of these government policies. Survivors have continued to resist the abusive culture of denial and silence through the Truth and Reconciliation Commission and successful class action lawsuits of the Indian Day Schools and the Sixties Scoop Survivors.[3]

Institutions of childhood confinement, forced family separation, and displacement from the land are part of the Canadian architecture of genocide against Indigenous Nations. Survivors who are houseless and enter the shelter system find no protection. Shelters are dangerous

The Anishinaabe Nation flag flies with pride in the Trinity Square encampment.
Credit: Zachary Grant

places, but, even worse, replicate the horrors of Indian Residential Schools. Shelters offer the loss of identity, overcrowding, lack of privacy, spread of disease, physical and sexual assaults, confinement to specific spaces, and lack of adequate nutrition, language, and self-determination over what one eats or communicates.

Though the Canadian government promotes a minimizing narrative that 150,000 Indigenous children were forced to attend Indian Residential Schools and Legacy Institutions, the actual number is more likely 1,000,000 children.[4] This disparity is because the Residential School Settlement Agreement only included 139 Indian Residential Schools, yet there were over 1,300 Canadian Indian Residential Schools, Indian Hospitals, Day Schools, and other childhood confinement institutions.[5] These institutions were part of a massive web of

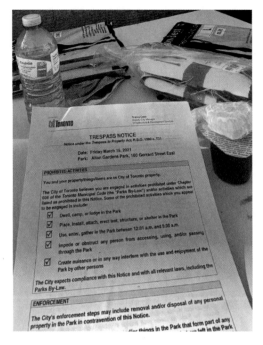

Eviction notice.
Credit: Greg Cook

genocidal intent. Indigenous children were forcibly apprehended and transported to confinement institutions where they were subjected to the removal of their names and separated from their beloved families, Nations, and communities. Children experienced torture for speaking their languages, were forced into child labour, and subject to mass crowding, the intentional spread of disease, physical and sexual abuse, and starvation policies. Indigenous children were often confined to indoor buildings, breaking their relationship to the land that resulted in the inability to harvest food to feed oneself. Survivors tell stories of scaling multi-storey buildings to find apples or other Indigenous foods for survival. Thousands of children died of forced starvation and starvation-related illnesses. Removing the right to choose what one eats and when and taking away the means to cook or make food for oneself are two of the ways the colonial system expresses control over another.

The prison, jail, and immigration detention centres of the state of Canada mirrors the logic of the Indian Residential School Legacy. The individual becomes a number, not a name. They are removed from their family and community and isolated for "reform." The person is confined to a small setting, subject to strip searches and other infringements on their privacy and self-determination. All contact with loved ones and support networks is cut off entirely or extremely restricted, the movement of the human being is controlled and dominated by those in power. The prison system, shelter system, courts, and probation system replicate the logic of the Indian Act and pass system, which controlled, restricted, and monitored every movement of Indigenous people.

During the Shutdown

The violence of systemic discrimination against Indigenous people was especially evident during the pandemic, when institutional and grassroots services were mandated to close and then were slow to resume or adapt their services to new conditions. Mental health services went online, cutting off those without access to technology from available supports. Prescriptions became difficult to fill in person. Access to critical information was online only. People were in crisis. Out of the Cold programs closed as well as many soup kitchens. The City forced people who were houseless out of tent encampments and into shelters and shelter-hotels, breaking up families and support networks. These shelters lacked services or trained staff to handle adequately the particular needs of Indigenous people experiencing trauma. Those who chose to remain in tents as COVID-19 ravaged the shelters, prisons, jails, and detention centres were subject to aggressive policing, criminalization, and arrests at the peak of the pandemic by police who would not wear PPE. The Toronto Urban Native Ministry and other grassroots collectives sought creative and in-person ways to address these discriminatory policics and bring technological access, information, and system navigation to displaced people, the elderly, people exiting prison or jail, and those living on the land.

In March 2020, we saw the mass closure of services across our city. The drop-in at the Church of the Holy Trinity went from seeing forty individuals daily to over three hundred. Together, we met the crisis seeking to support an increased sense of pride, self-determination, and sovereignty in our community members.

We witnessed community members lose a tremendous amount of weight as the resources they depended on disappeared overnight. With the Church of the Holy Trinity, we began Unity Kitchen to meet the nutritional needs of our community. People living in encampments would volunteer with the kitchen and give direction on the menu and program. We often used traditional recipes and Indigenous foods, such as Three Sisters Soup,[6] and bison or turkey dishes with wild rice. Through this work, we sought to support an increased sense of pride, self-determination, and sovereignty for our community members. Around Unity Kitchen and the Trinity Square encampment, a resource hub of relationships and networks formed. People supported each other in their choice to not enter shelters, which they felt were dangerous to their well-being and identity. Others seeking to enter the shelter system were supported in advocating for their access and rights. The leadership of Elders and community leaders from the encampment provided support to people experiencing trauma and crisis, from a position of self-determination that was outside the penal and policing systems.

Unfortunately, the Indigenous families that the Toronto Urban Native Ministry supports experience many barriers to the shelter system that has led to the continued breaking up of their families. Issues like this are part of a continuation of genocide against Indigenous families, nurturing communities, and Nations. An Indigenous couple who slept in Trinity Square before the pandemic became pregnant, yet they did not receive prioritization by the system or rapid access to family housing or services. Despite there being billions of dollars invested yearly in policing, uprooting, and displacing families and people who camp on the land for their survival, there continues to be almost no shelter options for houseless Indigenous families. The respite options that were extended to this couple would have enacted family disintegration. In one option, the mother would be allowed to take the newborn upon birth to a home for single mothers, and the father would be admitted to a separate shelter for single men across town. In a second option, the couple could move into a couples' shelter but surrender their beloved newborn baby to the state. In both options, they could not keep their baby, stay together, and be sheltered. These options were only temporary, with no offers for subsidized permanent housing. Both options would separate and force the dissolution of this newly founded family, so they continued to live in a tent. When supporting houseless pregnant people and families, we were able to mobilize support from Seventh Generation Midwives Toronto and the Call Auntie Clinic, who provided accessible and mobile health care from an incredible team of Indigenous birth workers and midwives. Throughout the pandemic, we witnessed the trauma of forced apprehension of newborns from their parents and a continued lack of emergency shelter options for families.

When shelter spaces are available, the environment and conditions of the shelter system often force people into crisis. Many Survivors of genocide use substances to cope and manage the impact of torture and the ongoing experience of criminalization, forced institutionalization, frequent experience of sudden death of family and friends, and lack of self-determination over one's life, safety, and privacy. A community leader and Elder remarks on these challenges:

> In the shelters, you can't have visitors, you can't drink or use drugs – everybody is going through problems, family problems, crisis, too many frustrations, so they use medicines to cope and get by, to have your rest, it eases the pain and frustrations and relaxes you after a while. With no visitors, being cut off from our families, can only use the phone at certain

times – we might as well be in jail! The shelters are prison. We have so much anger about what we have been put through in these places, some of us can't even speak about this. It's just like going to Residential School all over again, every time I see a police horse coming down the street … I lose it – I am right back to being taken. I am so scared every time I see them, I think to myself, "They're coming for the Natives."

The strict policies of the shelter system penalize people, and they are quick to withdraw their admittance when conflict occurs. If a person becomes triggered, is in crisis, or clashes with the staff, the staff will likely discharge them to the streets, pressure them to move to another shelter, or call the police. We have heard community members in distress refer to shelter staff as "the guards." The small, confined quarters of a bunk can trigger memories of being detained in an overcrowded jail cell or being placed in solitary confinement in the basement of a Residential School, or sedated and put in four-point restraints in their beds while in group homes. Elders experiencing post-traumatic stress flashbacks while staying in a shelter have had SWAT teams called on them. Some of our community members who are Survivors of childhood kidnapping, torture, and detention have died in and outside of shelters when they were forcibly discharged in the middle of the night. We have done many funerals for these brave souls, who are now buried in unmarked graves in empty barren fields located at the edges of the Greater Toronto Area, often hours away from where their families live.

We asked residents of the Trinity Square encampment to describe their thoughts and experiences about the shelter and temporary hotel system:

- Stop criminalizing us; stop with the empty promises, the housing list, the city statistics, the head counting, the profiteering off our bodies.

- We are still here; we take notice.
- Native and Black people get treated really bad; I get so mad when we get picked on! The racism from staff is really bad.
- The bodies of many that are unclaimed, that have died by COVID, murder in the shelters, or health complications have towered in the morgue. We have not been told of their deaths, or where they are. How can we grieve?
- When they [City parks department staff] slashed our tents, and with fences being raised around the parks, we now sleep in doorways.
- We need permanent rent-geared-to-income housing!
- You should see how they treat our Native women – I've seen security guards drag women by their hair. I've seen women being beat up. It took everything for me to not lose it.
- City housing workers are unreliable and miss appointments.
- I'm treated as a number and not treated as a human being.
- Shelters and temporary hotels still remain crowded and unsafe because COVID is everywhere in the shelters.
- Rotten food is served in the shelters.
- Poor services, not serving our people.
- Safety and privacy issues are just one concern from the women.
- We live in fear of being evicted or kicked off the housing list.
- I'm not a criminal but it's like take a number; sit and wait.
- We're tired of police harassment that uses tactics to humiliate and intimidate us!
- At night, teams of police circle our tents, flashing many bright lights throughout the encampment while tents are peaceful and asleep. We need sleep!
- Stop criminalizing us! We need respect and kindness!
- I have a right to self-determination!
- Don't shame me, I'm not a number!

Inside of a tent beside the Church of the Holy Trinity.
Credit: Zachary Grant

Despite families being broken up by a lack of affordable housing, and a dangerously full and overcrowded shelter system, the City of Toronto continues to invest in increased policing of houseless people. In the summer of 2021, many Torontonians questioned the millions of dollars spent on evicting three homeless encampments that formed within Trinity Bellwoods Park, Alexandra Park, and Lamport Stadium Park, and then on fencing off public spaces and parks across the city. The costs of these evictions were released by the City of Toronto, after such interventions failed to control and disappear houseless people. Fencing off public spaces; the theft, destruction, and bulldozing of people's homes; the criminalization of people living outside; the police raids on encampments; the militarized evictions and violent displacement of people who live on the land are part of maintaining the Canadian architecture of genocide.

Prior to the pandemic and during the COVID-19 crisis, our community felt that Mayor John Tory did not adequately respond to the concerns of the Indigenous houseless population, despite countless press conferences, petitions advocating for the health care needs of people living in encampments, and pushes to end the criminalization of houseless people. Our voices and those of our community members were either dismissed, silenced, or pushed out of dealings with City officials and Indigenous non-profit organizations. Yet on 21 June, National Indigenous Peoples Day, Mayor Tory issued a written proclamation stating, "The City of Toronto strives to strengthen the City's relationship with Indigenous communities and advance reconciliation. The City is committed to working with all Indigenous peoples in a meaningful way to help address their unique needs and work with the community to find solutions."[7]

The treaty and inherent rights of Indigenous peoples are not recognized or taken into consideration by the City of Toronto's enforcement of the "no camping" bylaw. As the needs of the houseless Indigenous population continue to grow within the urban setting, the consensus of this population is that their treaty and community rights as Indigenous peoples continue to be trampled upon. The violent raids on encampments lead to further displacement, the separation of people from their life-giving connections, and the criminalization of Indigenous people for applying their inherent rights. One of the Nishnaabeg Elders of our community, a leader at Unity Kitchen and a Residential School Survivor who lives on the land, stated: "The police are threatening everyone in their tents again with tickets. The cops are mad at me because I save more lives than they do. I go around at night helping people, saving people from overdose, helping them with anything – I serve and protect. They just serve tickets."

Community Well-Being outside Institutional Systems

The Toronto Urban Native Ministry supports people as they often cycle through living on the land, are forced to enter a shelter, end up in the hospital, are criminalized, detained in jail, sent to a shelter far from one's community, and then end up houseless in Trinity Square. We recognize how these institutions reflect the logic and practices of Indian Residential Schools and other colonial assimilation confinement centres. The Toronto Urban Native Ministry, in collaboration with the Unity Kitchen and other grassroots collectives, works towards mutual empowerment and offers support from a self-determination perspective. We follow the lead of our community members and work together to expand our connections and resources to meet the needs of one another.

The Toronto Urban Native Ministry has sought to support encampment residents, as they assert self-governance and self-determination on the land. During citywide closures, houseless people frequently visited the encampment Elders in Trinity Square for information exchange and emotional, physical, spiritual, and psychological support. Crises, conflict, challenge, and distress were handled through community care and without the intervention of police.

The Unity Kitchen continues to receive up to 200 people a day. On weekends, the Toronto Urban Native Ministry's Helping Hand Wagon goes out, meeting people where they are. Through this work, we have created a hub connected to collectives of front-line and community-based movements across the city. Our collectives collaborate through exchanging information, sharing resources and supplies, and collecting donations. Through the Unity Kitchen and our Helping Hand TUNM Wagon, our mobile services provide basic clothing, survival gear, water, knapsacks, traditional medicines, access to telephones or cell phones, traditional foods, hygiene supplies, PPE supplies with information about preventive measures to reduce the spread of the virus, spiritual support, referrals to mobile health care teams, and support in crisis, loss,

Sandra Campbell doing an interview about the escalating number of people without housing dying during the first year of the pandemic. The interview is for CTV following the Homeless Memorial on 12 January 2021. In 2019, 128 people without housing died in Toronto. In 2020, it was 144.
Credit: Leigh Kern

and change. Resource sharing and oral information exchange within the downtown core of Toronto are central elements for survival within our collective work, alongside access to harm-reduction supplies, Trans and Two-Spirit support, legal support, and care during crisis. Everything that is provided continues to be done through a collaborative lens of Indigenous world views, unifying within grassroots collectives and relationships with allied supporters and faith communities.

In March 2020, we began advocating for access to sanitation for those living outside and for the opening of public washrooms. Concerned about the lack of access to handwashing stations or protections for community

Unity Kitchen Toronto.
Credit: Zachary Grant

members, we coordinated volunteers to sew fabric masks for the house-less community until disposable masks were available for purchase. We purchased PPE from Indigenous-owned and -operated businesses and manufacturers while acquiring traditional foods from Indigenous busi-nesses. We procured ceremonial items and traditional medicines to sup-port people grieving, thereby offering hope and strength for community members enduring the hardship of the City's harsh tactics.

Without City support, we laboured around these obstacles and, through our networks, received volunteer suggestions from retired community nurses. We brought in Doctors Without Borders to assess our work and advise us on how to reduce COVID-19 community spread within the encampments and on-site. Through resource sharing and information exchanges, we became informed about COVID-19 and how to best serve the Indigenous houseless and internally displaced population. By pool-ing and sharing resources within collectives, grassroots organizations, and newly established networks, we were able to reshuffle resources with our constituents to meet the needs of the high-demand houseless regions within the Greater Toronto Area. This gave us the opportunity to concentrate on providing COVID-19 education to the community while handing out hand sanitizers and masks. With the knowledge that many of our community members have survived medical torture and abuse in Indian Hospitals, and cannot enter an institutional setting without becoming triggered, we successfully advocated for COVID-19 testing to become available in a mobile setting. In May 2020 in Trinity Square, in collaboration with the Church of the Holy Trinity, the Unity Health Network, Toronto Indigenous Harm Reduction, and the Giwaabamin Street Patrol, we held the first barrier-free COVID-19 on-site testing in an encampment. No encampment residents tested positive. People were able to receive COVID-19 testing in the encampment, without a health card or proof of status, in their own community and on the land.

In collaboration with community leaders and other grassroots organizations we were able to provide accessible regular testing and vaccination clinics in Trinity Square, while advocating for health care to be offered on-site to encampments across the City.

At our testing, vaccination, and health care clinics, we ensured that traditional medicines were available on-site and we opened every clinic with ceremony. These inclusive health care practices included traditional perspectives and the participation and direction of leaders from houseless communities.

The work of premature-death prevention in our communities has required mobilization around access to technology. Without access to technology, people are cut off from medical services, family, information, vaccination certification, and other supports. Many people, especially Trans people, youth, women, and Two-Spirit people experience high rates of hate crimes and violence in the shelter system and across the City of Toronto. For many houseless and internally displaced people, access to a cell phone can be a literal lifeline.

A community Elder offers traditional medicine at Yonge and Dundas Square.
Credit: Leigh Kern

For those we have loved and lost, we and our networks organize a monthly Toronto Homelessness Memorial. The support of a broader network within collectives strengthens and anchors us when hearing the many names of brave souls that have died during these difficult days. Houseless members of our community have created memorial art initiatives to honour those who have passed away.

The work of the Toronto Urban Native Ministry throughout the pandemic was shaped by the leadership of people living on the land. We recognize and honour their leadership exercised in encampment discussion meetings with stakeholders and the City, in participating in and providing feedback on advocacy initiatives, providing an emotional and cultural support network, attending Naloxone trainings and teaching others how to respond to drug poisoning and overdose, speaking at

COVID-19 information board at the Church of the Holy Trinity.
Credit: Zach Grant

events, contributing to the writing and review of this chapter, and drafting press releases. We recognize the creative and courageous leadership of our community Elders, with recognition of all Survivors of childhood confinement institutions, who continue to teach us how to support one another in the work of survival.

Conclusion: "This Is My Family, This Is My Home"

The current and dominant emergency shelter system in our communities reflects the culture and legacies of Indian Residential Schools. The criminalization and forced displacement of people who live on the land is a continuation of territorial dispossession and the theft of homelands. Currently, the Indigenous houseless population continues to assert their right to choose to live on the land and the right to permanent subsidized housing that prioritizes and respects their autonomy, their inherent rights as Indigenous people, and their right to self-determination. The grassroots community-based pandemic response of the Toronto Urban Native Ministry created small spaces of freedom, creativity, collaboration, and greater access to health care and survival supplies in the midst of the multiple ongoing crises of genocide, drug poisonings, housing shortages, and the ongoing Indian Residential School Legacy. When we support the self-determination of one another, grounded in love and respect, we can participate in the formation of community and justice outside of the colonial systemic formations of genocide. In the establishment of encampments, many Indigenous people have been able to keep their family bonds intact and survive during a precarious time during the pandemic. Through the work of sustaining an expansive network of mutual aid, kinship is strengthened. The bonds created through this time continue to be challenged by the ongoing pressures pushed on Indigenous people. An Elder and leader in the houseless community offers a reflection and conclusion:

> We're a family, but we are breaking apart – without housing or being allowed to camp, with the awful shelters, being pushed around by the cops, we have no home – so we end up stressed out and arguing. I hate seeing everyone argue, it is always about the same thing – we got nowhere to go. We survived through this though, we are a team and will always be family. I can't leave anyone behind. This is my family, this is my home – and they will never take them away. I'll always be there for my family.

SANDRA CAMPBELL Kanien'kehá:ka Wahta, Wakkwá:ho (English transla-
tion: Sandra Campbell is from Wahta, Mohawk First Nation, and Wolf clan).
Since 1992, Sandra has been an Indigenous Traditional Counsellor, special-
izing in supporting Survivors of Indian Residential/Day Schools, the Sixties
Scoop, houselessness, and other traumatic impacts of colonialism. Sandra has
worked at the Toronto Urban Native Ministry since 2010.

BLUE SKY is from the Whitefish River First Nation on Manitoulin Island and
currently resides in Toronto. He is passionate about living on the land and
supporting others who live outside. He believes in practising his culture
through sharing everything he has with others, helping others, checking up
on his friends, and offering smudge to those on the streets. He says "miig-
wetch" (thank you) to everyone who has helped these efforts over the years.

LEIGH KERN lives on the sovereign territories of the Michi Saagiig Nishnaabeg and is an Anglican priest who is committed to the work of repentance
and reparations for the ongoing genocide against Indigenous Nations.

 **CHAPTER 3**

Inconvenient Bodies and Toronto's History of Displacement

Lorraine Lam and Greg Cook

Lorraine:

In May of 2020, we were two months into Toronto's first COVID-19 lockdown and our team at Sanctuary was seeing triple the number of people accessing food, water, and showers. Services across the city were closed and options were minimal. Shelters were either full or unsafe, and Sanctuary's encampment located on Sanctuary property and the adjoining park was the busiest it had ever been.

That Tuesday was a busy drop-in day. During meal service, a community member yelled from his tent: "HELP! SOMEONE GET FUCKING HELP!" My co-worker and I bolted over. Cody[1] was ghastly blue and vomit covered one side of his face. My co-worker gave rescue breaths as I did CPR. We were not wearing all the necessary PPE, but the urgency to keep Cody alive was top priority. When Emergency Services arrived, a firefighter put a face shield over my head and told me to continue as he stood back.

Cody died.

I washed my hands and wiped vomit off my shoes after he was taken away, then raced to jump on a web call with the City Table[2] to discuss the need for harm-reduction infrastructures in shelters. That night, I facilitated a Zoom workshop for a Midtown Toronto neighbourhood group who wanted to learn de-escalation tips to navigate the new complexities of a shelter in their neighbourhood.

I did not stop all day to think about Cody – my first unsuccessful CPR attempt. I did not think about Cody for weeks, then for months. There was no time, no space, and no breathing room. There was so much work to be done. The housing crisis, the opioid epidemic, COVID-19 ... this lethal combination of crises created a reality that I never could have imagined.

Greg:

DISSONANCE

On 11 March 2020, I attended a meeting in a glass-walled room on the sixth floor of Metro Hall to talk about what the City's response to COVID-19 would be for those without housing. Yogi Acharya and Jessica Hales (both members of OCAP, the Ontario Coalition Against Poverty) were at the table, along with Mary-Anne Bedard and Gord Tanner, the two top managers of the Shelter Support and Housing Administration (SSHA), a representative from Toronto Public Health, and myself on behalf of the Shelter and Justice Housing Network (SHJN). Bedard and Tanner described the City's plans to open an additional eight temporary shelter locations so that the thousands of people in congregate shelters would be able to have their beds slightly further apart. This would hopefully mitigate COVID-19 outbreaks. Still the

City anticipated outbreaks in its shelters and predicted that as people sought safer options, the shelters might empty. They were confident that the necessary money would flow to cover what needed to be done. In this meeting, we had a short discussion about what outreach supports might look like with thousands of additional people living outside.

While I took notes and asked questions, internally I felt a deep sense of dissonance. The promises sounded surreal. Toronto has always been a tale of two cities with a booming economy, Rosedale old money, and proliferating luxury condos that soar over increasing numbers of houseless people in Rosedale Valley who have no prospect for housing.

A banner calling for the declaration of an emergency and an additional 2,000 shelter beds draped at City Hall by front-line workers on 26 November 2019.
Credit: Greg Cook

TORONTO: ONE CITY, TWO POLARIZED REALITIES

In Toronto, people who are poor have been living through crises for years. Prior to the pandemic, over a hundred people without housing were dying preventable deaths each year, many because of the overdose crisis. For years, advocates had been demanding that the City of Toronto declare a Homelessness Emergency and asking for additional resources.[3] Now, all of a sudden, there was a health crisis that would affect people with more privilege, and so poor people were promised more funding. Writer Arhundhati Roy sums up why governments were suddenly willing to spend money on poor people: "because now, in the era of the virus, a poor person's sickness can affect a wealthy society's health."[4] In the following months, I observed the municipal government deploy a massive amount of resources in the name of supporting people who didn't have housing, Indigenous and Black communities, and people with disabilities. Despite the volume of resources, these efforts never appeared to meaningfully reach the communities most impacted by the pandemic. Thousands of hotel rooms sat empty, relevant emergency equipment sat idle, and portable washrooms were deployed sparingly. Meanwhile, hundreds of police were assigned to issue tickets to people living in parks, erect fences, and evict people from apartments, tents, and Tiny Shelters.[5] While Toronto Public Health ran communication campaigns telling people to stay at home or socially distance, the City government continued to invest heavily in its infrastructure of displacement.

When faced with this overwhelming and terrifying global pandemic, why did the government repeatedly choose to respond with violence? What forces make it so difficult for government and industry to ensure each person has the essentials to live? The answer can be traced back to when white settlers first occupied this land.

One city, two polarized realities. Clarence Square, just west of the Central Business District. Credit: Greg Cook

FOUNDED ON DISPLACEMENT

The original settling, colonizing, and constructing of the City of Toronto required displacing and dispossessing Indigenous inhabitants. Violent acts of genocide and theft occurred that used logics of racial hierarchy and the invention of land as a private possession and commodity. The actions of the British Crown that culminated in the creation of the Toronto Purchase, Treaty No. 13, were riddled with dishonesty. At one point, the deed was found to be blank; the signatures of the Mississauga chiefs were on a separate piece of paper. The initial treaty was completed in 1787 but had to be renewed in 1805 thanks to its illegitimacy. Even then, the treaty was deemed to be so problematic that in 1923 and again most recently in 2010, financial compensation was granted to the

Mississaugas.[6] Wanda Nanibush, an Anishinaabe artist and community organizer from Beausoleil First Nation, writes: "We are always signing agreements with the government when we are backed into the corner of mere survival, without the strength to hold out for real justice."[7] In the midst of "mere survival," Indigenous Nations have continually found ways to resist despite section 141 of the Indian Act, "which made it illegal for First Nations to hire lawyers, obtain legal counsel, or raise funds for legal defence."[8]

As white settlers and the British government sought to appease an ever-growing appetite for furs, lumber, mined goods, farm produce, and real estate, more and more land was seized. To facilitate this further settlement, land was surveyed, Reserves created, and Indian Residential Schools built: the legal and cultural infrastructure crafted to dispossess Indigenous Nations. It is important to acknowledge the kind of narratives that continue to uphold these acts of genocide. Dara Culhane, a professor of anthropology who teaches at Simon Fraser University, states that for the British, colonialism was facilitated by the myth that inhabited lands "were simply legally deemed uninhabited if the people were not Christian, not agricultural, not 'sufficiently evolved' or simply in the way."[9]

The context may have changed throughout history, but the same tactics are used to facilitate dispossession today.

POOR HOUSES: TORONTO'S FIRST EMERGENCY SHELTERS

While the government of the British colony of Upper Canada was busy displacing Indigenous Nations from their lands and creating the Reserve system, it started to build the infrastructure for an expanding industrial economy and a system of private property. One of the facilities that helped to expedite this was the House of Industry, also known as "the Poor House." The first Poor House in Toronto was built in 1837 in response to the "new Poor Laws," which insisted that Britain's poor had to live in workhouses where they were forced to do manual labour to acquire shelter and food.[10] This same Toronto Poor House was later relocated to Elizabeth and Elm Street, just north of where the Eaton Centre is today. A *Globe* article from 1887 states: "They are kept warm and clean, but the hard boards of the floors are all they have for beds, and a range of boards, a little raised, for pillows. Last Saturday there were 125, and … they were lying as thickly packed as herring in a barrel. One could scarcely move without stepping on them."[11] The Poor House and its surrounding slum called "The Ward" provided "shelter" for the reservoir of labour that ensured profits for the growing crowd of capitalists that bought property and built mansions along Jarvis Street and in the new suburbs of Rosedale and The Annex.

Since its founding, the City of Toronto has always weaponized the legal system to dispossess Indigenous peoples, relied on the exploited labour of the poor, amassed property in the hands of the wealthy few, and housed landless people in miserable, inhumane conditions.

While the suburbs have multiplied and expanded, the conditions of emergency shelters have changed little. In 1935, John Bruce described the Wellington House, a shelter for men located just west of the St. Lawrence Market: "The men sleep in cots without mattresses or pillows. They are allowed two blankets … A short while ago, one man died. A number of other men who have received some treatment are now dead and buried. I can produce evidence of these cases to Commissioner Laver. I have done so and have received no satisfaction. There are men in the building who have tuberculosis and other infections mixing with 640 men in a building that is not equipped as a residence for anyone. There is nothing more abominable in life than this residence."[12]

For a short while, though, this changed. The number of people reliant on shelters diminished in the 1940s as people were either enlisted as soldiers or employed to build weapons.[13] Following the Second World War the government spent substantially more than it had previously on health and social programs. By the 1970s, the federal government had a robust national housing program: 12 per cent of the housing built each year was social housing.[14] Overall, housing costs were relatively low. As a result, there were fewer people without housing and in need of emergency shelters. This was a complex moment in Canadian history: it demonstrated that vicious living conditions and housing scarcity are the product of policy and are not at all inevitable. It is also important to recognize that much of the government's revenue came from natural resource extraction that continued to require the dispossession of land from Indigenous Nations.

THE CRISIS WORSENS

At the close of the 1970s a new cycle of dispossession and settlement was beginning in cities like Toronto and New York. In his book *The Creative Destruction of New York City: Engineering the City for the Elite*, Alessandro Busà writes, "the city has constantly endeavored to find new ways to create profit for land owners and developers through a relentless process of destruction and rebuilding."[15] This framework of destroying communities by confining and boxing in people – working to make sure they are invisible in both official narratives as well as along the main streets and sprawling suburbs – echoed the pattern that the British government instituted 200 years earlier when it set about selling parcels of land from the Toronto Purchase. If you weren't sufficiently wealthy, sufficiently white, or sufficiently able-bodied, this city was not for you. The government was too busy rebuilding it for landowners.

In the 1980s industrial jobs were decentralized in parallel with an upsurge of professional jobs in Toronto's downtown sectors like finance and real estate. Increased unemployment rates for Toronto's working class helped facilitate gentrification in the downtown core. In 1993, the federal Liberal government cancelled its affordable housing programs, followed in 1995 by the Ontario Conservative government that cancelled all new spending on social housing. In 1996 the Ontario government further doubled-down by cutting social assistance rates by over 20 per cent. These policy decisions left thousands without enough money to pay rent, increased the need for emergency shelters, and forced hundreds to seek refuge in Toronto's ravines and under its bridges.

In response to protests and film footage of the horrific conditions of the shelters that was shown in council meetings, the City's Community and Neighbourhood Services Committee (CNSC) agreed to a target of less than 90 per cent capacity for the city shelter system in March of 1999.[16] Despite this commitment, the city's shelter system was regularly found to be at 95 per cent capacity or above. Months later, the City decided to retire a temporary shelter at the Fort York Armoury. Both the Ontario Coalition Against Poverty (OCAP) and the Toronto Disaster Relief Committee (TDRC) pushed back against the premature closure.

OCAP brought a proposal to the CNSC for a "Safe Park" at Allan Gardens so that people without housing could sleep in a space without fear of police harassment. They argued that the shelters were full and people had to go somewhere. Kira Heineck, on behalf of TDRC, remarked, "We support it, but we wish we didn't have to … As one member of our community so eloquently put it, 'We used to demand housing for the homeless. They refused to build housing. Then we demanded hostels for the homeless. Now we are simply demanding a park. What next? That we demand heating grates on city streets?'"[17] The City refused to accept OCAP's proposal. In response, OCAP organized a sleep out at Allan Gardens with the support of "local health agencies, the TDRC, progressive trade unions, and the Mohawks of Tyendinaga."[18] They stayed there for three nights until the police raided the park and arrested thirty people.[19]

In the years since, the pace of gentrification has accelerated, the cost of rent has skyrocketed, and the number of people without housing has more than doubled. The need for emergency shelter beds has significantly increased. The City hasn't once met its shelter system occupation target of less than 90 per cent capacity, despite being reminded of the performance shortfall year after year.

In 2016, Cathy Crowe, members of OCAP, myself, and other front-line workers demanded that the City open the armouries. Cathy started a petition that tens of thousands signed. City Hall refused to listen to the thousands of Torontonians who were demanding shelter on behalf of their neighbours. As an outreach worker, calling Central Intake was hopeless: many of my friends living on the street would not bother calling, knowing that the chances of accessing a bed were most often slim to none. We knew that what people needed and deserved was housing; we also knew that was not realistically possible in the short term. Additional shelter beds would save lives in a society that was fixated on transforming homes into financial assets.

Lorraine:

It was a regular Wednesday morning in 2013. I was at Common Table, a breakfast drop-in program that operated in the basement of the Church of the Redeemer. I was in the middle of an intense conversation with a young woman named Terra, when Pierre came up to me and pulled a quarter out of my ear. We had never met, but it was clear he was not shy. He laughed gleefully after pulling off his trick, extended his hand to me, and said, "You're friends with my sis, Terra? I'm Pierre." We became quick and fast friends; it helped that we were the same age with similar interests. Pierre was from the Innu Nation, and had one of the brightest smiles in all of Toronto: his huge grin showed off his endearing front teeth as his eyes disappeared into crescent moons. A bit of a jokester, he had an infectious smile and personality: when he laughed, you laughed. He was laidback and easy going, which made him popular across the city. He had a gift of befriending everyone around him. Despite being homeless and having experienced so much hardship on the streets, Pierre was always optimistic, a cup-half-full kind of guy. Beneath the surface, he was a philosopher of life, and wrestled with internal hurts and demons. An avid hockey fan, Pierre grew up an athlete, and dreamed of becoming a musician. He always told me that when he was ready, it would happen. For now, he just wanted to take it easy, make people laugh, and roll with life's punches.

On 15 February 2016, Pierre Gregoire, then twenty-eight years old, died of a suspected fentanyl overdose in the bathroom of a KFC restaurant after being told there was no more room at the nearby respite. The respite was already ten people over its capacity.[20]

Pierre never saw his dreams come to fruition. His death shook the community across the city, especially the younger Indigenous community. My friend's death was a tragedy; it was real and personal to me. His death was also by design: the City of Toronto failed in maintaining shelter capacity at 90 per cent. He didn't have to take his last breaths in the bathroom of a fast-food restaurant.

Greg:

GIVE ME SHELTER!

As a result of Pierre's death and the ongoing experiences of not being able to find shelter beds for people, many of us gave deputations at City Council committee meetings, met with councillors, organized rallies and press conferences calling for the federal armouries to be opened. Despite our efforts, Mayor John Tory and the majority of City councillors voted against opening the armouries on 6 December 2017.[21] Mayor John Tory cited the cost and inadequate facilities as reasons he was against the opening of the armouries.[22] He also worked to delegitimize our demands by stating, "Why is it when it comes to opening armouries are these one or two people to be taken as having the gospel ... if I don't do exactly as they say ... that somehow that this means that I'm not doing my job."[23] At the end of that December, temperatures plummeted. I remember doing outreach when it was –20 degrees Celsius before the wind chill. Our team handed out Tim Hortons cards so people could purchase a drink and briefly warm up to catch a break from the deadly temperatures. Hospitals reported a spike in frostbite cases. Jen Evans, a local entrepreneur, used social media to crowdfund money from the general public to pay for hotel rooms for people left outside in the cold. On 6 January 2018, Mayor Tory relented to public pressure and opened the armouries.[24] That winter we agitated, held press conferences, and worked hard to make sure the public and City Council knew how horrendous the reality of the situation was. In the end, the City opened almost 1,000 additional indoor spaces. While these buildings saved lives, they were still spaces that – by design – robbed people of autonomy: the continuation of a settler legacy of shuffling inconvenient people out of sight for the sake of those with privilege.

Despite the addition of indoor spaces that the City labelled "respites," the housing crisis kept worsening. We demanded that Mayor Tory declare a homelessness emergency: that he use special emergency powers to expropriate buildings for use as shelters as well as for long-term social housing. We demanded that he meet with the other two levels of government and create a task force. He refused.

Lorraine:

WHERE DO PEOPLE GO?

Besides the lack of shelter beds, there were also many who refused to go into a shelter: the institutional setting was retraumatizing for many. The absence of privacy, the cramped space, and the prospect of living with strangers in dorms were enough for people to refuse to stay in a shelter. People were creative in finding alternative options: setting up makeshift homes under bridges, in ravines, or in alcoves of construction sites. Public transit, church steps, and park benches were sometimes the best options for people to catch a quick nap – though always negotiating the risk of police, private security, and city workers' harassment, forcing them to move along. Actual housing options were non-existent, and at Sanctuary, we began to see more and more of our community members pitch tents to create a sense of home, and a sense of privacy.

Over the years, our staff team at Sanctuary had many conversations about camping on our property: we would allow people to sleep on our space, but would ask that no permanent structures be erected, and that temporary structures be neatly packed up the next morning. In November 2019, we had seven people living in tents on our property, and this time we decided that the tents could stay. We knew there would be neighbourhood pushback, but without viable indoor winter options, we changed our stance. Because … where are people supposed to go?

As expected, we were summoned to meetings with our City councillor. These meetings involved Streets to Homes workers and our neighbours, including Children's Aid Society, local business owners, representatives from the condo association, and the Church-Wellesley Neighbourhood Association. The meetings culminated in a larger "Safety Meeting": a town hall panel that did not invite our homeless neighbours to the table. This panel was set up to discuss realities of homelessness and what were deemed "safety concerns" for the neighbourhood. Complaints about yelling, garbage, noise, and needles were raised.

At one point during a meeting, the condo board took the hard-hearted action of projecting onto the wall the slides of newspaper headlines reporting the murder of an Indigenous man. Jake[25] was a beloved Indigenous man who lived in the heart of the Sanctuary community for over ten years. His friends nicknamed him "Prez" because of the position of authority and respect that he held among them. Jake's murder was a horrific tragedy, yet in this "safety" meeting, it was nothing but a prop. Jake was an unwanted Indigenous body, like the unwanted Indigenous bodies that stood in the way of the Toronto Purchase. He was a poor man, like the people who slept on boards in the Poor House, and he was a scourge to the progress of real estate. His death is so personal to us, but it is also the product of 300 years of policy, choices, and structures that ruthlessly shape our city to favour the rich and brutalize the poor.

At the town hall meeting, there was little mention or critique about the larger systemic issues. There was no curiosity about why people ended up having to live in a tent in the first place, or why anyone would settle for this as their best option. There was zero willingness to engage in dialogue about how poor people are also members of the neighbour-hood and deserve safety and dignity. There was zero desire to engage the reality that gentrification and the condo boom on Charles Street had displaced many of the same people now living in the condo alleys. Charles Street once had a number of rooming houses, but they had been torn down and replaced by luxury condos. Many of those tenants had nowhere to go but to the street or a shelter. There were some empathetic voices present at the town hall, and there was a brief mention of the lack of affordable housing, but mostly the resounding message was, *"Thank you for your work, but do it somewhere else."*

In early January 2020, our City councillor, Kristyn Wong-Tam, de-termined that each of the seven people living in the tents at Sanctu-ary would be given a subsidy to supplement their social assistance, and each was assigned a Streets to Homes worker to support their search for housing. Surely this would mean these seven people would be off the streets in no time. The trade-off? They had to take their tents down immediately.

The tents came down on 10 January, though we warned the City that this immediacy could be deadly for our friends. All seven individuals were promised an indoor interim space until they found housing, but because couples were split up and people sent to unfamiliar parts of the city, the seven individuals simply slept on Sanctuary's front steps with just a sleeping bag.

A sleeping bag. In January. In Toronto.

Two weeks later, our councillor asked Streets to Homes why these seven people were not yet housed despite having a subsidy. She seemed genuinely surprised that it took much longer than two weeks for these individuals to get an apartment. It became very apparent to us that those in positions of power did not have any idea just how impossible it was to find any affordable housing in the city.

Two months after the City forced those tents to be dismantled, two of the seven people died. It was March 2020, and the number of COVID-19 cases was increasing dramatically in Toronto. The city went into lockdown just a day after we held a memorial for Chris, one of the two who passed away.

If Chris had access to a safe and dignified home of his own, would he still be alive today? If he had access to a safe opioid supply, would his future have been different? If housing costs stopped skyrocketing to a point of impossibility, would Chris have survived? If we as a society stopped enacting policies and practices of colonial violence and displacement that harm our poor communities, would Chris still be alive today?

PANDEMIC TRIFECTA

Toronto declared an emergency in response to the global pandemic. Shops, social assistance offices, and food banks closed across the city, and the meagre resources available to people before the pandemic became even less accessible. Many drop-ins closed because of a lack of staff or a shortage of personal protective equipment (PPE). Libraries and coffee shops closed. Community centres closed. Everyone in the city stayed home and the streets felt apocalyptic. COVID-19 was the third part of a trifecta of pandemics that was killing our vulnerable community; it joined the housing crisis and the overdose epidemic from a toxic drug supply. This new virus was suffocating an already under-resourced, under-supported population.

Public Health officials told us to keep our distance to stay safe; how do you stay 2 metres apart from your neighbour when you live in a congregate shelter dorm with bunk beds? They told us to wash our hands to stay healthy; where do you do that with no public bathrooms or sinks available? "Stay home," said the City; where does one go without a home?

Greg:

In order to highlight the severity of the situation and demand action, Cathy Crowe, Yogi Acharya, and Anne Egger, a nurse practitioner at Regent Park Community Health Centre, spoke at a press conference in front of City Hall on 8 April 2020 that OCAP and SHJN helped organize. At that time, there were eight reported COVID-19 cases in the shelter system. We made three key demands: hotel rooms or apartments for each person staying in congregate shelters and in encampments, screening and testing at all shelters, and a safe supply for people who use drugs. Just over a week earlier, the *Toronto Star* had published a story that quoted: "Modelling suggesting on average there could be, in several weeks, as many as 800 to 1,200 people in the homeless population testing positive for COVID-19 at any given time."[26] Despite this terrifying analysis, City leaders stalled and were sluggish to acquire hotels and move people still sleeping on bunk beds to living situations where they could safely self-isolate.

It was clear that the City was refusing to take a preventative approach to COVID-19 within the unhoused community. In the early weeks of the pandemic, most of the City's response to COVID-19 in the shelter system was to send those who tested positive to a Recovery Hotel program. Instead of focusing on the prevention of COVID-19, the City focused instead on limiting the virus spread beyond shelter systems. The City remained unwilling to acquire the appropriate infrastructure for safe social distancing. The City was prepared to let people remain stuck in congregate settings amidst outbreaks of COVID-19 and concerns the virus was airborne.

As open-minded as I had been during my meeting with the City on 11 March, I soon realized that what we were seeing was just more of the same. Poor bodies (which are so often Black, Indigenous, and People of Colour [BIPOC] bodies) are an interruption to the City's mechanisms of property protection and wealth hoarding. If COVID-19 and its deadly consequences could be contained among the bodies of the poor, the City had no interest in alleviating that suffering. It's the mentality of Poor Houses and of colonizers.

Lorraine:

People left respites and shelters to find safer and distanced spaces to sleep: outside. For many the impossible choice was this: stay in a shelter with guaranteed access to food and water but risk catching COVID-19, or sleep outside – safe from COVID-19 but with no access to your basic needs. Sanctuary handed out tents and doubled our efforts to stay open to provide access to washrooms, showers, food, and water to those left behind on the streets. Within days of the pandemic lockdown, an encampment grew on and around our property, at one point peaking at around seventy-five people living in Sanctuary's neighbouring parkette and our backyard. The increased visibility of tents and encampments across downtown was a glaring indicator that pointed to the failure of our governments.

Our neighbourhood's clamouring got louder. The loudest neighbours repeatedly complained to the City about the tents, garbage, and public defecation around Sanctuary. Sanctuary asked the City repeatedly to install public washrooms in the neighbourhood but they refused.

Sanctuary Toronto, 11 June 2020.
Credit: Greg Cook

With no places to sleep, with nowhere to use the washroom, with no access to food, water, or showers … Where do people go?
We are [not] in this together.

Greg:

In response to what was happening, people in the shelters took pictures of the crowded conditions. They spoke to the media. Others pitched tents in public parks only to be given tickets by Bylaw Officers and told that, if they didn't leave, the police would show up. We advocated at roundtables, spoke to the media, and amplified demands on social media. We organized press conferences and rallies. A coalition of legal groups and Sanctuary litigated the City to ensure people in shelters would be able to better physically distance themselves. During the first four months of the pandemic, the City was pressured to open over 2,000 new shelter-hotel rooms, moving over a thousand people out of congregate shelters into rooms where they could better self-isolate.

Lorraine:

The City regularly stated in advertisements and public-facing media that "We are in this together": it was this unity and this collective effort that would get us through the pandemic as healthy and as unscathed as possible. As the pandemic unfolded, it was clear that there was no room for poor people or people without housing in that collective "we."

With impossible options for those most vulnerable, front-line workers across the city scrambled. This already burned-out and overworked group of people doubled and tripled the hours they were already working. A weekly networking call began on 18 March 2020, just days after the first lockdown, and workers came together to share resources and support each other. There was a lot of anxiety and fear as we knew that this pandemic could be a death sentence for many of our community members. We created and circulated Google Sheets with different organizations' outreach schedules and geographic areas, as well as kinds of services offered. Emails flew back and forth as we worked together to cover as many gaps as we could in outreach and community supports. Callouts happened when organizations needed extra supplies, and mutual sharing of resources took place frequently. *This* community was in it together. This networking call continues to this day and has been one of the most valuable spaces that came out of the pandemic.

HE DIDN'T HAVE TO DIE

On top of trying to keep our communities alive, front-line workers were also engaged in behind-the-scenes advocacy efforts. We sat at City Table upon City Table, meeting after meeting, pleading with the City to listen to the voices of those without housing, and to those who had established rapport with these communities. We pushed for the hotel spaces that sat empty to be made available for people to safely isolate and pushed even more for the City to listen to community expertise regarding health care and harm reduction in these spaces. We asked the City to implement a robust infrastructure of harm-reduction supports before opening up these spaces and moving people indoors. Repeatedly, we witnessed the City being too slow to respond. They refused to listen and in so doing, gambled with people's lives.

Two apartment buildings in Midtown Toronto were some of the earliest spaces leased by the City as options for people outside. These apartments were slated for demolition but COVID-19 halted that. The developer leased them to the City, and the City began to move people from the most visible encampments into these apartment units. It was an exciting opportunity for many of the community who lived outside: their first opportunity to have their own apartment and keys – albeit temporarily. In addition to these apartments, more hotel-shelters began to open up. There were rules implemented that infantilized the community and many expressed how much they hated being babysat. Rules like 11:00 p.m. curfews, "no food allowed in rooms," and the constant security checks in people's rooms made people feel like they were in "a soft jail." A soft jail, a Poor House. We haven't stopped treating poverty like a crime. In addition, many of these settings were opening with subpar harm-reduction supports and resources – despite community insistence on how these need to be in place to save lives. Would the City permit a residential condo to exist without proper fire safety protocols in place? I doubt it. Harm-reduction supports are a life-saving necessity and yet the City did not implement these adequately before moving people inside.

When these spaces first opened, one of the rules in place for residents was no visitors in their rooms. As a community of workers and people with lived experience, we insisted the City change this rule, as it would mean an increased risk of people using substances alone in their unit, or people not getting help out of fear of getting kicked out for breaking the rules for visiting. This increased the chances of opioid overdose and death. The City refused, and days later, sure enough, a community member died in his room. It was then that the City decided to amend this rule.

My friend died before the City chose to listen.
He didn't have to die.

DO BETTER

Many of these new hotel-shelters were situated in some of Toronto's affluent neighbourhoods, historically isolated from the realities of the local poor. The response in these neighbourhoods towards the shelters varied: from compassionate church ladies who baked cookies for the shelters, to protestors who planned marches while insisting that homeless people were responsible for the rise in neighbourhood break-ins (no data supported this claim). On top of being front-line workers and advocates at City Tables, we were also now educators and workshop facilitators, trying to educate the wider community about the realities of the housing crisis in Toronto and offering de-escalation training in attempts to build bridges within the larger community.

In some of the vitriolic pushback against the shelters in different neighbourhoods, a familiar rhetoric sounded: if you weren't sufficiently wealthy, sufficiently white, or sufficiently able-bodied, this neighbourhood was not for you.

The founding of Toronto was rooted in colonial violence that made people invisible and displaced people deemed inconvenient to the privileged. This violence continues today. There are thousands of people across Toronto – and across Canada – who are houseless, and that number continues to rise. At the time of writing, the City's shelter data flow indicates that there are 200 new people who enter the shelter system every month.[27] The subsidized housing waitlist is over 81,000 house-holds long,[28] with an average wait of twelve years for a one-bedroom unit.[29] The rate of overdose deaths continues to skyrocket, and we still do not have access to a safe drug supply.

Over the last 300 years, policies and systemic structures set up and perpetuated by the privileged repeatedly favour the wealthy and discard the poor. These policies determine life or death for many. When policymakers fail to consult and adhere to the wisdom of relevant stakeholders, people die. The City repeatedly toys with the lives of vulnerable people. We carry our grief, mourn our friends, while we fight at City Tables and local neighbourhood associations trying to convince people with power and privilege that the lives of our vulnerable friends and

Lorraine Lam and Rob Dodds at Sanctuary.
Credit: Lyf Stolte

communities matter. The City of Toronto *can* do more to house people. They can raise taxes, stop policing the poor, and build more affordable housing. We know how to do better. The City *can* end homelessness and poverty-related deaths. Right now, the City refuses.

Greg Cook speaking at a news conference outside Regent Park Community Centre on 23 March 2020.
Credit: Cathy Crowe

LORRAINE LAM is an outreach worker at Sanctuary, a community in downtown Toronto that seeks to particularly value individuals who live on society's margins. Driven by her interest in social transformation and liberation, Lorraine spent her early adulthood pursuing an education in music, sociology, and social work. Motivated by hope and love for people, her life's work is to wrestle with the question, "What does faith, justice, hope, transformation, and collective liberation look like in our day-to-day?"

GREG COOK is a white settler who has been a drop-in and outreach worker in downtown Toronto for over twelve years, and at Sanctuary since 2009. Greg partners with community groups and agencies to agitate for a more just and equitable society. He is on the steering committee of the Shelter and Housing Justice Network, and he volunteers for the Toronto Homeless Memorial. He has worked on two documentaries: *Bursting at the Seams*, about the shelter crisis, and *What World Do You Live In?*, about police brutality.

 **CHAPTER 4**

Displaced There, Displaced Here

Jenn McIntyre and Steve Meagher

> no one leaves home unless
> home is the mouth of a shark
> you only run for the border
> when you see the whole city running as well …
>
> you have to understand,
> that no one puts their children in a boat
> unless the water is safer than the land
>
> Warsan Shire[1]

Human beings and the governments we elect love to create systems to solve "problems." We are also obsessed with collecting data, which we then turn into pie charts and bar graphs to monitor and analyse and evaluate how these systems are working. While data can be a powerful tool to help us understand what is happening in our society, an unfortunate repercussion is that the people affected most by these systems become little more than numbers and statistics.

It is quite common for refugee claimants to be relegated to statistical terms, particularly when we are talking about the emergency shelter system and how many people experiencing homelessness are "not from here." But far more important than counting refugee claimants is telling their stories. What we actually need to know is if these systems are failing them or serving them, particularly in moments of crisis.

As much as we love to count refugee claimants residing in shelters, we also love to blame them for straining the system – for simply arriving without a home to go to. Whether or not the scapegoating of refugee claimants has been an intentional or politically effective strategy, it is consequential. Fixating on the immigration status of shelter users is tremendously unhelpful. Beyond the racism, xenophobia, and entrenched marginalization that accompanies such public discussion, it also distracts us from a far more important question: *Why is this group of people forced to depend on the emergency shelter system?* And the even more important question: *Why, in a city as wealthy as Toronto, is anyone being denied the right to housing?*

Refugee claimants are not statistics or budget lines. They are not pawns to be used in political negotiations. They are human beings. They are mothers and fathers and sons and daughters. Teenagers and grandparents and newborn babies. Many have fled unimaginable persecution, danger, and poverty. And they have arrived in Toronto in a desperate search for safety and justice.

Moreover, refugee claimants are certainly not the cause of the long-standing homelessness crisis in Toronto. They simply draw our attention to an unacceptable situation that has persisted and worsened over the years because those in positions of power and influence have continued to favour profit over the rights and well-being of people.[2]

Although there are refugees and migrants facing many different circumstances within the shelter system, this chapter highlights some of the challenges particular to refugee claimants throughout the COVID-19 pandemic. As we push beyond the numbers and statistics, we have chosen to share the account of a family of five refugee claimants. Their story is a clear example of some of the barriers and hardships that many homeless and precariously housed refugee claimants have been facing since March of 2020.

We offer immense gratitude to the family for allowing us to share their experience, and we have removed any identifying information.

* * *

Our story begins in March 2020 when we were referred to a refugee centre office after landing at the airport. The person who attended to us at the refugee centre was very kind. I explained that we didn't have a place to stay and she found a temporary space for us in a shelter. Although we had to be out of the shelter each morning at 7:00 a.m. and couldn't come back until 6:00 p.m., we didn't think we would be able to find any help, so it was something beautiful that we had somewhere to sleep and food to eat.

The COVID-19 lockdown hit us fifteen days after arriving and changed everything. We had already been moved from the first temporary shelter into a shelter-hotel with hundreds of other people, and when everything closed we found ourselves stuck in two hotel rooms. Only one person from our family could leave to go and get our food and had to be wearing a mask.

For the first two months, there were no issues with COVID-19 outbreaks in the shelter-hotel where we were living. The numbers were still low in Toronto. But we still had very little contact with the shelter staff because of all of the precautions and fears of spreading COVID.

One of the hardest things was that the children weren't able to go to school for March, April, May, or June (three and a half months).

"Dream House" chalk-drawing by nine-year-old child living at an emergency shelter for refugee families in Toronto.
Credit: Photo provided by the family.

They weren't able to register because the schools were closed. We were told that if the kids had attended even one day of school in person before the lockdown, they could have attended online school. But because they hadn't been registered in school before it closed down, they didn't have access to online school. Everyone thought schools might reopen soon, so we still went through the complicated online registration process, which was difficult because we didn't speak the language. We were told "it will be two weeks," then "it will be a month." The days, weeks, and months passed. The children never started school. And then the summer break began and they ended up missing many months of classes.

∗ ∗ ∗

When Toronto went into an abrupt lockdown in March 2020, there were thousands of refugee claimants in its shelters. Given that many refugee claimants arrive in Canada with very few resources, they have often depended on short-term, initial stays in emergency shelters until they find their footing and are able to move forward. Leading up to the pandemic, the number of refugee claimants arriving in Canada was at historic highs, resulting in a significant population within Toronto's shelters. While they were spread across various programs throughout the system, the majority of refugee claimants could be found in the family sector. The family sector is a combination of shelters and temporary hotel programs designed to provide emergency accommodations for homeless families. It is remarkably distinct from the rest of the emergency shelter system for one simple reason: at any given time, roughly half of the residents living in these facilities are children. The reason that the family sector constituted the highest number of refugee claimants is fairly clear: when faced with the need to flee to a place of safety, families do everything in their power to stay together.

The lockdown of March 2020 led to a number of serious challenges for all people in the shelter system, not only refugee claimants. These challenges included a heightened risk of exposure to COVID-19; lack of access to appropriate isolation space; delays and barriers in accessing appropriate personal protective equipment (PPE) and COVID-19 testing; delays in accessing COVID-19 vaccines as they were being rolled out to other high-risk groups; and a significant reduction in access to essential services and supports that were available prior to the pandemic.

The lockdown measures were hard on everyone, but in certain ways they were especially challenging for families with children. Now consider the added stressors of living in a shelter and being a newcomer to Canada, which was the reality for many refugee claimant families who had been residing in Toronto's shelter system during the pandemic. School closures and online learning created massive access to education issues. And the transition to virtual service provision for health care, social assistance, legal proceedings, and recreational programming, among other things, has rendered many services totally inaccessible for some of the people who depend upon them the most.

* * *

We had to stay together in quarantine, stuck inside. This was new for our family, as we had never spent so much time together and hadn't all even lived together in a long time. We actually came to know one another so much better as a family in this time together.

We didn't have internet access in the afternoons, as everyone was using it in the building at the same time, so we needed to change our schedule in order to access the internet. I think that many people were taking classes online. We totally inverted our schedule to be awake at night and to be sleeping during the day.

Because of the size of our family, we had two separate rooms with the kids in one room and the parents in the other. The official rules were that we weren't able to be together, due to COVID-19. We were meant to stay separately in our rooms and not to visit our children in their hotel room. How did they expect me not to interact with my children? Of course, we broke the rules to be together.

The days were long and difficult. We tried to pass the time and not be so bored. We talked and played together. The internet wasn't good enough to watch TV programs or to take English classes online, so we read, we exercised, and we played games together. We took time to remember stories, things we had done when we were kids. We tried to occupy ourselves in any way that we could. We filled the hotel room with sticky notes with the English names of items and furniture that were in our room.

We were totally isolated in a brand new country. The only thing that we knew about Canada was what we saw out the window and the small store next to the hotel. All we saw in four months was the airport, the refugee centre, and the hotel.

* * *

Unless you have been a refugee, you cannot possibly understand the pain and hardship of the experience. Imagine being forced to leave your home and all you have known, being separated from your family and community support network, and navigating a new country when you may not understand the language and the systems are entirely unfamiliar. These overwhelming challenges can lead to further trauma and consequences that may continue to impact a person or a family for an extended period of time.

Recognizing this, it's nothing short of remarkable that so many refugees manage to build new lives for themselves and their families. However, the impact of the COVID-19 pandemic has compounded existing challenges. Offices closed, services moved online, and many immigration processes were put on pause. Overcoming the barriers that many refugees have historically faced became far more difficult. This left many people stuck in a purgatory of sorts – unable to return to the home they were forced to flee, and unable to move forward in this new and unfamiliar city.

For refugee claimants living in Toronto's emergency shelter system during the pandemic, every single area of their settlement process was adversely affected: housing, health, education, employment, immigration, social connections. Services were shut down so quickly that they were met with many closed doors and very few answers. They were simply told to wait. Wait for social assistance. Wait for medical care. Wait for the lawyer to call. Many families living in the shelter system had no choice but to stand by as any control or autonomy that they may have had over their own lives and futures effectively disappeared overnight.

* * *

The pandemic had a huge effect on our refugee claim. To start with, we had intended to make our claim in the airport when we landed, but unfortunately, we were so nervous that we didn't know where to go or who to say it to. We quickly realized that we should have made our claim with the customs officer, but when we didn't, there was no way to go back into the secure area of the airport to do so. Someone at the airport directed us to a refugee centre for help. The refugee centre explained that as we had failed to make a port-of-entry claim, we now had to make an inland refugee claim and they would help us find a lawyer to assist us. We were told we had to make our refugee claim online, which we did ten days after arriving in Canada. However, we didn't receive any sort of communication from the government until a couple of months later in May.

We also had issues with communication with our lawyer, probably because of the pandemic. We didn't actually meet with our lawyer until almost one year after our arrival. We also didn't realize that our refugee claim application was missing important information and wasn't processed. It took so long for everything to be sorted out, because we didn't understand how the processes worked.

We wanted to go to the government immigration office to try and understand what was going on. But there were so many rules put in place by the pandemic, and all of the offices were closed. There was no one that we could actually talk to. And it had huge consequences for our refugee claim process and our access to services. We were told that the only person who could help us find answers was our lawyer, but we couldn't get in touch with them either. Finally, things got sorted out, but it took a long time and involved the support of lots of community workers and ultimately a new lawyer. It took nineteen months to complete our eligibility assessment and receive our immigration IDs. Normally, claims are processed in a few months.

* * *

Newly arrived refugee claimants in Canada often find themselves in an extended limbo. On the one hand, they are told again and again about all the things they need to do to move forward: find somewhere to live, apply for this, register for that, go here, get a job, and so on. But even as they are bombarded by these various instructions and processes, many are haunted by a question that threatens to again upend the lives they are building: *Will my family and I be able to stay in Canada?*

The primary function of the shelter system is to provide emergency accommodations and move people from homelessness into housing. Although refugee claimants are certainly in need of housing, the main priority for many is to obtain Canada's protection and regularize their immigration status. The consequence of this misalignment in priorities is that the shelter system is meeting one serious need, but is not designed to effectively address their greatest concern. It is obvious that the shelter system's "Housing First" approach, as well as the government's continued focus on responding to "chronic homelessness," has not been designed with refugee claimants in mind. These families have serious legal and settlement needs to attend to, some of which have very short timelines and require technological, linguistic, and emotional support to navigate. We see far too many people at our refugee centres who encounter housing workers and security personnel in shelters, but have little to no support in accessing legal assistance, preparing for their refugee hearings, or meeting other pressing settlement needs.

In March 2020, Canada's immigration system effectively hit the emergency brake, leaving countless numbers of people in Canada and abroad without status or visas. This became an urgent concern for refugees in Toronto's shelter system. Inland immigration offices shut their doors, moving to fully online services. Refugee claims were to be submitted through an email address, often with months passing before hearing anything back. The collection of biometric data and conducting of eligibility interviews was halted before eventually resuming nearly a year later. This meant that many refugee claimants did not get their ID documents, which are essential for accessing supports such as health care, social assistance, access to education, and many other services. The immigration department improvised and released new documents, which were not always recognized by service providers and required education and advocacy by refugee organizations and community members.

In April, refugee determination hearings were shut down, as the employees of the Immigration and Refugee Board were not allowed in their building. Tens of thousands of families had their hearings postponed, family reunifications were delayed, and people were left in limbo even longer. A whole new system of virtual refugee hearings was created and debuted six months later. This virtual system has serious implications for refugee protection and should have been carefully considered and designed over many years with stakeholder consultation. Due to the pandemic, it was rushed into production. The shutdown of government offices and the subsequent shift to a virtual system was no one's fault, but the impact was amplified for a group of people who already face so many barriers in accessing technology, Wi-Fi, and accurate information. Frontline refugee agencies in Toronto took on the role of explaining to people what was going on, as most of the information about these rapidly changing systems continued to be inaccessible to the people who were actually being affected.

The challenges of Canada's immigration system shutdown were magnified for refugee claimants experiencing homelessness, who were forced to navigate these changes while simultaneously contending with the daily health-and-safety concerns that came with living in a shelter during a global pandemic.

We can't blame COVID-19 for all of the challenges that marginalized communities, including refugee claimants, have faced since March 2020. This pandemic has exposed wounds that were already there, long standing inequities and injustices that many of us have chosen to ignore for decades.

The list of injustices faced by refugee claimants and other migrants prior to and during the pandemic is a long one. It ranges from exploitative and unsafe working and living conditions for temporary agricultural workers to lack of access to pandemic aid programs for many precarious migrants. It includes the hardships of extended family separation for families with backlogged immigration cases, and higher COVID-19 infection rates amongst refugee and immigrant populations, as well as racialized communities more broadly. Although these issues go beyond the scope of this chapter, we mention them here to acknowledge the larger systemic discrimination faced by refugee and migrant communities.

We must proceed with some caution as we make the claim that the emergency shelter system does not respond adequately to the legal and settlement needs of refugee claimants. We are wary of the response that refugee claimants should be excluded from or segregated within the system. That is certainly not what we are suggesting, as it would be a serious misstep to restrict access to emergency shelters based on immigration status. Rather, insofar as refugee claimants have always been shelter users, the system must evolve to be more responsive to their particular needs.

To its credit, the City of Toronto has already demonstrated that this can be done. Specialized programs have been implemented in the past to respond better to the legal and settlement needs of refugee claimants living in shelters. The problem is that the capacity of these specialized programs has rarely lived up to the demand, with the majority of refugee claimants continuing to lack access to adequate supports. Rather than creating a separate system altogether for refugee claimants, these specialized programs within the system need to be enhanced and expanded. And shelter workers throughout the system need to be adequately trained to provide support to refugee claimants, to ensure that those who don't make it into specialized programs still receive access to appropriate services where they are.

As the shelter system attempts to rebuild itself for a post–COVID-19 era, the onus is on the City to be inclusive and to meet the actual needs of shelter users. This includes working with other levels of government and community organizations to offer accessible information and support to refugee claimants, regardless of where they enter the system or what facility they are staying in. A refugee claimant's path to achieving status and building a life in Toronto is directly related to the information and support they receive as soon as they arrive in this city. Therefore, the City of Toronto has a tremendous responsibility to see and meet the needs of this group of people.

Of course, the ultimate answer to homelessness must be housing. But we have also observed that refugees and migrants can be overlooked and left behind when access to housing is being advocated for.

"Freedom Dreaming" by an eleven-year-old child living at an emergency shelter for refugee families in Toronto. Credit: Photo provided by the family.

While the vast majority of refugee claimants tend to be homeless for a relatively short period of time after their initial arrival in the city, their duration of homelessness will be extended if they are not attended to with the appropriate support and resources tailored to their circumstances. This is the current reality in Toronto's shelter system, where refugee claimants are effectively being forced to live in shelters longer so they can meet the requirements to qualify for the rent supports needed to secure housing in the city's severely unaffordable rental housing market. This has created a manufactured situation of chronic homelessness amongst this group. That cannot be the way forward – not for refugees and migrants, or for anyone who is experiencing homelessness in our city. *Housing for all* must be the new standard as we press on. Let's do better, Toronto.

JENN MCINTYRE is a community practitioner and activist who has been living and working alongside refugee claimants in Toronto for almost a decade. She is a passionate collaborator who believes in the power of community to push forward real change. Jenn is part of several networks of people working to advance refugee rights, border issues, support for newcomer youth, and the treatment of detained migrants.

STEVE MEAGHER works as director at the Centre for Refugee Children, an initiative providing settlement and legal support for refugee and migrant children in Ontario. He has been involved in the Toronto shelter system for nearly a decade, both as an outreach worker and manager at a refugee shelter for families. Steve is an active member of the Shelter and Housing Justice Network (SHJN).

CHAPTER 5

Dystopian Realities

Michael Eschbach

It was strange that day. A simple momentary tilt of my head, a second of thought, that's when I realized I was suddenly at the last rung on the ladder: homeless. The realization shocked my belief system, which began to unravel almost immediately though I wasn't aware of it yet. Eventually, a catch basin for homeless people got hold of me, like a black hole swallowing the unseen ghosts of still-living vibrant souls. I was in the system, a system of promises that turned into lies later. Here it is now, after almost ten years homeless, a tattered mind trying to express itself like it used to but unable to do so. See, being homeless for two, three, four years, it's like doing a tour of duty in Afghanistan or Iraq. I've done two tours being at the bottom, not enough sleep, no proper nutrition, and shelters like prison camps instead of portals to get out. Unfortunately, I was in my fifties, and now my sixties, an easy time to shatter a mind and disassemble it. The younger people manage to absorb it, adapt to it, better than I could, though they still fall prey to trying to get out of an insane matrix of misinformation, outright lies, and an erosion of self-esteem and validity of their thoughts.

My mind couldn't handle it. It broke. I had so many layers of thoughts, walls, protecting me. Homelessness, and the human nature I've seen at its worst, ate through every layer, every boundary I had established like a caustic acid poured into my thought patterns. I wish I could have just run away. Get a job, control my path, but being on disability prevented that option. Not enough funds for the disabled to change one iota of their existence. The discarded and useless to politicians and the elite. At some point, after seeing too much of the dark side of humanity in the shelter system, and the indifference of the system itself, suicidal ideation set in. It's something I live with during every waking thought now even though I'm under the care of a therapist. Even the antidepressants seem unable to curb the thought patterns. The City and its policies are destroying real people, their thoughts, their dreams. I know; I'm one of them.

Lies. Everywhere. It's all you hear when you're homeless.

Early January 2020 came and with it the rumours of a virus, a new one. I'd always had an affinity for microbiology, so I followed, at first, the rumours, the spread, the death rate. When late January came along, I realized I was stuck in a death trap: a City-run shelter with sixty-five people in the basement of a church that shouldn't hold more than thirty people. An experimental rat cage of humanity, and I was one of the rats. It was something I was unprepared to see, and an anger arose within me to make sure I saw. I started to debate the staff about a pandemic getting in.

They laughed, seemingly unable to grasp the dystopian reality heading their way.

I tried to explain we are the same when it comes to something like this. They laughed, two worlds that will never see each other. I laughed too. Inside. At them.

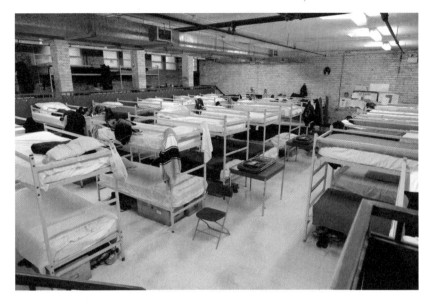

Inside St. Simon's Shelter months before the pandemic began. Michael believes he got COVID-19 here because of the City's failure to move people out of congregate settings despite many pleas and warnings.
Credit: Nick Purdon/CBC

Every day after that, I debated whatever shelter manager was on duty, whatever shift. Get out the old people, put them somewhere safe till we figure this out. We have ninety-year-olds, those who are eighty-five, seventy-nine, seventy-five, seventy … I didn't care about me, I was fifty-nine and thought I could handle this. February passed. I pleaded. March passed. I kept begging every day. April, late, the ranting stopped. Orders came, they were moving the older people to hotels for self-isolation. So we went, I made the cut. I caught COVID-19, and so did a lot of others sent to the hotel with me. A doctor came and tested us the second day we were here. The majority of us had COVID-19. Some of us got damaged, some were asymptomatic, spreading the virus. The government knew their homeless shelter system was vulnerable yet waited till it was too late. I still want to sue them, I really do. Two people died in the shelter I escaped from, many more got very sick.

A wildness encompassed my sense of self. I was being sent to places with no say in the matter, to a fourteen-day isolation centre for COVID-19 positive homeless people. I felt insecure. Food insecurity, sleeping insecurity, all the insecurity homeless people feel overwhelmed me all at once. And I had the virus I caught in City-run shelters. I thought strange, impossible thoughts on the drive to another new facility. Is this it? Did the City succeed in killing me by waiting too long? Are they trying to save me now to save face? Will COVID-19 kill me or is my body strong enough to resist? So many thoughts manifesting themselves at once broke my emotional barriers. I cried on the ride to a new shelter, broken again. When we arrived, we waited one by one to have our intake done. I was surprised to learn during the meeting that harm reduction was provided among many other things. After that I was escorted up to my room. I couldn't help feeling strange, I had COVID-19, everyone around me had COVID-19; shit, whole families with kids had it, everyone but the staff. Who are these crazy workers that would do this? I thought. There were no vaccines in sight, those were months and months away; in fact, it wasn't even a truly formed concept yet. Over the next fourteen days, though, I came to know the staff at the Four Points Sheraton Hotel recovery and isolation site and realized there were still heroes left on this blue dot of ours called Earth. Eventually I got to my room, was checked in, and finally left to my own devices. I sat on the bed and looked around. It's a room I thought, four walls, floor and ceiling, washroom and lock on the door; yep, it's a room like every other room. Bed and television. I didn't really care though. I had COVID-19 and no idea what to expect but, if the worst outcome evolved, I thought this would be as fine a room to die in as any other.

It came to pass over the next few days that the original version of COVID-19 had no effect on me physically. I was asymptomatic, but a spreader of a killer virus. The very thought made me ill to my stomach.

Most people don't understand, but homeless people give a shit, from politics to asking others "how are you actually doing today?" After the first few days, I started to wander, talk to people and staff, generally unafraid of COVID-19. I saw many different people there from many different parts of the world, all Canadianized like me and all living with very little money like me. It really made me think, meeting families with two or three beautiful children, if this was a virus for the poor in a great country like Canada.

After fourteen days, it was time for me to leave. But I want to tell you about the staff and nurses and doctors before I depart. These people were, not just the bravest, but the strongest of lighting to illuminate the darkness people go through when they first catch COVID-19. The nurses checking me fully twice a day, the cook who understood that nutrition helps fight COVID-19, and those that joined me outside for air. I had COVID-19, they didn't, so why bother with me? They cared. For whatever reason, they actually cared.

I was then sent to this hotel-shelter right when it opened, when COVID-19 began to open eyes.

I realized after a few days, that this was just another shelter, not a home. The same old nonsense had followed me here. The violence, the hate some people have for others and society, the prejudices, and worst of all, the hate people have for themselves that makes them want to die instead of trying to change things. The pain inflicted by your status in society. Drug overdose deaths every other day, stabbings, fights, the bullying, the worst humanity had to offer. Here it was all over again.

I had been judged, I thought to myself, while gazing out the COVID-safe window in my room at the inn. Venomous storm clouds lurked, all about, green, twirling, like all my emotions about humanity. I had come out of COVID-19 unscathed, but I was going back to the City's shattered shelter system. I was a victim who survived the politics of uncaring elected people. Something has judged me, I believe, to scream back at a system ravenous to eat itself, to scream at the insanity of a system that has lost compassion. I watched the storm clouds, their ire, march across my eyes while the vast city served as a backdrop. Yet I did nothing, just storm dreams that coalesce into nightmares when I finally sleep.

I awoke, looking at my surroundings. A room like any other but a room to shelter from COVID-19. Something better than the shelter death trap I was webbed in by the poisonous fangs of bureaucracies. My anger was gone but my energy level was drained. I rested over the next few days. I had caught COVID-19 and, though asymptomatic while I had it, there seemed to be many after-effects. No energy at all, pains in my body that weren't there before, a heart that jumped beats of life-giving blood, shortness of breath, and a loss of taste and smell that affected my ability to bother eating. You would be surprised how much a lack of smell and taste bothers you when you try to eat food. I lost some weight, forced myself to eat, and somehow maintained a balance. It's been a year and a half since I had COVID-19, but some of the after-effects still linger. At some point, I finally stored enough energy to explore the surroundings of the COVID-19 safe shelter and define what a fully functional room for myself meant to me. I was surprised to find that a door and a washroom for myself made me feel like a human being again. Such simple things and I felt alive again. Away from the danger and stress of Toronto's policy on homelessness, or affordable housing, I felt like a person again. I began to think like someone who had a structured belief system with all the mental safeguards in place. I felt like I might actually scream, scare myself, or just laugh hysterically and feel normal. I didn't do any of that though, I was still simply in a shelter, albeit one that let me think like a normal person when my door was closed.

I met the staff, the security, and many of my fellow shelter residents. I felt more secure knowing I had my own space to go to, which made me feel more open and receptive to other people and their problems. That was what eventually led me to believe that nothing had really changed. Interaction, listening, watching, news, rumours, information.

I've been here a year and a half now (as of November 2021). The City ran it for the first six months and then handed the reins to CONC, the Christie Ossington Neighbourhood Centre. They are good at having all their systems running. I still believe, though, that they will help me find subsidized supportive housing. I have to hope. If I don't hope, I have nothing.

Sublimation

IT'S 14 FEBRUARY 2022

5,183,042. That's how many grains of sand I've counted on this tiny beach. Twice. You can count them yourself if you like if you don't believe me. It's a small beach, room for two, perhaps three. A small creek adjacent to the beach imitates the susurrus sounds a larger river might make. All around this beach and creek a shimmering haze surrounds me. I've tried walking towards the haze, but I never seem to be able to get any closer to it than I am just sitting on the beach. I believe the mist represents people. Sometimes I see shadows and outlines in it, feel empathic probes. I still don't understand how you circumvented the mist and ended up, here with me, on this beach I thought my mind created. Your company is welcome, though. It's been a long time since I conversed openly with another person. I hope we can exchange thoughts, but my nature is to dismiss threats, gnaw them down to their fundamental building blocks, and digest them. What's that you ask? Am I insane? I believe I am now, hiding on this beach I created. My sense of self is tattered and frayed and hard to control. I still have memories though. Snippets of knowledge that seem to keep my sense of self afloat in a miasma of chaotic thought. I ask you if you've had COVID-19 yet, but you seem to shy away from the question. I tell you, in trust, that I've had it twice now. I ask you what you think but you remain silent, you dumb down your empathy, and send me reeling into nothing. Memories

overpower me, though, and I fall into a daydream about my second infes-
tation with the virus.

* * *

It came as a surprise, my second time getting COVID-19. I had followed all the right protocols. Self-isolation, mask wearing, distancing. None of it mattered, COVID-19 seemed able to circumvent all the scientific knowledge with every new variant. I was sent once again to the Four Points Sheraton Hotel recovery and isolation site, which has ended up with my believing that we are just animals. What's that you say? We're above being animals? I don't believe that anymore. I've been on the bottom for a long time, seen things that a structured person would never understand, lest it break their belief system.

So, I'm back at Four Points, isolating. Things are different, though, from the first time. The hospital has been severely slashed by budget cuts, and two-thirds of it have been turned into a shelter. My vital signs were taken once on the first day, that's it. I was called every morning at 10 a.m. to see "how I was feeling." It took two days for me to get a pillow. Tough time for a disabled person. My room had no clock, making it hard to relate to people on schedules. The room had bed bugs. People from the shelter somehow managed to come up and knock on my door, maskless, looking for something or other. A contradiction to all safe mandates. My isolation got terminated early with instructions to self-isolate at "home." The hospital was flooded by the fast-spreading Omicron variants, and we were sent back to finish isolation … wherever. For me, that was the shelter-hotel. Toronto Public Health, and you'd be surprised, phoned me. They threatened me with $7,500 in fines if they found out I didn't comply with self-isolating. They also have, apparently, a special division to deal with the homeless, many of whom are disabled and trapped within an uncaring system. Why are the homeless and disabled relegated to a different protocol? Why are we seen as different? Lesser? Animals?

Michael, after his second
COVID-19 infection.
Credit: Chris Young

That brings us back to here. *Who are you and how did you get past the mist that surrounds me? I hear no reply. I look deeply into your eyes for an answer, yet you start to fade out of my sight. Before you are gone, I implore you to share your secrets of the mist that surrounds me. I watch, as you implode before me, go back to your existence.*

I sit once again on this small beach wondering if I should count the 5,183,042 grains of sand again, or if I should fight the stigma disabled people face. I don't know what I should do anymore. My inability to relate to the animal nature of ourselves has cast me adrift. Perhaps one day, I will go to sleep and not awake. It would help with all these conundrums floating within my sense of self.

MICHAEL ESCHBACH has been homeless for over ten years. He is disabled and can't earn an income, apart from panhandling, which he refuses to do. Trying to find housing on the pittance allocated to him is like trying to find the proverbial genie in a bottle. All he really wants is a place to call home.

PART II

FIGHTING BACK

 **CHAPTER 6**

Responsibility Downloaded: How Drop-In Centres Stepped Up and Pushed Back during the Pandemic

Diana Chan McNally

How do you stay at home when you don't have a home? For unhoused people, the pandemic starkly demonstrated how seemingly innocuous public health protocols, such as staying home, became both immaterial and taunting in the absence of brick-and-mortar housing. How do you self-isolate? How do you practise proper hygiene in the face of a deadly virus? How do you get the uninterrupted rest you need if you do become ill? With restaurants and coffee shops shuttered, how do you keep yourself fed without a kitchen and a fully stocked fridge? Where can you panhandle for change, or even use change with an accelerated switch to card payment only? Where do you go and what do you do to survive? How do you stay healthy and safe from COVID-19?

It was immediately clear to me that as the city shut down in March 2020, the hundreds of unhoused Torontonians sleeping rough were being shut out. As a coordinator with the Toronto Drop-In Network (TDIN), a coalition of daytime drop-in centres across the city of

Toronto, I knew our drop-ins would have to step up. Our work has always been to provide the necessities of life, reduce systemic barriers, and provide community and care for low-income, precariously housed, and unhoused people. We exist in tandem with an integrated network of supports but function largely as a starting point: a place where people can access emergency needs and the basic necessities of life, as well as get support for their health needs, harm reduction, housing, employment, financial trusteeship, and recreation. We offer everything from community kitchens, to on-site podiatry, to storage lockers, to free legal support – essentially, whatever the community needs, drop-ins aim to provide it. I have always posited that drop-ins are the last rung on the ladder before people slip through the cracks entirely, as well as the first step back into a different life. We are, for many people, a home without being a home. A place you know will always be filled with friendly faces and chosen family to support you through whatever comes your way. With the onset of the pandemic, this meant more than we could have ever imagined.

Toronto has long had encampments. From the time of St. John's Ward, the disappeared neighbourhood bounded by Queen Street, Yonge Street, College Street, and University Avenue, people have been building their own tenement housing in this city for over 100 years. During the post–Second World War era, there were year-round lodgings on the Toronto Islands for people who could not find housing on the mainland, and during the early 2000s, there was Tent City on Toronto's waterfront. While much of the discourse during the pandemic has focused on the phenomenon of encampments, the fact is there have always been people living outdoors in Toronto. Since the creation of the city's first drop-in centres in the 1980s, folks sleeping in stairwells, on the street, on park benches, under bridges, and in ravines were part of the fabric of our communities. In a sense, this made the appearance of encampments at the start of the pandemic nothing new for us. What was different, however, was the sheer number of people and their visibility in prominent

Toronto parks, including Trinity Bellwoods, Alexandra Park, Moss Park, and Lamport Stadium.

What wasn't evident to the public was why these parks were considered to be apt locations by encampment residents. While this depended on a number of factors, including the social make-up and dynamics between the residents themselves, each location existed within a nexus of social services, drop-in centres in particular. Lamport Stadium residents could access round-the-clock services from the on-site homeless respite, operated by TDIN member St. Felix Centre. Alexandra Park and Trinity Bellwoods sat within walking distance of several drop-ins, including West Neighbourhood House's The Meeting Place, Evangel Hall, St. Stephen-in-the-Fields' Safe Space drop-in, St. Felix Centre's 25 Augusta drop-in, and St. Stephen's Community House's Corner drop-in and overdose prevention site. Moss Park sat across the street from Fred Victor's Open House drop-in and supervised consumption site, and close to All Saints and Margaret's at Dundas and Sherbourne. With the exception of Evangel Hall, which shuttered briefly at the start of the pandemic, and Fred Victor, which remains closed for indoor services, every other drop-in located close to Toronto's major encampments remained open. In fact, this handful of drop-ins, alongside Sanctuary and St. John the Compassionate Mission's Broadview and Scarborough sites, represents the only publicly accessible, indoor spaces that never closed during the course of the pandemic, and which welcomed unhoused people.

Even as City-run facilities, such as community centres and libraries, closed for long periods of time, encampment residents were welcomed inside open drop-in spaces for hot meals, clothing, on-site nurses, harm-reduction supplies, as well as washroom, shower, and laundry access – and the most basic need of escaping the elements. To the question, "Where did unhoused people go to access the most fundamental resources available to those in brick-and-mortar housing?" They went to drop-ins, their closest facsimile to a home. And as the only social service within Toronto to recognize the full weight of the pandemic on unhoused people, we at the drop-ins obliged.

At TDIN, my work pivoted to ensuring that the spaces that remained open could do so safely and with sufficient resources. I stayed abreast of COVID-19 policies and created numerous online guidance documents, often updating them multiple times a day. Those drop-ins that didn't have the resources, staff, or capacity to maintain a COVID-safe indoor space, I helped transition to takeaway and outreach services to support those living outdoors and in encampments. For drop-ins with more technological capacity, services and recreation turned to phone lines and Zoom groups as a means of ensuring the well-being of precariously housed service users with phone and internet access. Of our drop-ins across Toronto, only one shuttered fully, and permanently: North York Women's Centre. Every other drop-in organization – fifty-six in total – stepped up in unprecedented ways, and we became the de facto emergency resource for people living in encampments.

We also became a lifeline for people in shelters and those with drastically reduced income to access free, hot and homemade takeaway meals. Both TDIN and the food bank sector recognized that food insecurity was a major concern. In just the first six months of the pandemic, TDIN drop-ins served 963,168 takeaway meals between them.[1] Who was hungry? Unhoused people, as well as those living in low-income housing and supportive housing, which features wraparound health supports. However, we also saw many people coming from shelters where the food was subpar or not enough, as well as front-line workers, including Uber Eats drivers and cyclists, and people who were out of work. At The 519, a drop-in and community centre located in Wellesley Village, people who had never experienced a drastically reduced income or used social services were coming from nearby condos to line up for a bag lunch. Families were also coming, particularly those that had previously relied on school-run breakfast programs. We also piloted a new program, the TDIN Meal Voucher Program, which allowed unhoused people to use chits at local BIPOC-owned restaurants to secure a free meal. Overall, the need for meal programs increased dramatically, and the demographic of those in need diversified in unprecedented ways. Even today, with the return of a modicum of stability, little has changed for drop-ins preparing takeaway meals: the need and the diversity of those in need remain. While there is no shame in an individual needing food, what is shameful is that drop-ins and food banks were forced to step up beyond their capacities to address a clear failure by government to ensure people's right to food.

Another public policy failure that drop-ins attempted to address was the dearth of public bathrooms throughout the city. At the beginning of the pandemic, there were a handful of bathrooms the City was operating, most of which were clustered in the centre of downtown (e.g., Nathan Philips Square, Union Station, and the St. Lawrence Market) and only accessible during certain hours of the day. Park washrooms were unavailable, as service by Parks, Forestry and Recreation staff was suspended, as were bathrooms located in shuttered public libraries and community centres. As well, with the closure of malls and coffee shops – those private sources we rely upon as stand-in public infrastructure – there were no other toilets open to the public. Toronto had less than a dozen functional bathrooms and no public showers for five months. Again, drop-ins stepped up, and those that were open indoors maintained publicly available bathrooms, including accessible bathrooms for people with mobility needs. We also maintained the only public showers in all of Toronto, with hygiene products and towels provided.[2] Three of our drop-ins also made free laundry service available, understanding that clean clothing and bedding is imperative to people's good health and hygiene, especially in the context of a pandemic. Even drop-ins offering no indoor services made some of their bathrooms available, recognizing that there was nearly nowhere else for people to go to access a toilet.

This remained the situation until late June 2020, when park washrooms were reopened. But even then, not every facility was accessible for people with mobility needs. As well, more than half of all park washrooms were not open during the winter months, and no facility   besides those on

Toronto Islands – operated twenty-four hours a day. Instead, portable toilets became the default "bathroom" for park users, despite the fact that they were poorly maintained. As well, a few portable hand-washing stations were installed, including in Moss Park, but these were often filled with dirty, stagnant water. In sum, the City's clear lack of investment in ensuring functional washroom facilities was overt negligence. It showed a blatant disregard for the primacy of good hygiene required to stay healthy and safe from COVID-19. This is true for all park users, including middle-class Torontonians getting outdoor exercise, as promoted by the City's ActiveTO program, but was an absolutely urgent concern for people living in parks. It must also be recognized that given the over-representation of Indigenous people among Toronto's encampment communities, this denial of access to fresh, clean water can be traced to a larger colonial project.

Of equal concern was the lack of running, drinkable water available to the public. Indeed, beyond the lack of washrooms, the City withheld the most basic necessity of life – water – from encampment residents and the park-going public more broadly. Drinking fountains were not turned on until the summer of 2021, following a Twitter scandal created by journalist Shawn Micallef – and even then, not universally. In light of this, and alongside the grassroots mutual aid group, the Encampment Support Network (ESN), and the individual efforts of advocate Rafi Aaron, TDIN's drop-ins once again stepped up to fill an egregious gap. Between March and August 2020, drop-ins distributed a total of 185,300 bottles of water – a necessary endeavour, but an onerous one entailing immense labour and incredible amounts of plastic waste.[3] While TDIN, alongside groups such as the Interfaith Coalition to Fight Homelessness, advocated for over a year for the City to deploy its two mobile "HTO To Go" water trailers, the City never obliged – even after Councillor Kristyn Wong-Tam's motion requesting their deployment passed. Because there is no consistent running water available in parks, TDIN drop-ins are still distributing bottled water at the time of writing, twenty-one months into the pandemic.

Everything TDIN was doing represented a downloading of responsibility from all levels of government directly on to the front line. Drop-in staff were burning out and they were falling ill. Outbreaks and positive cases of COVID-19 among staff and service users resulted in an ongoing cycle of temporary drop-in closures. TDIN was asking for an incredible amount of work and fortitude from its front-line workers who were underpaid, undervalued, and enduring immense personal sacrifices to do what the municipal, provincial, and federal governments failed to do. For myself, as TDIN staff but also as a front-line worker at one of our drop-ins, it wasn't enough to simply "keep us going"; I had to commit to fighting for systemic change for all of our workers. I also felt a moral imperative to do better for unhoused and street-involved people, whose unpaid labour supporting one another to survive was the most egregious downloading of responsibility of all. Too many weren't surviving the untenable burden we were placing on them, including several people I knew well: Natalie Boyer, Doreen Upson, Darryl Monast, Quincy Williams, Paul Le Gresley, Oliver Dick, Angela Cromarty, and Kyle Bye. I couldn't watch the level of death and abandonment continue, and so I stepped up as an advocate.

In February 2021, I authored an open letter, *Demands for Immediate Action to Address COVID-Related Risks and Harms for People Experiencing Homelessness,* which argued for action from all levels of government to commit to housing and health supports for unhoused people, as well as support for front-line workers. Following the March announcement of the City's Pathway Inside program, which aimed to render the coercion of encampment residents into shelters as official policy, the letter was updated to demand an end to encampment evictions.[4] To be clear, the City had been evicting encampments throughout the pandemic – and, quite frankly, for many years prior as an extension of the provincial Trespass to Property Act and Safe Streets Act, especially encampments under the Gardiner Expressway and in Toronto's ravines. It was, however, more urgent than ever that the evictions end, as outbreaks in the shelter system were constant and the risk of infection high. This letter was signed by fifty-eight organizations and culminated in a press conference with representation from executive directors, faith leaders, medical doctors, front-line workers, and people with lived experience. Unfortunately, our demands went unheeded.

On 19 May, Toronto saw the situation with encampments escalate. I was present that day at Lamport Stadium, the site of a small community of tents and Tiny Shelters in Toronto's Liberty Village neighbourhood. The mood was tense, and the situation new. Police, out by the dozens, had been deployed to Lamport Stadium to enforce the removal of encampments. For the first time ever in an encampment eviction, we saw police on horseback and others forming blockades with their bicycles. One officer, later identified on Twitter as wearing a "thin blue line" badge, inexplicably rammed me in the leg with a bike. TDIN's manager, Susan Bender, can be seen being assaulted in media footage. A member of the Bike Brigade, a volunteer group helping TDIN distribute meals to encampments, was forced to go to the ER with a head injury after being pushed by an officer onto the road. Reverend Maggie Helwig, who operates the Safe Space drop-in at the Church of St. Stephen-in-the-Fields, risked her body by sitting down on King Street to create a barrier against horse-mounted police, who legally cannot trample people on the ground. Members of ESN attempted to support Lamport residents during the melee, and ultimately just one side of the stadium's tent community was removed that day. However, I recognize that this was in no way a win; it was, in fact, the beginning of the City's escalated, paramilitary response to encampments.

As a reaction to the events at Lamport Stadium, I authored *COVID-19 Response Update: Protecting People Experiencing Homelessness and Ensuring the Safety of the Shelter System*, which was signed by the Shelter and Housing Justice Network (SHJN) and which addressed elected leaders at all three levels of government.[5] This letter expanded upon my open letter from February/March and incorporated our demands to increase safety in shelters, adopting many of the principles and recommendations outlined in *A National Protocol for Homeless Encampments in Canada*, authored by Leilani Farha, the UN Special Rapporteur on the right to adequate housing, and Kaitlin Schwan of The Shift, an international organization focused on realizing the human right to housing.[6] Another press conference ensued, with another lacklustre response – although the letter was instrumental in influencing Councillor Kristyn Wong-Tam's motion to deploy water trailers to encampments. Our advocacy and that of others, including ESN, did impact other motions, however: Councillors Mike Layton and Josh Matlow both produced motions specific to safety in encampments and shelters. Layton's motion, however, did not succeed in full, and Matlow's motion failed entirely while Etobicoke councillor Stephen Holyday's motion setting a goal of "zero encampments" passed. Although weak as policy, Holyday's motion was overt in its ideology and spoke to the desire of those in power to invisibilize, if not outright eradicate, people living in parks.

It was clear to me at this time that Mayor John Tory had a personal desire to see encampments removed. This was especially evident in the failure of Councillor Matlow's motion, which sought to improve conditions in shelters and establish an advisory committee of shelter residents. I was a key informant on Matlow's motion, which was notable for being the first working relationship between a homeless advocate and City Council since before the pandemic. Mary-Anne Bedard, the former general manager of the City department overseeing homelessness services, was also an informant. By all logic, the motion should have passed, as both activists and senior City staff had come to a consensus on shelter safety. Moreover, if the City was going to continue removing encampments, didn't it have a responsibility to ensure that shelters be made safer and healthier? Evidently not.

On 22 June, Trinity Bellwoods Park was targeted for encampment removal. Despite the display by police at Lamport Stadium in May,

On 22 June 2021, the City used this 721G wheel loader to pick up and remove the Tiny Shelters at Trinity Bellwoods Park once the residents were violently cleared out by police.
Credit: Greg Cook

nothing prepared us for the events at Bellwoods. I was again present, called early to the scene by volunteers with ESN. When I arrived close to 8:00 a.m., police were already present, alongside staff from Parks, Forestry and Recreation, and dozens of private Star Security staff hired by the City. No social workers were on-site. There was, however, a police drone, two helicopters, and a seemingly endless procession of officers. By 9:00 a.m., City staff had erected fences around the two encampments at the north and south ends of the park, caging in encampment residents and their supporters. I immediately called it "kettling lite"; instead of unlawfully trapping people inside cages to be assaulted or arrested ("kettled"), those inside would be deprived of rest and resources to essentially tire and starve them out.[7]

In the afternoon, with supporters inside the caged off area periodically linking arms in defence of encampments, crowds on the outside attempted to dismantle the fences. In the mayhem, pepper spray was deployed, and more people entered the cage. I watched the tensions rise as nearly 100 officers, clad in riot gear, flanked us. I assumed the worst. However, a violent clash was eventually averted, although those actually living in the park were coerced into the shelter system and their encampments removed. This included Jimmy Pudjunas, a former IT professional and a creative and gracious soul who I've known for years. Jimmy didn't want to go into the shelter system, but he felt like he didn't have a choice – and he was not alone in that sentiment. What Jimmy and many others experienced – being cheated of making a free and informed decision about where they felt safest to live – was violence. Full stop.

What Toronto witnessed in Trinity Bellwoods Park in June 2021 was a dark stain on its history. Understanding that this violent approach to encampments needed to stop, I began the process of writing *A Path Forward,* a set of policy recommendations for the City of Toronto that presented an achievable, human rights–compliant roadmap for working with unhoused people.[8] Between a clandestine park meeting with key informants and a flurry of Signal online chats, *A Path Forward* was crafted with input from key homeless advocates and former encampment residents.

The document specifically prioritized the agency of unhoused people to determine the supports that work for them, underscoring that they are currently given no control over how encampments are engaged, or how services are offered in the shelter system. It also asked for members of City Council to reconsider their votes on the failed motions of Councillors Josh Matlow and Mike Layton to promote safety and transparency in shelters and in encampments. Thanks to my network of contacts in social services, *A Path Forward* was signed by sixty-one agencies and organizations – including Sistering and Warden Woods Community Centre, both homeless respite operators – and forty-one community leaders, including former Toronto mayor John Sewell, and former MP and City councillor Olivia Chow. From my networking in the music industry, I also pulled together signatures from an additional ninety-eight

A Path Forward

A Path Forward advocates for the following:

- A human rights–compliant approach towards encampments, including meaningful, ongoing engagement with encampment residents and the deployment of the necessities of life (e.g., running water and fire-safe camping equipment) where they live. This entails the recognition of unhoused people as rights-holders. That is, encampment residents must be presented with full information surrounding housing and shelter space options, and they must be given the time and space to make informed decisions regarding their living situation without the threat or use of force or coercion.
- A safer, more welcoming environment in shelters for residents. This includes creating an advisory committee of current and former shelter residents to have meaningful input into and control over the design of the shelter system. Currently, the shelter system offers no avenues for control over service delivery by the people who use the services. It also entails appropriate harm-reduction supports, services, and spaces specific to Indigenous, Black, and gender-diverse populations, and transparency around the amenities (e.g., where and what they sleep on, how many people are in a room with them, and if non-binary washrooms are available).
- An investment in permanent housing. This means rent-geared-to-income rental housing, individualized mental health and disability supports for those that require them, and the creation of eviction prevention plans and upstream supports like drop-ins.

creative leaders, including musicians Cadence Weapon and Serena Ryder, and renowned sculptor Shary Boyle.

In all, 206 organizations and leaders supported *A Path Forward* and collectively demanded that the City of Toronto stop the forcible removal

of encampments. It was the strongest effort yet to leverage the senti-
ments of the public, who found the situation in Trinity Bellwoods untenable. As well, it served to concretize the expert voice of homeless service
providers who understood that encampment evictions pushed people
further away from the grounding relationships and programs they relied upon to survive. With a social media campaign and an associated
petition, I sought to force Toronto City Council to consider and adopt
A Path Forward as official City policy – a policy I knew would be less
harmful and more successful in reducing the number of encampments
by prioritizing residents' real, expressed needs. What was the mayor's response? Our collective voice was unwelcome. In short, the public – from
sector professionals, to political leaders, to artists, to unhoused people
themselves – was to be given no say over the City's approach to encampments. *A Path Forward* was not even brought to City Council for debate.

On 20 July, people were evicted from Alexandra Park. While I was
outside the modified kettling cage built around the perimeter of the
park, I saw and hugged Sam, a woman I knew from drop-ins who was
being evicted from her tent. Sam merely moved on to Queen Street, and
she is still living there today, effectively abandoned by the City. Beside
the Shoppers Drug Mart at Queen and Ryerson Avenue, I co-hosted with
journalist Desmond Cole a counterdemonstration on behalf of ESN,
where street-involved people, including residents of Alexandra Park,
were given a platform to speak. Many of my street friends spoke and
listened, including Dave Swan, Dave Saban, Matt Le, Dreddz, Robert,
and Brad. While overt violence at the hands of the police and the City
was minimized that day, every person evicted from Alexandra Park experienced the stress and violence of unnecessary displacement.

On the very next day, 21 July, residents were evicted from Lamport
Stadium for the second time. I arrived around 7:00 a.m. to a procession of horse-mounted police. Without detailing the now infamous
events, what we saw in Lamport Stadium represented an egregious
use-of-force by police and the City. I was indirectly pepper sprayed,

and my right wrist was sprained after being pushed to the ground by a police officer. Encampment supporters and unhoused people alike were assaulted en masse, including MPP Rima Berns-McGown, who came into contact with pepper spray. City workers impeded the media in their attempts to document the chaos – a dubious action we also saw in Trinity Bellwoods and Alexandra Park. On-site sector representatives and experts in homelessness services, including FoodShare's executive director Paul Taylor, St. Felix Centre's executive director Brian Harris, and myself, were ignored in our calls for the violent evictions to end. Instead, the violence was grossly escalated, and many were injured and traumatized that day, especially the residents of Lamport, none of whom were housed. Of course, this was the case in every encampment eviction: nobody received housing from the City, and the majority of people did not end up staying in the shelter system. To be absolutely clear: the evictions did nothing to address homelessness, they only traumatized people and made homelessness less visible.

Immediately following the events at Alexandra Park and Lamport Stadium, I crafted a statement decrying the evictions, which I include here:

To say the least, the events of this week have been devastating.

On Tuesday, we saw the residents of Alexandra Park forcibly removed from their encampments, and a community of people providing mutual support to one another and attempting to survive razed. While Mayor John Tory has touted the removal of Alexandra Park's encampments as a success,[9] we must understand that the outcome of the City's approach was unsuccessful, and moreover harmful. Indeed, no one was housed, 15 people were displaced to other locations outdoors, and the Park has since been made inaccessible to the general public – not just to former residents.

Less than 24 hours after Alexandra Park's removal, we saw unprecedented violence enacted by the City through the grossly disproportionate police use-of-force deployed against peaceful civilians. This includes un-housed people and people living with disability who were both physically and emotionally harmed during the incident. While the events in Alexandra Park were shameful and deeply damaging to unhoused people, what we witnessed at Lamport Stadium goes even further and constitutes a lasting stain on the City of Toronto. That all City councillors and the Mayor himself have not denounced this violence is a shameful abandonment of the public. It is also tacit support for the approach that we saw, including throttling and pepper spraying civilians, as well as beating subdued individuals with batons. This is not a City that can purport to be compassionate and inclusive when law enforcement, deployed by the hundreds, beats its residents unprovoked. Most important to remember is that the result of this horrific exercise resulted once again in no one being housed. Beyond egregious, the approach of the City is also ineffectual. It must end immediately, and a public inquiry must be initiated regarding the events at Lamport, including police use-of-force. Furthermore, police must not be deployed to encampments, and encampments must be allowed to remain with adequate supports until residents freely accept suitable indoor spaces and housing options.

Beyond the unconscionable and indefensible violence perpetrated at Lamport Stadium, the attempted removal of the media – including issuing trespass warnings to journalists on the scene and preventing access to Alexandra Park – is deeply unconstitutional, and extremely telling. Without their eyes and cameras documenting the situation at Lamport, would the violence have been further escalated? If the City's strategy for removing encampments is compassionate and "human services" oriented, why would the media be disallowed from documenting it? It is a deeply important question, and we denounce attempts by the Mayor and the City to prevent journalists from performing their duty, which is essential to a free, functioning democratic society.[10]

What is most important to realize about the events this week is that none of it was necessary – ever, but also since we at the Toronto

Drop-In Network, alongside 207 other signatories, presented a letter we co-authored to Mayor Tory, *A Path Forward*. Informed by experts in homelessness service delivery, as well as unhoused people, this letter is a roadmap for the Mayor and the City, which not only espouses a more compassionate, human rights–compliant approach to supporting unhoused people, but an effectual means to reduce the number of people living outdoors.

Councillors Matlow, Layton, Perks, Carroll, and Wong-Tam have openly supported this letter, and have called upon the Mayor to adopt it as City policy. We agree, as do an additional 2,400 members of the public who have signed on to a petition.

Violence does not end homelessness. A human rights–compliant approach can. Mayor Tory: adopt *A Path Forward*, and end the violent approach to encampments – now.

While the media was in contact with me to discuss *A Path Forward* and how it could have prevented the evictions of Alexandra Park and Lamport Stadium from happening, the City itself remained reticent to engage. I co-authored an op-ed in the *Toronto Star* with Dr. Naheed Dosani, which reiterated the need for *A Path Forward*, and which gained some political traction.[11] Indeed, five City councillors – Josh Matlow, Mike Layton, Kristyn Wong-Tam, Gord Perks, and Shelley Carroll – aghast at the violence seen at Lamport Stadium, called on the mayor to adopt *A Path Forward* as City policy. The mayor, in his obstinacy, refused to consider our demands or decry the excessive violence wrought by the City against unhoused people and their supporters. *A Path Forward* remained unrealized.

Yet something did change as a result of the events at Lamport Stadium. Residents of Moss Park, who had already been issued "No Trespass" notices, never faced their "eviction day" and remain in the park at the time of writing. A moratorium on large-scale encampment removals seems to have ensued, although this has done little to quell the collective unease of the unhoused, or the dogged pursuit of encampment supporters by members of Toronto Police Service 14 Division.

From the side of councillors, with whom I had established a working relationship, and government watchdogs, a call for public inquiries into the actions of the City and Toronto Police Service was put forward. Ombudsman Toronto was the first to oblige, announcing it would investigate the City's clearing of encampments.[12] Councillor Wong-Tam also filed an administrative inquiry requesting information on the cost of, and logic behind, the militarized encampment evictions of Trinity Bellwoods, Alexandra Park, and Lamport Stadium.[13] The total expenditure of public dollars? $1.3 million to carry out all three evictions, plus an additional $792,668 to "remediate" the park grass post-eviction.[14] The logic? Inscrutable. Councillors Josh Matlow and Mike Layton put forward a motion requesting a judicial inquiry – necessary for holding police accountable for their use-of-force in encampment evictions, but which the Ombudsman cannot investigate due to its mandate. Unsurprisingly, given their record of voting against actions such as defunding the police, City Council did not pass this motion, and as it stands, the Toronto Police Service will not be held accountable for its actions that injured dozens of Torontonians – myself included.

August 2021 passed, and Moss Park remained untouched. While smaller encampment sites on Beaty Avenue and in the Parkdale Amphitheatre were removed, growing encampment communities at Dufferin Grove, Randy Padmore Park, and Bellevue Square Park were undisturbed. These sites housed some of the former residents of Trinity Bellwoods, Alexandra Park, and Lamport Stadium, and they were certainly visible enough to make them targets. But the City did not serve "No Trespass" notices to residents en masse; instead, they seemed to be leaving people mostly alone. Dreddz, a contributor to this volume, was an exception, having been served a flagrant "No Trespass" notice barring him from any City-owned property. As September advanced, outreach volunteers from ESN began to see a shift in the City's approach to Dufferin Grove Park. Streets to Homes, the City's homeless outreach service, was working one-on-one with residents and giving people time to make free, informed decisions about accessing housing and shelter space. Indeed, people were being expedited into housing, and not being coerced into shelters – the first time since the start of the pandemic that such an approach had been used in an encampment.

This approach, deemed a "pilot" program and extended to Kensington's Bellevue Square Park with the support of Councillor Mike Layton, appeared to derive significant influence from the recommendations of *A Path Forward*, as well as from the work of groups like The Shift. Nevertheless, it was wildly imperfect. For instance, why was the approach limited to just two parks? And why was it not made available to new people inflowing into the parks hoping for housing? Still, it showed promise, and a tacit understanding that the City's former militarized and extremely violent method did not work. But Streets to Homes needed further guidance from TDIN, as well as from other service providers and advocates, and from unhoused people themselves. Sadly, like many others, I am still waiting on this call for consultation. And I am waiting for the establishment of a truly human rights–compliant, city-wide policy for supporting people living outdoors – one that recognizes the full humanity and dignity of unhoused people, and one that helps expedite them into what they really need: affordable, appropriate, accessible, safe, healthy, and sustainable housing.

Until then, drop-ins will continue to step up and push back, although – and I cannot stress this enough – we never should have had to.

A 2016 portrait of the author created by Jimmy Pudjunas, a former resident of the encampment in Trinity Bellwoods Park.
Credit: Jimmy Pudjunas

DIANA CHAN MCNALLY (she/they) is a community worker employed by the Toronto Drop-In Network, where she oversees advocacy initiatives and learning opportunities for fifty-six organizations across the City of Toronto supporting unhoused people. As someone with lived experience of social services and being unhoused, Diana's work focuses on human rights and equity issues for people who are experiencing homelessness, and she is particularly invested in rights protections for residents of encampments.

CHAPTER 7

Surviving COVID-19 in the Shelter System

Brian Cleary

I had been homeless for almost two years when the first news of the pandemic began to spread. I have struggled with mental illness all my life, but I had a full-time job and was slowly recovering from a difficult divorce. In 2018, I lost my job and apartment. After two years in the shelter system, I'd had several suicide attempts, been formed[1] several times, and been beat up and sedated by hospital security once. I'd been charged with mischief for cutting camera and communications wiring at my first congregate shelter and had been wrung through the court system after a year of hearings and delays to have the charges dropped. The stress of the shelter system was a burden and more trauma at a time when I desperately needed to heal. It changed me as a person long before the pandemic hit.

I had spent the last six months staying at the twenty-four-hour respite site run by St. Felix Centre,[2] which was designated as an emergency shelter space when it opened, but quickly became a long-term shelter

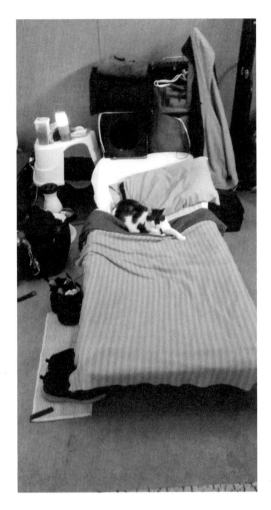

Brian's cot at the St. Felix
Centre respite site.
Credit: Brian Cleary

with most residents staying for months or even years. One hundred souls packed into a tent in a parking lot on cots 18 inches apart. Aside from the washrooms at one end, the entire structure is open, and only rolling office walls separate the dorms from the kitchens and storage and dining areas that make up the rest of the vast open space under the tent. We were watched day and night by staff, security, and cameras. The lights only ever dimmed, and the noise never stopped.

My tiny cot area contained all my belongings in two bags, my cat, his litter and sleeping box, and a CPAP machine.

I had yet to meet with a housing worker since becoming homeless, my medications were barely controlling my mental illness, and I was drinking and smoking pot regularly to numb the chaos and boredom of this hopeless existence. Shortly after Christmas, a friend died in the dorms, surrounded by residents, staff, and security who failed to notice her passing. Police, ambulance, fire … the whole circus came, her body was hauled away, the area around her cot taped off, detectives and staff consulted, and then the circus moved on and someone else was in my friend's cot eight hours later. The staff promised to hold a memorial, only to use her dead name and image on the posters announcing it. This was my life in January 2020.

I had always been an avid news reader and followed the beginnings of the pandemic with a combination of worry and curiosity, like most, but was soon dreading what a virulent airborne disease might do in the environment I was in. The HVAC system was designed to circulate and recycle the air and featured one giant fan hung in the middle of the structure that was already attracting and shedding clumps of dust and was nearly impossible to clean. Dorm cleaning consisted of daily mopping, but many residents failed to properly clean their cot area, and cleaners would skip the worst offenders. Cots were supposed to be sprayed daily with a hydrogen peroxide solution, but many residents refused to have their belongings and area sprayed. Spills involving animal and human waste, including blood and feces, were common and mopped up indifferently and infrequently. There was no health team on-site. I was not willing to accept the risk of staying in that environment and began to actively seek another less crowded shelter to stay in. Because of my cat and my CPAP machine, there were few other spots in the shelter system available to me. Had I not been burdened by the need to care for my cat and the need for electricity for the CPAP,

Homes First shelter on St. Clair Avenue East, aka "The Swamp."
Credit: Brian Cleary

I think I would have chosen to live outdoors at that point out of sheer desperation.

In early February 2020, I found an available spot at a newly opened, City-run men's shelter, Junction Place. It was a recently renovated Goodwill store that had been converted into a series of dormitory-style rooms with four or five beds per room, common bathrooms, a common dining area, as well as a kitchen and offices for staff. Much design planning and consultation had gone into opening this shelter, and it was intended to offer many programs and services to integrate residents into the community. I had a housing worker for the first time since being homeless. The shelter and dorms were cleaned regularly and properly. I had a sense of hope for a short time. Unfortunately, this shelter was part of the George Street revitalization project, and most of the staff and clients were directly moved from Seaton House to this new location. No one had considered that poor staff attitudes and performance might have been part of the problem with Seaton House, and the new location quickly became another Seaton House–style nightmare, with staff supervisors running the shelter based on arbitrary rules that had no basis in reality.[3]

As February turned into March, the only response to the growing pandemic was to cancel all programs and services as the rest of the country slowly went into lockdown. The residents' committee, our only form of feedback and communication with staff, was the first thing to go. Coffee and juice machines were taken away. Food was served from behind barriers and all staff began wearing face masks. No changes were made to our living or dining arrangements, and the City would not institute a mask mandate for clients in shelters until late September 2020. When a resident meeting was finally held to explain these changes a month after they were implemented, we were told everything was fine, but we would now be subject to daily temperature checks. For these, they lined us up in a hallway 3 feet apart, without masks. We lined up for every meal as well, sitting four people to a table instead of six. We were told that only two people could sit at once at the only picnic table outside. All these rules seemed as arbitrary and pointless as everything else in the system. Rumours had begun to spread that the Shelter Support and Housing Administration (SSHA) had opened shelter-hotels, yet when I asked management at Junction Place about this, I was told that such accommodations didn't exist and that management knew nothing about them.

In April of 2020, my temperature was elevated for three days in a row. Staff simply noted these readings and suggested nothing, even though I reported other symptoms. After questioning staff and hearing that they would take no further action, I called Telehealth Ontario and explained my situation. Telehealth told me to go to the nearest ER and get tested. I relayed this information to the shelter staff, who told me that they would not provide me with a mask or transportation to the hospital, and that I was responsible for these things. I went maskless on the TTC to the nearest ER, where they quickly tested me and then were left with the quandary of returning me to a congregate space without knowing the results of the test. After deciding they had no other option, they discharged me back to the shelter where isolation would be impossible. Thankfully, my test results eventually came back negative.

I complained loudly and often to staff about policy irregularities, and in June 2020, I was kicked out for these complaints. Since this was in itself against shelter regulations, it took them three days to discharge me, and during that time I was able to speak directly to several senior staff at SSHA, who agreed with my critical assessment of the situation. I was asked what I wanted. I told them I wanted a shelter-hotel. Within twenty-four hours, I found myself at the Comfort Inn Airport North shelter-hotel in Etobicoke. I would spend the next eight months there until I was finally housed in rent-geared-to-income (RGI) housing through the City's Rapid Rehousing Initiative[4] in March 2021. Ironically, shelter

Brian's room at the Comfort Inn Airport North near Toronto Pearson Airport.
Credit: Brian Cleary

residents became eligible for the first dose of the COVID-19 vaccine the week after I moved into my new housing.

I lived my life with a bit more relief in the spring of 2021 and enjoyed my new apartment. However, in late April, I woke up one Sunday feeling achy, exhausted, and with absolutely no sense of smell. Thankfully, a testing clinic was available the next day in the lobby of my building, but it confirmed what I feared: I had tested positive for COVID-19. I spent a miserable week in self-isolation feeling completely exhausted until I recovered. At this point, I had been visiting often with my old friends from the shelter system who were staying at the Trinity Bellwoods and Lamport Stadium encampment sites, riding the TTC there and back, and living in a large apartment building with over 2,000 residents. I'll never be sure where I picked up the virus, but I suspect the TTC. My visits to the encampments were mostly spent outside, unmasked but physically distant from my friends. I never feared the virus in the encampments and always viewed them and the residents there as low risk.

My second dose of the vaccine (both Moderna) came from the Anishnawbe Health Toronto mobile unit when I was visiting my friends at Trinity Bellwoods in May of 2021. It was a wonderful sunny day, and I finally felt safe and secure. That September, I turned fifty.

I don't know what to think of my experiences being homeless. I certainly don't know what to think about the COVID-19 outbreaks that raged through congregate shelters after I left them. I'm still processing the trauma of being with my friends as police in riot gear brutally pushed and beat them out of three parks where they were living peacefully. I live my life surrounded by other unhoused folks who, like me, are still living with trauma every day, and the strange and wonderful assortment of folks who try to support and advocate for us. I'm still numb. I still drink and smoke a lot of pot to cope. My mental illness is better medicated now. My cat lives and is happy. I have a nine-year-old son who gives me hope and purpose. This is my little lonely existence. It's better than it was.

Brian Cleary.
Credit: Brian Cleary

BRIAN CLEARY lives alone with a large cat in downtown Toronto. He is currently recovering from his time spent in the shelter system and seeking meaning and purpose in his life through homeless activism. It's been a rough year.

 **CHAPTER 8**

Social Murder: We Need More Than Band-Aids

Roxie Danielson

Hope in Hopeless Times (1)

in a city where only the rich can thrive
as people made to feel hopeless
endlessly pushed just to survive
so we aren't
able to fight the greed and power
because people rose to be
among those hoarding all the money
fighting to take down the rest of society
continuously demanding more prosperity
now we are left
believing we are worthless but still
they're ripping us apart

through social murder
the rich have blood on their hands
because money doesn't care
never again will greed matter
about the lives of you and me
for all the people who've died on the streets

Roxie Danielson

On Friday, 24 January 2020, the City of Toronto held one of its first press conferences to give an update on the pandemic that was only then beginning to circulate throughout the world. The chair of the Toronto Board of Health and the chief medical officer of health were both present. Toronto was told that its leaders were well prepared because they had learned from the 2003 SARS outbreak and that the City had many resources and experts ready. More importantly, the people of Toronto were reassured that there were no COVID-19 cases in Canada. The next day, the Government of Canada confirmed its first case at Toronto's Sunnybrook Health Sciences Centre. Street nurses knew exactly what this meant: the inevitable devastation for people living in shelters was coming.

Almost two weeks earlier, a rally at Toronto City Hall was held by the advocacy group Shelter and Housing Justice Network (SHJN) to mark the shameful addition of the one-thousandth name of a person who died homeless to the Toronto Homeless Memorial. SHJN demanded that there be 2,000 shelter beds added to the shelter system since we knew that many people were being turned away from the overcrowded system. At this point, advocates had been pleading for years for homelessness to be declared an emergency in Toronto as we watched the number of homeless deaths continue to mount from lack of adequate government support. This rally saw supporters leaving 1,000 small paper cutouts of bodies outlined in chalk to show the City of Toronto just what their policies were doing to the homeless community. I gave a speech at that rally, part of which I reproduce here:

> I have worked as a street nurse in downtown Toronto for almost six years, and since that time I have known many people who have died as a direct result of homelessness. I never imagined that as a nurse I would be dealing with this level of death, nothing prepared me for this. Living without a home kills. Poverty kills. We need homelessness declared an emergency because what is happening in our community is unacceptable. It really is social murder.[1] 1,000 names are officially on the [Toronto] Homeless Memorial and we know so many more will soon be added if we don't act.

This was only one of many warning calls we gave. The situation was bad before the pandemic and it was going to get much worse.

By 17 March 2020, Ontario had declared a state of emergency as community transmission of COVID-19 continued to rise and people began to die. Services and businesses were beginning to close, and people who were homeless had nowhere to go, making it clear how much people relied on twenty-four-hour fast food and coffee shops for shelter and washrooms. Services homeless people depended on for their survival, such as drop-ins, harm-reduction services, shelter beds, and even some health services, had started to scale back. Many community clinics rolled back their services as they tried to do as much work as possible by phone to protect both staff and patients. Workers started to get exposed to the virus and had to isolate for two weeks at a time, and increased workloads and fewer staff resulted in reduced access to care for people who relied on these health services. Within many organizations, workers with the most precarity and lowest pay, such as front-line workers and harm-reduction workers, struggled to provide services with decreased capacity and resources. As well, many street

Some of the 1,000 paper cutouts placed on the carpet outside Mayor John Tory's office on 14 January 2020.
Credit: Roxie Danielson

nurses were told that they could not work at multiple locations or do outreach beyond their base clinic location, leaving many of their clients feeling abandoned. Often people would call for an appointment but would only be offered a phone appointment a few weeks later with no help until then. At one point, people were even camped right across the street from health centres they had been going to with no idea how to access them.

It was obvious to those of us on the ground that health care needed to become nimble and responsive to people without homes. People who needed health care the most faced the greatest challenges in accessing that care. We needed to provide more outreach outside of

Roxie Danielson speaking on 14 January 2020 at the protest outside the office of Mayor John Tory.
Credit: Paul Salvatori

clinics to see people where they were living. That included support for people staying outside to get to their medical appointments safely, especially to specialist appointments or to surgeries where accompaniment and transportation were needed. It was also critical during an airborne pandemic that people had the option to be seen outside in well-ventilated areas rather than in small clinic spaces with poor air circulation.

There was, however, a shocking lack of accountability from all three levels of government to provide safe shelter, housing, and services for people experiencing homelessness during the pandemic. Many well-established and well-funded organizations with a mandate to provide care to unhoused people were not able to meet the needs of the community. Early on, many people lost contact with their primary care providers as barriers to connecting with health and social services piled on, and especially as more people began to live outdoors in response to information about how COVID-19 spreads and their realization that congregate settings were not safe places to be. Inevitably, we saw a proliferation of encampments across the city. Street nurses and other outreach workers went to encampments to support people living there while also trying to source sleeping bags and tents from community partners on social media, something nursing school never taught us. At one point, we were appealing for supplies on Twitter and people were offering to pay for taxis to deliver tents and sleeping bags where they were needed most. However, because of the dramatic rise in people sleeping outdoors and organizations being unable to meet the needs of the community, street nurses were contacted to address the health concerns of people living in encampments and would outreach on their own time.

Despite there being so few of us, the Street Nurses Network began a phone line for people to call to dispatch a volunteer nurse to see someone in the community. Nurses signed up to be on call and gave their phone numbers to outreach workers and encampment residents. We saw wounds and dog bites and were asked questions about how to best take care of infections while staying in a park with limited supplies. The phone line quickly became defunct, however, as many of our workplaces did not allow nurses to work in multiple locations out of fear of spreading COVID-19. There was a major gap in care for people sleeping outdoors, and more mobile health care was desperately needed – not to mention safe and affordable housing options to avoid this need in the first place.

Providing nursing outreach means a nurse works more autonomously and makes critical decisions on the spot. For example, sending someone to hospital is usually a last resort. Hospitals have never been

Street Nurses

Street nurses have the flexibility to work in shelters, in encampments, on sidewalks, under bridges, in ravines, and potentially in the bathroom of a Loblaws to meet clients wherever they happen to be. Many of the people we see have little or no money for transportation, are not able to leave their belongings unattended to go to medical appointments, or have a physical or cognitive impairment that prevents them from travelling alone. This makes it especially important that we be mobile in our care. Street nurses are accustomed to having limited medical supplies on hand, with no physician or nurse practitioner nearby.

It is important, however, for health care workers to recognize the structural violence that is inherent in medical systems, which are rooted in anti-Black and anti-Indigenous racism, and to appreciate that people experiencing homelessness often face discrimination when encountering the health care system. Therefore, street nurses should outreach with someone who has a meaningful connection to the community, never force or impose nursing care on people living outside, and accept that many people may not want to receive their care. Knowing that the relationship between health care professionals and patients is inherently not an equal one, outreach should be done by slowly building organic and mutually supportive relationships with the community, and it should be grounded in partnerships with people with lived experience, mutual aid, or peer support.

that welcoming towards people who are homeless and became even less so as restrictions around accompaniment, visitors, and smoke breaks were enforced more harshly during the pandemic. A long-time client of mine required routine hospital follow-up three times a week but could only go with accompaniment. Due to the restrictions, he was forced to go alone at a time that did not work for him and was denied necessary accommodations despite advocacy from his health care team. He died shortly after not being able to make it to his appointments. His death was just one of many that resulted from the pandemic's impact on an already inequitable health care system. Another life tragically cut short.

Many of our clients were admitted to hospital during the pandemic but then prematurely discharged to the streets because their hospital bed was needed for someone else and there was not enough time or staff to arrange for proper housing or shelter accommodations after discharge. Even pre-pandemic, many of our clients have talked about the judgemental care and unfair treatment they experienced from hospital staff. We often heard of homeless people accessing the emergency department of a hospital for a physical issue only to be accused of drug seeking or to be told to cut down on their substance use instead. There have also been many reports of people experiencing homelessness being targeted by security and thrown off hospital property without any instigation. During the pandemic, hospitals were one less resource homeless people could rely on when there was already a mountain of pre-existing systemic obstacles they had to face. This made the role of street nurses all the more important in ensuring people in the community received care where and when they needed it the most.

Throughout the pandemic, we provided wound care, access to medications and injections, and health information about the COVID-19 virus, always with our masks and hand sanitizer in tow. We provided the latest COVID-19 news and information on how people could protect themselves and friends, what to do if they felt sick, and where to go to get tested. Street nurses also tried to bring people much needed supplies such as socks, snacks, harm-reduction kits (including needles, pipes, alcohol swabs, tourniquets, cookers, vitamin C, and condoms), warm weather gear in the winter, and cool water in the summer. Although people living outdoors were exposed to the elements and at risk to weather-related injuries, it was our experience that the people we saw outside were better protected from COVID-19 than those who were living in shelters. In the shelters that we visited, the infection prevention and controls that were put in place were often inadequate. We saw broken thermometers for temperature checks, lack of personal protective equipment (PPE) for staff and residents, and even some shelter workers who admitted they did not feel adequately trained to be a COVID-19 screener. At one shelter, the screening staff said that they had tried to speak to their management about some of the issues they were facing, but nothing changed. The staff had reached a point where they felt there was no benefit in speaking up, and some were afraid of being reprimanded. The result was limited space for people to safely isolate and protect themselves from the pandemic.

Here was the absurd paradox: To prevent the spread of COVID-19, we were all told to stay home, wear a mask, practise proper hand hygiene, and stay at least 6 feet (2 metres) apart from other people outside of our households. But what if you did not have a home? What if your household included hundreds of other people, such as the case when living in a congregate setting? What happens if you didn't have access to masks? To hand sanitizer? The messaging coming from our government leaders simply did not address the realities of what homeless people had to face.

By the end of March 2020, the City had started leasing empty hotels to create shelter-hotels, where many people experiencing homelessness were moved for the purpose of creating safe distancing within the remaining shelters, and to provide shelter-hotel residents private rooms and bathrooms to minimize the risk of contracting COVID-19. Many of us were excited at the thought of our clients living in these hotels where they would have their own rooms with doors that locked, real beds, hot showers, and functioning TVs they could watch freely: the very basics of a safe and dignified space. However, this excitement soon turned to frustration. The shelter-hotels were run like regular shelters with bed checks and unnecessary rules, such as not allowing couples to room together and not allowing guests to visit. Moreover, when front-line workers tried to get people into the shelter-hotels, it was nearly impossible. In fact, most times when we called for a shelter-hotel bed, we were told there were no beds available and to call back in an hour. And not only was it difficult for people to get into the shelter-hotels, but the people in the remaining congregate shelters were still reporting that there was no safe physical distancing or barriers between the beds, and that many people around them often sounded sick. Shelters quickly started experiencing outbreaks, and people were being brought to a "Recovery Hotel," a hotel repurposed as a medical facility where people without homes would stay for the duration of their isolation period.

The Recovery Hotel itself was far away from people's resources, and while staff did their best to provide harm-reduction services for the people staying there, it was no match for the toxic drug crisis that was worsening across the country. Pre-pandemic, Toronto was already seeing a continuous rise in overdose deaths, which only worsened once the pandemic hit. In particular, there was a dramatic rise in overdose deaths among shelter residents, which contributed to the increased number of deaths of homeless people in Toronto. Disturbingly, the City later designated one of the shelter-hotels for certain encampment residents only and kept beds empty and inaccessible to other people who were homeless, despite knowing those beds were desperately needed as more unhoused people than ever were dying in the city.

As the pandemic wore on, it became clear that safety within shelters was becoming an afterthought, and not because of a lack of resources but because of a lack of prioritization. Many advocates and front-line workers began speaking out to improve shelter conditions as COVID-19 cases within congregate settings began to rise. We knew from past outbreaks just how easily diseases spread within the shelter system and that people experiencing homelessness were especially vulnerable given that many live with comorbidities (i.e., one or more health conditions). Initial testing for COVID-19 was also clumsy and did not benefit people who were homeless. Testing involved waiting for hours in a long line only for people to be shuttled to an off-site location to await test results or, in some cases, back to the shelter where they came from. Test results took days to return, so people could easily spread the virus without knowing if they had it.

There was also no sentinel surveillance (i.e., monitoring of a disease within a population to understand its rate of occurrence) within the shelters and no accessible on-site shelter testing, so timely testing if someone was showing symptoms was not always happening. The Street Nurses Network wrote a letter to the City in April 2020 that read, in part, as follows: "Public Health measures to stop the spread of COVID-19 need to ensure the safety of all people, especially for those who are homeless. Without sentinel surveillance with physical distancing for shelter users, widespread outbreak and death is inevitable. We are demanding a prioritization of testing for people experiencing homelessness with accessible on-site testing at shelters and respites for everyone who needs it." Around this same time, Willowdale Welcome Centre, a shelter for refugees in North York, started to show signs of a COVID-19 outbreak. Roughly two weeks later, provincial guidelines changed to allow mass testing at homeless shelters. While this appeared to be a step in the right direction, too much time had already passed since the first positive COVID-19 case at Willowdale, resulting in a massive outbreak and over 180 people eventually testing positive for COVID-19.[2] The warnings that advocates had been sounding were largely ignored, and much-needed changes were happening too slow. On 8 May, our worst fears came true: the first homeless person in Toronto died in hospital from COVID-19.

By the summer of 2020, Ontario was starting to reopen parts of the province, ignoring the advice of public health experts. More people than ever were living in encampments as word was they were safer than shelters, with respect to COVID-19, and no real affordable housing options were available. There was no mask mandate for shelter users to wear masks indoors, unlike the mandatory mask policies in virtually every other public place, and there was little to no additional support for shelter staff to ensure that all shelter residents had masks available, a common concern that was brought forward by many of our clients. Clinics were seeing many people testing positive for COVID-19, and much of our work shifted to checking in with sick patients while doubling down on screening and cleaning procedures. One of my clients who tested positive for the virus said that he was constantly seeing people without masks at his shelter and often heard people coughing around him. He knew getting sick was inevitable. Once he recovered from COVID-19, he left the shelter system to protect himself from contracting the virus again.

Given how bad the rollout was for the protection of shelter residents and workers alike, advocates predicted that eventual vaccine access for the homelessness sector would be equally poor. When the first vaccine was finally announced, there was no mention of homeless people being part of the initial vaccine rollout and another battle was fought. The Street Nurses Network wrote to the Toronto Board of Health in April 2021:

Public health measures to stop the spread of COVID-19 include having your own space to physically distance, wearing proper PPE including N95 masks, practising infection control and getting the COVID-19 vaccine when available. Since the start of the pandemic, folks who are homeless were not given adequate support to enforce these critical public health measures, despite many front-line workers and homeless people speaking out. There has been difficult access to safe shelter beds, limited access to masks and now a slow vaccine rollout. With over 300 COVID-19 cases within the shelter system, things have gotten out of control.

By the end of the month, there were nearly 400 active COVID-19 cases within the shelter system. Five months after that, only 47 per cent of shelter residents had two doses of the vaccine compared to 78 per

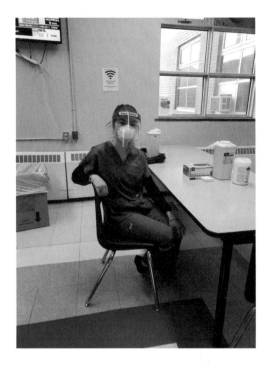

Roxie Danielson in a shelter
preparing to vaccinate
shelter residents.
Credit: Jo Connelly

cent of the general population of eligible Ontarians. It was clear that we could not rely on government support and that politicians were not listening to us.

By the summer of 2021, things went from bad to worse for encampment residents. The City was actively trying to push encampment residents out of parks that were visible to rich neighbourhoods while claiming that the City cared about the well-being of people who were homeless. One client I was working with was living in a tent tucked away in an alley and needed help moving indoors into a shelter-hotel. When we called Streets to Homes, a City service designed to help move people off the streets, we were told that it would be weeks before someone could come to see him because they were busy trying to move encampment residents inside instead. This man eventually found his own housing months later with no help from the City.

While the City of Toronto's communications team was working hard to convince the public that it was helping, the City began a violent attack on encampment residents with the help of the Toronto Police Service and private security in an effort to clear encampments. Eventually, the clashes became so intense that street nurses and other medics were called in to provide aid and tend to the injuries of the encampments' residents and supporters. I posted the following on social media after witnessing the forced removal of encampment residents at Trinity Bellwoods Park on 22 June:

> I watched as people's homes were being destroyed and their community being ripped apart with nowhere to go. I watched as my friends and allies were being pushed and sexually harassed by the cops and threatened with a fine of up to $10,000 for defending the site. There was such a pain and heaviness in my chest that I just broke down in tears. It was so sickening to watch. When I arrived, mounted police were moving through the crowd on their horses and people were being shoved and pepper sprayed while encampment residents and supporters were already caged in. There were also drones flying above and police and security lining the entire perimeter. All of this to "safely" move 25 residents into housing that doesn't exist.[3]

Encampment residents were forced out of the parks with the unkept promise of housing. The City did not care. The homelessness and housing crisis remained critical. People were dying like never before.

Which brings us to today. Many street nurses had already been hardened to the fact that the government was not listening to us, but the pandemic brought activists and advocacy groups together to work to get what was needed for the community. We knew from the first official announcement about COVID-19 back in January 2020 that the

Die-in at a rally at Toronto
City Hall, 14 January 2020.
Credit: Cathy Crowe

pandemic was going to hit the homeless community hard, and that pre-
diction unfortunately has come true. Despite becoming burned out and
demoralized at times, street nurses have continued to work on the front
lines throughout the pandemic, and we have no intention of leaving our
community to stand alone.[4] We will not stop advocating for those experiencing homelessness. We will not back down.

Hope in Hopeless Times (2)

for all the people who've died on the streets
about the lives of you and me
never again will greed matter
because money doesn't care
the rich have blood on their hands
through social murder
they're ripping us apart
believing we are worthless but still
now we are left
continuously demanding more prosperity
fighting to take down the rest of society
among those hoarding all the money
because people rose to be
able to fight the greed and power
so we aren't
endlessly pushed just to survive
as people made to feel hopeless
in a city where only the rich can thrive

Roxie Danielson

ROXIE DANIELSON has been a street nurse in downtown Toronto since 2014 and has worked on the front lines since the beginning of the pandemic. Roxie supports people experiencing homelessness by not only providing hands-on clinical care but by also actively advocating on issues of homelessness, poverty, and harm reduction. In addition to providing care in clinic and out in the community, Roxie enjoys working with students and hopes to inspire other nurses to become street nurses and activists as well.

CHAPTER 9

Slipped through the Fingertips of the System

Dreddz and Greg Cook

Greg: What would you like people reading this book to know about you?

Dreddz: That I am one of them. That I'm one of the grains of sand that slipped through the fingertips of the system. Someone who upholds good values against outrageous odds.

Greg: Did you grow up in Toronto?

Dreddz: I grew up in Jamaica and Toronto.

Greg: Can you tell me what it's like staying in Padmore Park versus when you stayed at Alexandra Park?[1]

Dreddz: Padmore is a small space with a lot of people. You can fit like thirty tents. Alexandra Park was like Skydome, right? You have the space to stretch out, be yourself, not have so much clutter near you. We had more space to be ourselves, and we had our tiny homes. The Tiny Shelters that Khaleel [Seivwright] built.[2]

Greg: For people who have never slept outside, what are the pros and cons for a Tiny Shelter versus a tent?

Dreddz: Well, it's tiny so you gotta be ready to go to bed once you are going in there. So that's definitely a con. But it's a box, you're outdoors. As long as you know where there is a bathroom that's close by. You can lock your door, [but] Tiny Shelter owners usually have a way you can get in if you forget your key or something. You gotta devise how you might adapt your Tiny Shelter for your specific needs. Some people customize their tiny house by cutting an emergency exit in the floor, and others took out the insulation so they weren't as hot in the summer.

Greg: Did you find they were warmer than a regular tent? Or not really?

Dreddz: They were warmer. They had a smoke detector, they were insulated, that kind of stuff. It was easier to keep the food away from the rodents, the rats and the skunks. We had seasonal changes. You could hold stuff like extra lawn chairs when people decided to visit, we had tables, we had extra food and we could serve people.

Greg: So they allowed you to be more hospitable, make it more like a home. Sort of?

Dreddz: That's it. It was easier to make it like a home. Make it like a home feel.

Greg: What ways did COVID-19 change your experience of being outside?

Dreddz: It made it harder to do certain things, but easier to do others. If you are someone that's displaced, COVID-19 changed everything. It became more of a control thing. Where we could go and couldn't go. Like the library, which was always a public domain, a place we could go and get warm or use the computer. The drop-ins were cut out. There are less places to go shower. The Out of the Cold programs, they're gone. So instead of getting a church floor to sleep on, this is what made people have to go to the park. There was nowhere else to go.

Greg: Can you tell me a little about when they went in with all the cops to clear Alexandra Park? What was that day like for you?

Dreddz: I was up at like six in the morning. There was just a march of police going by us. I was at the north end of the park. They went on by, so we just thought something was happening in the park. Then we noticed they were surrounding sections of the park. We were noticing they were making sure to have enough officers to cluster off each set of areas. Then they told us we had about an hour to pack up all our stuff. Then while we did that, they started looking up people's names in the Canadian Police Information Centre [CPIC] database. To see who had warrants. Then coming back in for people. If they were just there for clearing us out, the warrants and stuff shouldn't matter. They arrested one of the volunteers that was helping us. They had come to give us food supplies and stuff. The police ended up releasing them and giving them a trespassing ticket. My neighbour got arrested. The police said that we were lying about the conditions of the shelter-hotels and that we chose not to accept the help offered to us. Versus the truth, which is we had been asking about the safety of the shelter-hotel program since it had been offered to us.

The city workers nor politicians had any answers, they just kept coercing us to go into these institutions. We had friends coming to the parks saying how unsafe the shelter-hotels were. We saw documentation, pictures of documentation, that showed that the shelter-hotels aren't safe, that people are dying, and we are trying to find out why we should be accepting these spaces instead of tents. You go from having whatever you think you can keep in a tent to only having two bags in a hotel, and then getting babysat or checked on three times a day. There have been incidents of staff harassment, client harassment, theft, there has been assault, I can go down the list. On top of that, there are the overdose type deaths, fires, and other situations. A solution would be to offer a counsellor where people live and helping them on a caseworker-like basis and find out what the gaps are that are keeping each person here.

Greg: What I am hearing is that the City workers aren't sitting down at different encampments with people and checking in on what it is that is going to work for them, and making a plan that is going to get them to where they want to be.

Dreddz: They're not. What they are doing is coming around taking pictures. We are asking why. They are lying to say it's to figure out what services are needed, and they are taking pictures of how many tents and people. They come every day except when the police come. Then there are no City workers there to help quell the situation like at Alexandra Park.

Greg: Why do you think some people have been volunteering to support you?

Dreddz: They were doing it because they were seeing a big gap. They were going around saying "Why are there so many people outside if I am being taxed?" There is supposed to be welfare, subsidized housing, all these things. They want answers, and so instead of waiting for their politicians to lie, they decided to go out there to educate themselves. We've had every kind of person, landscapers … we've had people that are trying to turn themselves into lawyers, counsellors. These volunteers have supported us in a lot of ways. That includes defending us when the City workers targeted us. For example, some of those that spoke out or did something on camera were given letters banning them from all the parks. They accuse you of a set of crimes. They just say you are banned for a year or six months.

Greg: Did this happen to you?

Dreddz: I just woke up one morning and I got a letter. That letter said what I was accused of. And that I was doing things to make the environment unsafe for the community. All these accusations claimed to have witnesses and they have it in writing, but if I do get a drinking ticket from the police, for example, it would tell me I was drinking, it's a public intoxication, whatever. It would tell me a time and place I could go and voice my defence against that. That hasn't happened here. You are just flat out accused of a crime and given the punishment.

Greg: Have you ever stayed at a shelter or shelter-hotel?

Dreddz: I cannot stay at a shelter-hotel as it may compromise the tenancy rights I have at my TCH [Toronto Community Housing] apartment. I'm trying to get back into my apartment. It's subsidized housing. When you are poor like I am you have less housing options. I can only afford subsidized housing. So, when I found myself in a conflict with my neighbour, I applied for a transfer to another TCH unit. I am still waiting. I can't go back to my own apartment at the moment. I'm working with the lawyer now to try and get that settled.[3]

Greg: Can you tell me about how Toronto Community Housing is run?

Dreddz: The government tells us to build a sense of community, yet at almost any TCH building that I've been to, the neighbourhood classifies us as criminals or addicts. It's like at what point do you accept us as people, people you can give jobs to, people you see as just your neighbour, right? It's kinda a calamity. They want to make it look like we are criminals, but we aren't. There's a lot of neglect there on the part of management. Meanwhile, when you look at people living there, people turn around from being addicts and operate community gardens and go around rescuing pets and things of that nature. We want to become part of a community. We are citizens, we are tenants, and yet we are being ignored. So now what's gonna make you go out there and do a lot of good? What's the point?

Greg: Just to finish, what are one or two things that you would, if you could, tell Toronto's mayor, the premier, or the prime minister? What would you say to them?

Dreddz: Honestly! Don't talk to us like you love us. Don't talk to us like you are being honest. Do not bullshit us – be real! Right? If you are gonna sit there and be like, this is gonna happen, that's gonna happen, right? That is bullshit. There are reservations out there still without clean functioning water. Why would I believe the promises you are trying to make in the city? You can't even take care of the original people that were here. So, anybody else that comes after, you promise freedom, rights, a fair trial all these things and they don't exist. So, who do we complain to? So many people are having so many chaotic things happening in their lives. There's no one to complain to. Suddenly you got to have money, but guess what, when you come from [social] housing, you don't have money, so you can't get a lawyer. You may do nothing and get a bunch of time for something you didn't do. So now when you go to jail it's fucking with your psychology. You didn't do this so now you're getting punishment for it, so fuck it, I might as well be bad anyways. For some people that's snapping them from a good path they are already on. Where they were self-sustaining. They didn't get in trouble, but they weren't dancing in the eyes of the justice system either.

The right people need to hear the truth while they are listening to this or reading it … whatever intake method they are using. It needs to be done. If the reader doesn't hear the truth, the world won't be able to sustain itself. They have people living in the fantasy of going to space and all that. It's cool, it's achievable, but what is happening to the things on earth? You're letting your fellow man die. People are getting fired from work for trying to bring extra Tim Hortons donuts for when they see hungry people in their neighbourhood. We live in the Western Hemisphere where we throw away bundles of food like that and in the other half of the world people are dying and are starving. Sometimes it's one bowl of rice for the day. Does it make sense if you have resources to share, and you decide not to share them? We are supposed to be a privileged nation. We're supposed to share. We're supposed to be looking out for our fellow man. We are supposed to be seeing through the eyes of justice and all this stuff and when it's not happening, who do you complain to? If you complain when the police mistreat you, you are complaining to the police about the police. So how are you certain you are getting justice? It might get examined or looked at, but how are you so sure you are getting justice? The city is a business. And all they want to do is keep the different components of the business running. My life doesn't mean anything to them.

Dreddz in Alexandra Park.
Credit: Ginger Dean

DREDDZ is an advocate for the streets and an anti-poverty and anti-suffering activist.

GREG COOK is a white settler who has been a drop-in and outreach worker in downtown Toronto for over twelve years, and at Sanctuary since 2009. Greg partners with community groups and agencies to agitate for a more just and equitable society.

 **CHAPTER 10**

Report on Toronto: The Encampment Support Network

Words by Simone E. Schmidt, photos by Jeff Bierk

As I write this in early November 2021, Toronto is still reeling from the militarized encampment evictions at Trinity Bellwoods, Alexandra Park, and Lamport Stadium. Media has focused on police violence at the evictions rather than the ongoing housing crisis or daily police violence towards un-housed people living in encampments. This chapter will focus on the City's other strategies to evict encampments from May 2020 to May 2021, and the way in which the Encampment Support Network (ESN), a volunteer group of over 180 people, pushed back through a combination of mutual aid, public education, art, and direct action. This account is necessarily partial given the wide range of perspectives held by a group so big and the limitation on the word count. I have also underemphasized information that is inextricably linked to encampments but will be covered in other chapters of this book, namely the overdose crisis and the shelter-hotels. Thank you to AK, Amie Tsang, Andrew X, Anthony Brown, Derrick Black, Domenico Saxida, Ginger Dean, Les Harper, Zoë Dodd, Nichole Leveck, Jeff Bierk,

Marcel North Gallant, Jesse Crowe, Nathan Doucet, and Lil Man, all who contributed to this chapter in the form of interviews or notes.

This chapter is dedicated in loving memory to Domenico Saxida, mayor of Alexandra Park, who welcomed me into his home and reshaped my understanding of care.

* * *

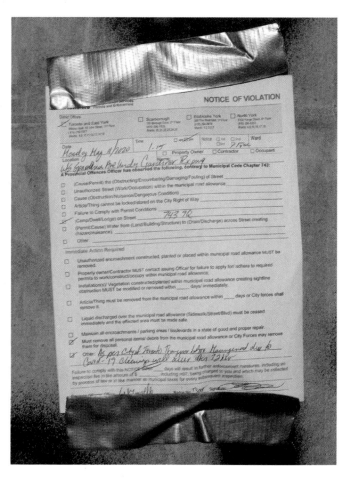

Notice of Violation posted under the Gardiner Expressway.

In the early lockdown of May 2020, harm-reduction workers Zoë Dodd and Tave Cole called me, Jeff Bierk, and Ginger Dean down to Bathurst and Queen's Quay. We met up with about twenty-five other people, most of whom we didn't know. What we witnessed there were City housing workers from Streets to Homes (S2H), backed by Parks Ambassadors, Toronto police, Bylaw Officers, and bulldozer and dump truck drivers, enforcing a Notice of Violation and forcing the relocation of the people who had set up tents in visible spaces under the Gardiner Expressway. It was an eviction. Advocates had called the media to the scene. Our presence staved off the enforcement for the day.

Zoë Dodd berates a Toronto cop and a City official about the eviction.

When I introduced myself to the others there, it became clear they were mostly harm-reduction and outreach workers on their time off. If they were burned out and grieving the preventable deaths of the overdose crisis in their community before the start of the pandemic, now they were also rocked and disoriented by the closure of overdose prevention sites, community health centres, drop-ins, as well as cuts in capacity to shelters. The total upheaval of the systems and spaces in which they worked compelled them to try to enact harm reduction as best they could in this fresh hell. Church of the Holy Trinity, Sherbourne Health, Sanctuary Toronto, and Parkdale Queen West Community Health Centre had been doing tent drives and handing them out to people in need, so encampments had sprung up all over the city that, due to stay-at-home orders, otherwise felt like a ghost town.[1] Jeff, Ginger, and I organized to support the tent drives through our own social media and built relationships with seasoned outreach workers from there.

People set up homes under the Gardiner Expressway. In May 2020, the City moved to evict them and trash their belongings.

Early Eviction Response: Can't Stay Home without a Home

We learned very quickly from Greg Cook and Doug Johnson Hatlem, outreach workers at Sanctuary, that even before COVID-19, the City was posting notices at encampments, giving people seventy-two hours (or less) to move out or be removed by police and have their worldly belongings trashed. It was cruel, inhumane, and traumatizing, and it denied the reality that people were making the safest situation for themselves. The practice of evicting people from the only homes they had contravened Centers for Disease Control and Prevention guidelines and denied people's right to self-determine where they live. Indeed, when you have no indoor space, encampments are the only practical way of abiding by stay-at-home orders.

On 15 May, a school teacher named Anna Jessup stood in front of a bulldozer under the Gardiner. The image attracted media attention, and at the press scrum that night, Deputy Fire Chief Jim Jessop had to answer to the eviction of unhoused people. But it was clear that the City was not ready to back down on these evictions or be honest with the public, and we sensed our sustained presence as witnesses might be the only thing that would force the City to be accountable for its actions.

It was still early lockdown, and my musician and artist peers were gigless, bored, and thrashing in the vacuums of their own homes, so I put out a call on Facebook for people to come down to witness subsequent evictions. From there, we organized a scouting schedule to monitor if notices were posted at different encampments. We gathered a list of people who would be willing to show up to at least observe and mitigate the harm caused during an eviction, and at most, stop it. We did a basic training on Zoom, with Mac Scott of Movement Defence Committee detailing our legal rights at an eviction, and with Greg Cook, Zoë Dodd, and Les Harper describing the history of outreach in Toronto and how to be in an encampment. Les emphasized the point that we should ask permission to be at an encampment and remember we were guests in people's homes: "'What do you want?' 'What do you need?' And that's the key thing – it's asking each other 'What do you need?' I'd never want someone throwing stuff at me and saying what I need." This proved to be crucial advice for what was to come.

As our yet to be formalized group attended evictions, we exchanged information with Amanda Leo and Lorraine Lam, outreach workers who were already speaking with officials from Shelter Support and Housing Administration (SSHA) at the City's weekly emergency harm-reduction tables. The pushback against evictions was felt on the ground, in the media, and also at a bureaucratic level.

Eviction under Any Other Name

The City's crisis response unfolded before our eyes, and throughout the next year and a half its attempts at evicting people took on many names and forms: "cleanings," "clearings," and coercive relocations. Toronto's top priority seemed to be to invisibilize the housing crisis rather than to actually house people. Gradually, the non-congregate spaces in the shelter system increased as the City opened more shelter-hotels, and the City's encampment team focused its efforts on getting people inside from the encampments that were receiving the most 311 complaints.

The eviction at Little Norway Park, a small plot of land on the lake-shore right across from Billy Bishop Toronto City Airport, serves as a good example of what we were seeing at the time. The breeze off the lake and the park's tall pines provide a relatively cool place to wake up in the heat of summer. But the park is also located at the foot of a bunch of condos, where people want to walk their dogs. There was a community of about twenty-five people living there in sixteen tents when the City posted notice in early June 2020. We asked the residents whom we had just recently met if they wanted our support. Many of them did, and so we waited until City officials came.

Because of the previous pushback, this eviction looked different than what had happened under the Gardiner. No cops came initially. Instead, Streets to Homes workers went around and told people they had the option to move to a newly opened shelter-hotel or to just leave. Police would follow. S2H communication was confusing and imprecise. They didn't seem to have any relationship with any encampment residents, nor did they have brochures outlining the conditions, rules, or locations of the shelter-hotels. Imagine being told you had to move somewhere by people who couldn't tell you anything about the place. We remained and asked questions so that residents could make the best decision for themselves. All S2H could tell us is that residents had two hours to pack up a maximum of two bags' worth of their belongings (the rest of their stuff would be trashed) and board a chartered TTC bus to the Delta shelter-hotel run by Homes First at Highway 401 and Kennedy Road. We were able to buy people more time, but not much else.

Most people took the City's offer. A few people who wanted to stay in the park held out until the end of the day. We offered to mobilize a larger group to come down and help support them in staying, but when faced with the eviction of the rest of the camp and the threat of police enforcement, they packed up and moved to another location. After all, we had no pre-existing relationship with these residents and hadn't built the trust necessary to provide that kind of support.

Throughout the week, we returned to scout the neighbourhood every day and realized that eleven of the people who had accepted shelter-hotel offers had returned. By public transit, the Delta was fifty-one minutes away and required three transfers. The people returning said that they were too far away from their health services, that they couldn't abide by the shelter-hotel rules, that security and surveillance and bed checks made them feel like they were in prison, and that they missed their communities. Former residents of Little Norway Park moved their camps to new places scattered around the area, and for the next several months, those encampments were largely left unvisited by S2H because they were not in green space coveted by condo residents.

The experience taught us five things that shaped our understanding of the City's approach and our own response going forward:

1 Shelter-hotels were not working for people. People should have been able to try out the option being offered to them and, if it didn't work, return to their tent and belongings.

2 The imminent threat of police enforcement, whether or not it comes at the same time as S2H, makes any decision coerced.

3 The City would try to use us to do their job. For instance, the head of Parks, Forestry and Recreation gave us plastic gloves to clean up peoples' belongings after they were coerced into taking the shelter-hotel offers.

4 Like every other battle within the settler state, this is a fight about how authorities conceive of land, and who gets to live on it. Indigenous and Black people are overrepresented among unhoused people and are forcibly displaced by both police and the soft arm of social work. Private property owners' rights to green space are valued over all others.

5 If we were going to assist people in self-determining and make sure we weren't just another crowd of housed people lending to the chaos and trauma of the situation, we would have to become literate in the City's crisis response, and most importantly forge sustained relationships with encampment residents. Showing up only in a moment of conflict to fight with authorities would not be consensual solidarity and could cause more harm to people in the long run.

Daily Outreach

Throughout this early eviction response, we were horrified that people didn't have water or access to sanitation. The brutality of the situation cannot be overstated: people were suffering, they were hungry, they were dehydrated, they were in distress. "If there had been a tornado that had wiped out ten city blocks during a pandemic, the City would have stood on its head! Why was it so hard to get people food, water, first aid and porta-potties?" recalls Ginger Dean with incredulity. I had never seen so many open and infected wounds in Toronto. COVID-19 had not only decimated the pre-existing services for unhoused people – not even the mobile health busses were visiting encampments – but had also shuttered the informal spaces like Tim Hortons and public libraries where people used to go to the washroom, cool off or warm up, and rest.[2] Mobilizing a public that was afraid of catching a deadly virus to demonstrate was difficult, and so we organized a car caravan to try to pressure the provincial and municipal governments to change their response. But Ginger thought this action lacked pragmatism and suggested that we bring people the stuff they needed. It made sense to try to provide basic humanitarian aid, and to do that, we formed neighbourhood committees (NCs) in five locations: Moss Park, Scadding Court, Trinity Bellwoods, Parkdale, and Little Norway Park (LNP). (When winter hit, we were made aware by outreach workers that Cherry Beach was in need of assistance, and a sixth committee was created.) We called ourselves the Encampment Support Network (ESN).

Every morning for the next fourteen months, ESN NCs would undertake outreach to unhoused people living in encampments in their neighbourhoods. We introduced ourselves and asked people permission to be in their space. If they wanted us there, we asked about what they needed. ESN started Instagram and Twitter accounts and got an official email address. ESN used social media to crowdsource and organize the delivery of survival gear, asking housed neighbours to drop off Gatorade, trail mix, protein shakes, first aid kits, hand sanitizer, tents, sleeping bags, socks, underwear, and grocery store gift cards at different addresses. We picked up harm-reduction kits from The Works and Parkdale Queen West Community Health Centre. The Interfaith Coalition to Fight Homelessness and Toronto Drop-In Network provided us with water. The Ice Man provided ice and coolers free of charge, and local coffee shops donated carafes, cream, sugar, and cups. Eventually, a deeply industrious committee was formed to centralize the donations process, initially spearheaded by Hally Levy and Tom Hobson, who had previously organized a local community TV station, BUMP Television. Most of the original ESN organizers were artists, musicians, and non-unionized gig workers, familiar with creating our own infrastructures. COVID-19 and the Canadian Emergency Response Benefit (CERB) allowed us to embody a different way of being in a city where rent is so high we were normally forced to squander our time and energy on meaningless hustles to keep the rich entertained.

After ESN's donations operation grew too big to run from a porch, Why Not Theatre loaned us their space that was sitting idle due to COVID-19. Pictured here, a donations committee member organizes stock for daily pickups by neighborhood committees.

Lil Man in Moss Park puts up signs at his encampment reading, "We Need to Take Care of Each Other" and "Can't Stay Home without a Home." The signs' slogans were contributed by encampment residents at Queen Street and Dufferin Street. ESN sign painters organized by Sarah Creskey kept people stocked with signs for the year.

"Mayor Tory? He didn't come through here. He didn't check us. He didn't come see. This guy ... we're some of his biggest constituents, and we vote. Don't get it twisted. We vote, and I voted for that asshole, and he hasn't come here once. Not once. My boy over there had the cops come and rip his shit down. He ain't doing nothing. He wants his rights. We're all entitled to some housing, some cleanliness, some showers, some food. That's not a privilege, eh? That's a fucking right."

Lil Man

Different Communities, Different Calls

Over the course of the year, each NC developed differently, as each re-sponded to the needs of their respective communities. Encampments are shaped by the people living in them, and people choose to live in different locations for different reasons, such as proximity to agencies, services, nature, family, their jobs, histories, and the presence or response of their housed neighbours.

For example, Lamport Stadium encampment in Parkdale was right next to St. Felix Centre's respite, so it was built by people who were used to, and interested in, accessing shelter services. The tents were often used by people who stayed in the respite part-time, especially as a place to use drugs together more safely given that the respite had inadequate over-dose prevention services. The culture of the encampment was shaped in part by the constant presence of the respite's community safety team, which meant more cops were called in the event of overdose and con-flict. Ultimately, proximity to the institutional authority of the respite impacted the culture of the encampment.

In stark contrast, Cherry Beach was renegade. People who lived in this remote location had no easy access to basic amenities or stores and did not want to be found by the world. Public transportation to the lo-cation was cut off during the pandemic. No one living there wanted to publicize their lot, regardless of how brutal it was. This committee had to be more intrepid than most.

Little Norway Park NC supported people living in encampments along the waterfront who were choosing to live in smaller groups and were more easily targeted and displaced. It was virtually impossible to garner any community support in the neighbourhood. Housed neigh-bours threw paint, hot oil, golf balls, and ice at people's tents and actively harassed them. And like everywhere else, park residents were regularly

"We have the number one view of Toronto. That's why they want to kick us out of here." – Encampment resident down by Lake Ontario, Bathurst Street and Queen's Quay

subject to enforcement by police and private security, who were called by affluent condo dwellers.

The encampment at Trinity Bellwoods was first established by people who had been part of the overflow from the shelter system and had been moved into the temporary respite that the City had opened in the park's community centre during the early months of the pandemic. People had been trying to find space away from the risk of COVID-19 in that congregate setting. Tents were tucked away in different areas of the park, some hidden, some bordering the main streets. A large group of Trinity Bellwoods encampment residents were artists self-organized as the "White Squirrel Brigade," managing their own donations from the surrounding community of renters and homeowners.

The Alexandra Park and Scadding Court encampments were in close proximity to the Alexandra Hotel and the Women's Residence shelter, and people who stayed there also found community in the encampment, sharing in daily outreach and community meals organized with the This Way Up Collective. The Scadding Court library workers were hospitable and organized a free box of food and survival gear for the local community. Surrounding renters practised tai chi and played soccer in the park. Some of the bordering townhouse residents called 311, while others joined ESN and organized to support the encampment. Many Alexandra Park residents grew up around the park, worked downtown, and wanted to stay in the neighbourhood close to their services, families, and community.

Similarly, Moss Park is home and community centre for many people who are proud to have grown up in now gentrified Regent Park and the surrounding public housing projects. It is also the epicentre of the overdose crisis, and the location of the first unsanctioned supervised consumption site, organized by the Toronto Overdose Prevention Society in 2017. People living there have a long history of organizing within the community and many joined the NC.

All of these factors would influence what ESN NCs were asked to provide, their varied memberships and ways of organizing, as well as their regular activities and responses to crises.

Andrew ran a free store at Alexandra Park and connected people with donations from the community. This photo was taken on one of many pizza days, when Maker Pizza donated lunch to ESN.

"I came down to Alexandra Park and helped all those people, cuz I had all this free time and staying home feels lonely. I met a lot of new people down there, made a lot of friends, saved a lot of lives, which made me feel good, saving lives. Doing good, just doing good.

I feel that the City could have done a lot more. Like me, I went down there with nothing and did something. They got hundreds of people working for the City and they should have been able to do more."

Andrew

Reporting on the City's Organized Abandonment

Although service providers in the homeless sector did have to recalibrate during the pandemic, the City might have made life safer for encampment residents by allowing them access to basic amenities in the form of public washrooms, running water, clean electricity, and fire safety. Instead, Toronto's strategy seemed to be to squeeze people out of their communities by making life impossible and unsafe. I say seemed, because we could never get a straight answer about the City's plans, and all official channels funnelled us into bureaucratic sinkholes. When we came upon City employees who were interfacing with encampment residents – be it Parks Ambassadors or fire, S2H, or Parks workers – we asked them about improving conditions, because that's what encampment residents were saying they wanted. We were ignored, told it wasn't in the budget, or accused of harassing them. All the while, the City's mouthpieces – Brad Ross, Toronto's chief communications officer; Jim Jessop, Toronto's deputy fire chief; and Mayor John Tory – would adopt the language of care and cite safety as the main reason that encampments had to be evicted.

Crowdsourcing on Instagram was a good way not only of providing for people but also bringing to attention the reality of the City's organized abandonment. For instance, encampment residents were regularly targeted for producing garbage, but in most places the City refused to provide regular trash disposal and sharps containers.[3] So ESN put out the call and got some volunteer truck drivers to do dump runs. Out of respect for encampment residents' privacy, we didn't document our efforts, but our public ask for assistance revealed and shamed the City's neglect. Eventually, SSHA organized garbage service.

As we continued our daily outreach, the toll of structural violence on encampment residents showed itself. We were seeing people return to encampments from shelter-hotels grieving from the loss of their friends to overdose, or injured from being beaten by security guards, or evicted for breaking petty rules like swearing or not showing up for curfew. At encampments, people lived in physical danger and psychological terror as the police conducted night-time raids on bogus warrants. Parks Ambassadors, who were supposedly conducting wellness checks, would break residents' Charter rights and enter tents without consent and document their contents, clearly more a method of surveilling residents than anything. If they found an empty tent, it might get deemed abandoned and cleared by the City's Parks workers. People would lose their cookware, IDs, clothes, and tents and have to start back at zero. ESN outreach found people dead in their tents. There was literally no recourse for any of this. We called the City's Central Intake to try to access detox beds and shelter space for residents who wanted it but were told there was no room. Meanwhile, the City denied that the shelter system was full. So we kept records. Outreach volunteers would write daily reports about City activity, and NCs shared weekly reports to compare notes on the City's response.

No Go Zone

Almost everyone who took up the authority to report on and decide things for encampment residents used COVID-19 as an excuse to not actually go to an encampment and speak with them. Journalists working from home simply regurgitated the City's PR. University professors who had received funding to run clinics and do studies on legal rights of encampment residents couldn't send their law students on-site. Right-to-housing academics and members of not-for-profit organizations who made their careers evaluating the City's response to encampments didn't visit and would call us to feed them information. Any hope that publicly funded agencies and health advocates might speak out on this public health crisis was dashed. It took two and a half months of advocating for health professionals to do medical outreach in encampments before mobile teams finally arrived. When we asked them to use their status as experts to advocate for improvements in this public health crisis, we were told that their employer, Inner City Health Associates, was playing a long game, trying to secure contracts in the shelter-hotels, which they risked losing if they spoke out.

So, we doubled down on our communications by making video and audio recordings in collaboration with residents who wanted to speak to their experiences. Many residents feared the repercussions of speaking out and instead directed us on our messaging. Podcasters Aliya Pabani and Allie Graham produced two episodes of the *We Are Not the Virus* documentary, which shared the voices of encampment residents with a broad public that had no real-life knowledge of the context. The ESN media committee pitched stories to news outlets and connected journalists with encampment residents.

Artwork by Michael Deforge for the podcast *We Are Not the Virus* by Aliya Pabani and Allie Graham.

Kassie holds up a spread of photos taken by Jeff Bierk in collaboration with herself and other Moss Park residents published in the *Globe and Mail*.

We recorded and compiled what we were seeing and sent out (almost) weekly newsletters to people who donated to ESN. We encouraged everyone who donated to write to and call their City councillors with a regularly updated list of demands that focused on:

- consulting directly with encampment residents about what they need and want;
- repealing the bylaw that criminalizes people living in encampments in city parks;
- providing encampment residents with survival gear, such as tents and sleeping bags, and access to basic sanitation;
- opening more shelter-hotels and providing robust overdose prevention services; and
- opening rent-geared-to-income housing in the downtown core.

These postcards (made in collaboration between Jeff Bierk and Title King) were handed out to ESN donors who came to action events to write on and mail to City councillors.

City councillors stonewalled both ESN and the public for months. Amie Tsang, a journalist who eventually joined the ESN Explainers (a group of policy analysts who were tasked with explaining the larger political context to people on outreach), recalls trying to get an interview with Councillor Kristyn Wong-Tam: "I naively handed over the questions I intended to ask about encampments to her staff, and they never got back to me." Finally, a snarky tweet from the ESN Twitter account forced Parkdale–High Park's Gord Perks to speak with me. He repeated the screwy logic we would hear over the next year in canned emails from other City councillors and out the mouth of Mayor John Tory on the news: encampments are not safe, and providing people living in them with basic sanitation is "enabling homelessness." Mr. Perks refused to even visit an encampment, and pitted investment in supportive housing and shelter-hotels against the provision of porta-potties and water trucks. Never mind that we were about to see an increase in COVID-19 evictions. Never mind that the shelter system was full and people had nowhere to go. He told me that City staff were doing a great job, and that this was the most significant investment in the shelter system and housing we'd seen in years. And then he said that Toronto's housing advocates had to stop sending mixed messages to City Council, and that ESN had to come into alignment with a group called Toronto Alliance to End Homelessness (TAEH). Over 100 volunteers were doing the City's job of responding to a humanitarian crisis during these "unprecedented times." I was talking about people dying, and somehow the problem was that we couldn't fall in line with what appeared to be professional lobbyists?

This dynamic, which would extend throughout 2020 and beyond, clearly demonstrates how the City values the feelings of its staff over the lives of encampment residents, and how it designates who it will listen to when it comes to housing advocacy. On 7 December 2020, we organized deputations at the City's Economic and Community Development Committee. Joe Cressy, City councillor for Spadina–Fort York, where three of the major encampments were located, talked on his phone while forty people gave impassioned deputations about the carnage of the year thus far, demanding that there be a moratorium on evictions and that encampment residents be provided with survival gear. When Kira Heineck, executive director of TAEH, began to speak, ears perked up. "We [TAEH] do not yet have an official position on a moratorium on evictions from encampments," she said, and went on to give her deputation. Committee Chair Michael Thompson replied, "Thanks, I imagine you're an absolute expert, you are not someone who just came to this a few months and seeing it and wanting to sort of bring solutions that are not necessarily founded but solutions that are basically rooted in data as you point out, and facts, and having information that helps to address the issue around long term housing."[4] This obsession with data-driven solutions and long-term housing solutions is not a substitute for crisis response. Furthermore, it misses the important reality: You cannot house people who are dead.

Pushing Back against False Narratives

"The consistency of doing outreach every day, and the building of real relationships through our presence in the park with people allowed us to organize directly with encampment residents as an act of resistance to the City's false narratives," says Jeff Bierk of ESN Moss Park. We privileged the voices of encampment residents over non-existent data.

As our Instagram account crested to 20,000 followers, the City ramped up its PR battle against encampment residents through misleading data and false narratives.[5] The City underestimated the number of people who were unhoused and held back data they did have around deaths in shelters. John Tory claimed there was room in the shelter system[6] despite the fact that most days when we tried (and we tried most days) we couldn't get people who wanted a room inside into one. This bolstered perceptions of unhoused people as irresponsible and ungrateful. The City pitted housed people against them, saying encampments impeded the public from using the parks. But who were encampment residents other than the public?

The City was artful with its language. City spokespeople called shelter offers "housing" and "hotels." They said that S2H was on the ground every day 24/7, which may have been true, but with a small staff and hundreds of encampments, they simply weren't developing consistent relationships with residents. We would often hear from residents that they'd been put on the list for shelter months ago but had never been revisited by S2H. Every tragedy and opportunity the City might have used to improve people's conditions was held against them.

One of the most classic false narratives is that Toronto Fire Services responded to 253 fires in encampments in 2020. Through a Freedom of Information (FOI) request, FactCheck Toronto found that there were only 132 encampment fires in 2020, almost half as many as the City claimed, and that this figure included fires where there was no property damage and no injuries.[7] False alarms, controlled campfires, BBQ smoke, steam from a pot on a cooking stove, or even someone setting off fireworks were counted as "fires." The City inflated the sense of danger in encampments by including all emergency responses to notifications of a suspected uncontrolled fire as actual fires in their press releases.

Of course, fire does pose a safety threat to people living outside, but that threat might have been mitigated by providing people with fire extinguishers (as recommended in the Faulkner Inquest)[8] or safe electricity, fire pits, and cooking facilities. Or housing. But for all of Toronto Fire Services' visits to encampments, they never seemed to ask people what they needed. Instead, ESN would regularly see Toronto Fire workers walking through encampments with S2H and Parks Ambassadors, confiscating propane. This amounted to encampment residents concealing their life-saving heat sources, which of course is more dangerous.

In the aftermath of a serious explosion at an encampment down by the lakeshore, Sarah Rehou, a burn specialist at Sunnybrook Health Sciences Centre, teamed up with ESN volunteers, encampment residents, and Greg Cook of Sanctuary to design a fire safety workshop and create a "best fire practices" manual. The first outdoor workshop was at Clarence Square, an encampment surrounded by townhouses and commercial real estate where, ironically, across the street the CaféTO program allowed a restaurant to spill onto the sidewalk and operate a heat lamp right inside a dining tent.

By September 2020, it was clear the City was vastly underestimating the number of people living on the street and had no winter plan in place for them. Material conditions in encampments had hardly improved, and people were returning from shelter-hotels. The ESN sign committee calibrated to the season.

Winter is coming. Moss Park, September 2020.

The Housing Crisis Is a Real Estate Game

ESN and residents of the Moss Park encampment organized a Meal and March event on 23 September 2020. Starting at Moss Park, the march ended at the WE Charity Foundation properties, which ESN demanded the City expropriate. An architect provided plans for a redesign of the grounds that would create living room for fifty-three people. Seeing that the City would not consult with encampment residents, ESN did its own consultations and projected them on the walls of the building. Nichole Leveck, who led the march with her family, recalls the power of the action: *"One of the moments when I felt it the most was when there was the rally and we took it to the streets. There was that projection of people at Moss Park on the WE buildings. I felt so proud in a good way to be part of it all. You were actually amplifying the voices of people in the park. If you're not going to listen to their needs, then we're going to put it on the wall."*

The Meal and March for Housing, departing Moss Park on Shuter Street, led by Les Harper and Nichole Leveck.

Despite the very achievable solution of expropriating buildings to create housing, ESN had to accept that the City was not about to invest in solutions that would disrupt the real estate market that winter. So how could we provide warmth to people living outside? We organized boot drives and warm winter clothing drives, but we knew it wouldn't be enough. Inspired by a French architect who built sleeping pods, we organized very public foam dome builds in encampments. Every dome was outfitted with a carbon monoxide detector and "No Smoking" signs. They kept people warm enough simply with body heat.

Residents of Moss Park, ESN volunteers, and architectural students build foam domes at the encampment.

AK, a Moss Park resident and ESN Moss Park volunteer, reflects on the foam dome builds and the City's response: "*See how we built it? We had 100 people. It was a good day. Cuz people were sleeping outside, they*

had nowhere to go, just to make a small place they can sleep at night time.
They cover themselves. And thanks you group, helping people when the
government didn't. I don't know what they say to them. But they take it
back and they throw it in the garbage. What they say:

'What is this?'
'This is house!'
'This is a garbage!'

What do you mean it's a garbage? Two people can sleep there. No one
can come in. No rain can come in. No snow can come in. Two three blan-
ket, you be sweating. The first time I had it, I sweat through the blankets.
Thank you god. Thank you families."

By October 2020, we were in a second lockdown with COVID-19
numbers increasing. Shelter space was still limited and difficult to access.
The City's infrastructure of displacement remained relentless, pushing
out people in the small encampments along the lakeshore and in Rosedale Valley and creeping around the larger encampments at Alexandra
Park, Trinity Bellwoods, Lamport Stadium, and Moss Park, scooping up
people's belongings and homes when they were left unattended. They
called it "cleaning," and every few weeks they devised new metrics for
measuring whether a camp was abandoned. The City said it tagged and
stored belongings, but when Ginger Dean went to go collect a resident's
things, she was directed to sort through a dump pile.

Then, they started trying to confiscate people's foam domes, calling
them fire hazards.

As the City opened the Canadian National Exhibition's Better Living
Centre, a respite with a capacity of 122 people divided by plexiglass cubicles, residents of Alexandra Park were being told they might be subject
to a mass eviction any day. Former Alexandra Park resident Anthony
Browne leaked a photo from inside the Better Living Centre (taking
photos of the respite goes against policy), which caused an uproar in the
media and had people who had never seen the inside of such a facility
calling it a "dystopian hell." Later, Anthony would speak out about the

experience: "I'm actually still traumatized by the experience that I had at the Better Living Centre. It was horrible. There's no privacy, there's no sense of security, you're sleeping in a glass cubicle where everyone just walks by. They're looking at you, staring at you, and every time you have to leave to do anything important, there's always a fear that your things will be gone. There's no locks on the cubicles … You can't have food on the cots. Not even a glass of water is allowed."

ESN Scadding Court organized a press conference on 8 November, and hundreds of people in the community came to listen to the experiences of residents. Advocates, librarians from the Scadding Court Community Centre, and sympathetic neighbours spoke too, and local children made signs in support.

Soon, carpenter Khaleel Seivwright started to build Tiny Shelters, and we teamed up with him and the Toronto Tiny Shelters to do nightly drop-offs.

Khaleel Seivwright delivering a Tiny Shelter.

The City tried to remove people's Tiny Shelters at all costs. When Sean Boyd died in his friend's Tiny Shelter at St. James Park encampment on 24 February 2021, the City swooped in to remove the structure within hours, despite asks from the grieving community that it be left there. ESN volunteers would block City trucks, get in the way of Tiny Shelter removals, engage in high-speed chases with City staff to try to track the Tiny Shelters, record conversations with Parks supervisors who directed removals, and publicize the callousness of an administration that would take no responsibility for the violence of its actions. We galvanized thousands of people to sign public statements in support of residents in our #NoEncampmentEvictions campaign, and many academics, health providers, musicians, actors, artists, skaters, and service workers issued their own public statements. Celebrities such as Colin Mochrie, Ennis Esmer, Leslie Feist, and Leanne Betasamosake Simpson signed on to them and posted about them publicly. We reiterated our demands and pressed for a moratorium on evictions so that encampment residents might make decisions for themselves without the threat of eviction.

Police raid the encampment at Moss Park in November 2020 during a healing circle, terrorizing and arresting Black youth.

When people died in encampments, it was Indigenous knowledge keepers who created the space for grieving and ceremony in parks. Les Harper and Nichole Leveck's family regularly brought ceremony and healing circles to Moss Park and to encampments where people had died. Nichole Leveck: *"This is the day there was a raid on AK's spot in Moss Park, and this was just after Les had stopped the circle. We had witnessed that violence there. And I think I had talked about how it was in the past, under the Indian Act, illegal for us to be on our own land and to do ceremony. And there we were witnessing more colonial violence."*

Suspiciously, in December 2020, a string of seven arsons took place in encampments within seven days.[9] Brad Ross, the City's chief communications officer, tweeted out a photo of a charred foam dome down at HTO Park. No one was hurt, though the well-being of encampment residents was not the focus of this PR. Despite an October motion by Kristyn Wong-Tam for City staff to provide fire safety equipment and survival gear in line with the Faulkner Inquest, we saw no such things delivered.

City Tables

By the end of 2020, the City had a public relations nightmare on its hands. City officials asked to meet with encampment "stakeholders" who had signed on to the campaign against encampment evictions, including executive directors from social agencies, academics, outreach workers of conscience, and ESN delegates from every NC. Chris Brillinger and Leila Sarangi from Family Service Toronto were brought in for the purpose of building trust between members of the community and the City administration by conducting separate meetings with each and returning with recommendations. The narrative that this was a conflict between people with hurt feelings rather than a real humanitarian crisis seemed to be the very premise of the meetings. Community members stressed that a moratorium on evictions would be necessary for trust to be built between encampment residents and City staff. How could the same people intent on evicting encampment residents also be offering them a safe place to stay? ESN asked why encampment residents weren't at the table and refused to speak on behalf of residents. At a second meeting on 22 December, Alykhan Pabani with ESN Parkdale joined the discussion via Zoom from an encampment where he was doing outreach and put a resident on the line to explain residents' demands. Then there was radio silence as the bitter cold swept through the holidays and on through January. In February 2021, eleven months into the pandemic, Dan Breault, one of the leads at S2H, announced by email that he would be conducting consultations with encampment residents. On 18 February, between 9:00 a.m. and 4:30 p.m., he intended to visit Moss Park, Alexandra Park (and Scadding Court), Trinity Bellwoods, and Lamport Stadium and lend his ear for a whopping two hours at each encampment. There was already a foot of snow on the ground, and residents were paid in cash to come out from their tents, shivering, and speak to their experiences. ESN volunteers monitored the meetings as per request of those who participated. The next day, on 19 February,

Dan Breault's name appeared on affidavits against Khaleel Seivwright. The City had filed a Notice of Application against Seivwright, barring him from building or giving away lifesaving Tiny Shelters. The entire City Table and consultation process had clearly been conducted in bad faith.

On 28 February 2021, following the Notice of Application issued by the City against Khaleel Seivwright, ESN worked with other advocates to organize an action where about 1,000 people lined up around the block at John Tory's home to sign and deliver their own "Notice of Action" against the mayor. John Tory would not come down from his condominium on Bedford Road.

Pictured here are Mayor of Moss Park Derrick Black and ESN's John Fox delivering notices to Tory's cardboard surrogate.

The third and final City Table meeting wasn't until 5 March, and at this meeting ESN came asking questions. Dan Breault was asked if he would live in a Tiny Shelter if he had nowhere else to go. He refused to answer the question. This was recorded by artist Yuula Benivolski of ESN Scadding and shared via social media. Shortly after, we stopped seeing Dan in encampments, and SSHA replaced him with Mitchell Lamont.

Pathways Inside Program

On 16 March 2021, the City of Toronto sent out a press release announcing the Pathways Inside Project (PIP): "Pathways Inside, a new City program, is focused on those living in encampments at four priority sites, namely Moss Park, Alexandra Park, Trinity Bellwoods and Lamport Stadium, that are subject to increased health and safety concerns. The City has secured safe space inside hotel programs for everyone at these four sites."[10] Media celebrated that the City had secured enough inside space for encampment residents. The next day, flyers describing PIP, along with "outreach schedules" detailing the hours when Parks Ambassadors, Albion Neighbourhood Services, Toronto Fire, The Works, and Streets to Homes would visit the encampments, were plastered on poles and taped to trees in these four parks. Then, on Friday, 19 March, trespass notices were posted on all the Tiny Shelters and tents at the encampments, and in some cases hand-delivered to residents by Mitchell Lamont, flanked by security guards in bright yellow uniforms. Tensions in the encampments mounted as people were given until 6 April 2021 to move their homes or be criminalized under the Trespass to Property Act. The psychological terror of this threat of eviction caused some people to move. Others refused to leave.

Domenico Saxida, mayor of Alexandra Park, at his compound.

On 21 March 2021, there was a three-hour joint press conference held by ESN Alexandra Park, Trinity Bellwoods, and Moss Park with fifteen speakers, including encampment residents, shelter residents, and community supporters. Alexandra Park resident Domenico Saxida described his experience being vilified by the City and the anxiety we all feel about the future of the shelter-hotel system: "The way the City describes us is that we're rodents, rats, roaches, a menace, harassing – who are we harassing? No harassing. And we're not a menace and we're not harassing, we're human beings. The City has expanded their shelter system to include hotels. Okay so what happens when you're discharged from the shelter-hotel? Where you going to stay? Where do they expect you to go? I'm telling them now: every discharge is another person coming back to the parks."

"The Pathways Inside Project was just an extension of all the bullshit leading up to it," says Nathan Doucet of ESN LNP. "We watched the City try to reframe their actions in light of our messaging, and it was the precursor to their most brutal evictions of all." Two hundred and fifty spots were opened in the downtown Novotel shelter-hotel, but they were only available to people in the four "priority parks," despite the fact that hundreds of people who may have wanted a shelter-hotel space were living outside in ravines, stairwells, other encampments, or riding trains. The City's policy was that no one who had accessed any kind of shelter, including respites, within thirty days of the notice would be allowed access to Novotel. It was clear that the parks were a priority because they were the sites of organized community and resistance.

ESN NCs galvanized more public support against the encampment evictions. In collaboration with encampment residents, we organized press conferences, BBQs, yoga classes, and concerts in encampments to provide opportunities for the public to show up and show support. We printed 1,000 lawn signs and countless window signs saying "I Support My Neighbours in Tents," and within two weeks they were posted across the city. NIMBYs (Not In My Back Yard) had 311 to call; kind neighbours had ESN.

ESN Trinity Bellwoods and This Way Up Collective organized a BBQ and concert with encampment residents at Trinity Bellwoods Park on 27 March 2021 to rally community support against impending evictions.

The City did not enforce these trespass notices at the time. On Thursday, 1 April 2021, a press release announced that "no enforcement action to vacate parks will occur on April 6." The Novotel had become the latest site of a COVID-19 outbreak within the City's shelter system, forcing Toronto Public Health to temporarily suspend intakes at the PIP's main referral site. The City, however, refused to revoke the notices, maintaining the psychological pressure on encampment residents.

Later that month, the downtown City councillors – Josh Matlow, Mike Layton, Joe Cressy, and Ana Bailão – felt the pressure mount, as their homes were visited by "People's Ambassadors" posting notices similar to PIP on their homes and recording mock wellness checks. These were recorded in a series of videos that would detail the record of inaction of these councillors on both encampment and housing files. As some political traction was gained with Councillors Matlow and Layton, who opposed the City's approach to encampments, the Tory administration seemed to tire of the way in which the encampment file was being handled and it was moved from the jurisdiction of SSHA to an emergency management taskforce, directed by former police officer Joanna Ruth Beaven-Desjardins.

On 12 May, the City brought twenty-five security guards to clear three smaller encampments at George Hislop Park, Barbara Hall Park, and on the University Avenue median. Some people declined the City's offer of a shelter bed and were forcibly displaced to unknown locations.

On Wednesday, 19 May, the City showed up at Lamport Stadium encampment. The community and ESN mobilized to defend the encampment while roughly sixty City of Toronto corporate security guards and Toronto Police Service officers (including eight on horseback), six people in hazmat suits, a handful of other City workers, two "claw" heavy excavators, and three dump trucks tried to clear the encampment. By noon, they realized they had no shot, and the City gave up. The media attention from this eviction was enough to stave off evictions for another month.

The eviction of Trinity Bellwoods on 22 June, and the evictions of Alexandra Park and Lamport Stadium on 20 and 21 July, respectively, saw the City spend nearly $2 million on personnel, including militarized police and Star Security, and fencing for the parks. The force was brutal, fascistic in a way I hadn't seen since the 2010 G20 Toronto summit protests. While John Tory claims that the police presence at Lamport Stadium was due to "protestors," equal force was on hand at Alexandra Park, where residents asked for safe passage. The eviction of Lamport Stadium and Trinity Bellwoods were well documented in independent and mainstream media. Press were barred from the eviction at Alexandra Park, but it is described in a detailed report from the Scadding Court NC, which is available to the public.[11]

A combination of direct action, public outcry around encampment evictions, sustained pressure from right-to-housing advocates, and the push for a human rights approach to encampments spearheaded by Toronto Drop-In Network's Diana Chan McNally[12] have pushed the City to take a different approach for the time being. While some City councillors have condemned the violence of the latest evictions, we should not forget that their inaction and refusal to engage directly with their unhoused constituents for the entirety of 2020 is what paved the way for the City to use such force.

There Is No End

How do you finish something that's not over? I can't think of a good way. I ask my collaborator Jeff Bierk how to end this chapter, and he responds: "*It feels like a circling back now. The city is opening up and things have changed drastically since the beginning of the pandemic. We are returning not to a robust, compassionate shelter system, but to a decades' old problem and fight: a shelter system bursting at the seams, a housing crisis, a city that is uninhabitable for a lot of people. The major encampments have been dismantled, and smaller, more hidden pockets of tents remain. People are still riding the bus and sleeping in stairwells. People are still dying in shelter-hotels or leaving with nowhere to go."*

ESN volunteers calibrate to what we've learned and experienced. Many NCs continue to do outreach in a very different context than how we began. We grieve for the many people who've died this past year and anticipate another winter's carnage. As sure as the snow falls every year, the City still has no plan to house people permanently.

* * *

For a vivid record of the Encampment Support Network's communications, see ESN's social media archive at www.encampmentsupport network.com.

JEFF BIERK is a self-taught, multi-disciplinary artist working with photography, sculpture, video, and paint. Through a practice of collaborative photography, Bierk and his collaborators disrupt the formal definition and economics of photojournalism and problematize the idea of the photographer as sole author of the photograph.

SIMONE SCHMIDT is a multi-disciplinary artist, musician, songwriter, and writer. Born and raised in the settler colony of Toronto to parents of Gottscheer, Irish, and Scottish descent, Schmidt has contributed to social justice movements for the past twenty-two years.

CHAPTER 11

Wish You Were Still Here

Zoë Dodd

14 November 2021

Dear Cuz,

I often watch this video of us in the injection site when I want to see you. I'm playing Womack & Womack "Teardrops" for you. It's the first time you've heard this song. Marjie is there and we're all dancing and you're yelling "alright, you go, you go, you go …" We're all laughing. It's the end of the night, and the site's closed. I love watching this video, though when I do my eyes well up. I try not to cry. I don't know why? Maybe I know if I do, I might not be able to stop. I'm so grateful Sarah captured this moment of us.

Every Black Scotian I've ever met was deep into music, just like you. You always brought a huge vibe everywhere you went. The other day, I was walking along Sherbourne Street and people were all spilled out on the sidewalk outside of the Salvation Army Maxwell Meighen shelter. There was an ambulance parked outside, like there often is. I heard someone playing Eric B. & Rakim "Paid in Full" from a portable speaker. I looked across the street to the people on the hill outside the community centre. It wasn't you.

I feel like I personally let you down. I feel deep sadness about that. You praised me all the time for what we all did together, but it wasn't enough. So much is stacked against us at every turn. The indifference to human life is absolutely unbearable. Especially from those who purport to be our allies and "champions." They've really shown their true colours through this whole pandemic. Not a shred of urgency runs through their blood like it does ours – as people drop over and over and over. Even Councillor Joe Cressy, who came to our closing party in the park when we were moving the overdose prevention site into a building – legal and funded. You hung out with him there. He helped us with the campaign for supervised injection sites. I don't think he has spent any time in the encampments, and he seems to think the City's proposed "decriminalization model" is going to be a tool to help us get out of the overdose crisis. It's a total joke. It's basically being led by the police. It's not what we've been fighting for. It's not rooted in racial justice, human rights, or defunding the police and reinvesting in communities most impacted by the drug war. Framed as a health issue and not also an issue about the laws, you can imagine where that's heading while people die all the time. Alternatives to possession – a "pathway to health care" ... like imagine getting caught using and then having to go to a doctor and that ending up in your medical chart? The police back it so ... you know they're just going to ramp up their focus on dealing and trafficking. The relief communities are asking for from the harms of criminalization won't materialize. Cressy as the chair of the Board of Health barely speaks to the deaths, especially the ones in the City-run shelters, or to how encampment evictions increase overdose.

It would be hard for you to witness the carnage that is happening and the complete social abandonment of people on the streets whom government have left to die, control, harass, and clear like garbage. It's actually gotten worse since you passed, which may be hard to believe. You missed the whole violent paramilitary operations to evict people from some parks, and they have fenced off the south side of Moss Park so people don't try and live in the whole park – tents are still there on the north side near the tennis courts and close to Shuter Street. The fencing makes it so unsafe; you could totally get trapped in there. You would be fucking crushed by how many friends of yours have now died. Shit, eight people are dying a day in the province of Ontario from opioid overdose – the majority from fentanyl and all the other drugs that have been added to the dope.

Your memorial was beautiful – it wasn't the party you would have hoped for. We had a send-off for you and others in the park, and there were drummers and dancers and singers. It's completely surreal that you died, especially how you died. Rumour is, people tried to get to you, but they couldn't, they were blocked by security. We said goodbye to you and others who died around the same time. A lot of tears were shed. You were so well loved by everyone. I miss you all the time. I lurk on your Facebook to remind myself you're really gone, though I try to stay off of it since it's post after post about people who've passed. Every month we're gathering to have a healing circle. They're led by Les Harper; his mom Elder Pauline Shirt has been at the last ones co-leading with him, and the circle is named after Nichole Leveck – Waskastaw Kakak Iskwado. You've met Nichole. She dances with her family for our healing in her jingle dress. Her partner Isaiah drums and sings and her daughters Indiana and Nazarene dance with her – they've all been coming to the park since last summer.

I was thinking about this time last year, when you were still alive, when I witnessed a body lying on the ground with a yellow sheet covering them outside the porta-potties, near the BIXI bike racks and the broken water fountain in Moss Park. Their body on the cold hard concrete, lifeless, waiting for the coroner to arrive. You know, as I know, that sometimes this can take hours. Weeks before, a man OD'd and died in an encampment in Alexandra Park in the west end of the city – he was left there for five hours. People living in the encampment, people who were friends with him, had to watch his lifeless, covered corpse for hours. It's not like people can really go anywhere. They need to watch their stuff, their homes, their tents, and there's nowhere to go inside. I was surprised to hear they came in a couple of hours; to be honest, that's never been my experience. AK told me what happened. His home is right there in the park. This was the second man to die in those last few weeks, their last breaths taken in these filthy toilets. I'm guessing from the description people offered that he was a man in his early fifties, but it's hard to say. This life can age a person. He wasn't anyone I knew, but maybe you would have, as you always knew everyone on the block.

Since that day so many other people have died outside – Sketchy, Damien, Caleb, Shawn, countless others. It's like a horror movie, really. Our friends have found people right out on the street, dead, lying across the sidewalk, in doorways, trying everything they could to revive them. I think of those who go unidentified, hundreds of unclaimed bodies in this province. Their corpses put into wooden boxes – John and Jane Does buried in cemeteries outside of the city, their loved ones never knowing that they're there. How many people do we know who might be one of them? For a whole month I couldn't stop thinking about it. It made me sick. I pictured the field of markers up at Highway 7. I was walking through it to find our friends, but nothing identified the next grave to the next. Just a sea of dusty blue coffins, lined up to be lowered into the earth, the cheapest kind, paid for by the City.

I'm not doing outreach anymore. I had to take a break. You don't know I took a new job. You left us before I started it.

The last time I saw you, I was visiting the Moss Park injection site, and even though we were supposed to be social distancing, we hugged. I'm glad I embraced you. I never thought that would be the last time I would.

I want you to know though that we tried. Maybe I'm saying this to remind myself. When I say "we" I mean all of our dedicated harm-reduction friends. The ones who didn't want to abandon people to die. The ones you worked with at Street Health. The ones who helped set up the tents in the park, which you were so proudly a part of. I loved that time. I loved getting to know you there. I loved that we were all in it together, running an illegal overdose prevention site in Moss Park, the first in all of Ontario.

We tried. We fought for shelter-hotels because we thought it would be the best solution so people could physically distance and not get COVID. The City had no plans to move people from shelters or even space out beds. They didn't care. They had to be forced to do something so people without a home could physically be safe. I guess I didn't think that they wouldn't include overdose death prevention as one of the most important components of the shelter-hotels. We didn't fight for the shelter-hotels so people would go in them and fucking DIE!!!

Amanda Leo, Kris Guthrie, and I started organizing these weekly front-line worker calls so we could all coordinate our efforts. And the City was meeting with their community partners and shelter operators to discuss health care and harm reduction in physical distancing sites. Amanda, Lorraine Lam from Sanctuary, and I got ourselves on those City calls too. In April 2020, Amanda, Liam Michaud, and I presented to the group a range of options that they could implement from peer witnessing, to opening overdose prevention sites, to having a system where people could just call staff on-site to check on them. We tried.

You never heard a shelter operator or the City on any of those calls talk about the catastrophic emergency in the shelters. While many of us have asked the City to release overdose data from the shelters, they have in past years refused. They finally released the numbers this year. It's shocking. They knowingly let people die. They knew overdose was going to kill people when they couldn't access what they needed. It took to the end of 2020 for some projects to get off the ground. Funding didn't flow in like it did to the Inner City Health Associates (ICHA) or the Multi-Disciplinary Outreach Team (M-DOT). We had to form a small group and ask a foundation to fund peer witnessing. It still isn't funded properly and it's only in a few shelter-hotel sites. I know you tried too. Your stickers with "Knock, Knock, Naloxone," illustrated by Verity (Junkie Rat), are amazing, and it was such a good idea to hand them out so people could put one on their doors to let each other know they had it. It's not like Naloxone is readily available in the shelter-hotels – well, it wasn't for a whole year.

A group of us, on our own, off the sides of our desks, formed the Toronto Shelter-Hotel Overdose Action Task Force and conducted assessments of the shelter-hotels. We visited the shelter-hotels in October and November 2020 to help them with their overdose response and to assess the gaps. We even included your stickers in the package. The Delta, run by Homes First, was the last one we went to because the executive director was angry that we called our visit an audit. We didn't want people to die. That was our intention. Exposing people wasn't our goal – even though they should be called out for their neglect. We really wanted to work together with the shelter-hotel staff.

A report was written up of the findings – a series of recommendations. It was finished in January 2021, but the City didn't release it until June.[1] They called it a guidance document.

These bureaucrats don't act like we're in a fucking emergency.

If the City had an emergency management system or a coordinator to actually respond to the overdose crisis, maybe it would have been taken more seriously and 521 people wouldn't have died last year.[2] But they don't and they never have, despite our demands. We've been in this overdose crisis/toxic drug death massacre for almost a decade.

When the pandemic hit, and we were told to shut everything down and people couldn't come inside our workplace, I sat at my desk and cried. I packed it up, I don't know why. I knew I wasn't going to be working from home. I turned to Les Harper and said, "We have to go outside, people are going to die." And we did. We started collecting tents and sleeping bags and hopped on every call we could. Those first days were intense.

Remember at the beginning of the pandemic when The Works closed its doors? The busiest safe injection site in the City closed its doors for weeks! When they re-opened,[3] it was by appointment only. Appointment to use an injection site? This was completely unheard of. Over time that changed, but the perception was that The Works turned its back on the community. I personally find it so unforgiveable, and not what harm reduction is even about. Staff wanted to open but apparently the higher ups at Public Health had other ideas. We all knew what was going to kill people was going to be overdose. Little did we know it would increase by 80 per cent during the pandemic. But of course, it did. It crushes me that you're one of them.

The day The Works closed, staff put a sign on the door telling everyone to go to Fred Victor, to their supervised injection site, despite Street Health, Regent Park, and Moss Park also being close by. A staff member from Fred Victor called me out of desperation and said people were using in the parking lot and overdosing. I ran to The Works at Victoria and Dundas to find out what was happening: they had closed to figure out their COVID protocols. Everyone was scrambling to figure them out since we use aerosolizing procedures (oxygen) to reverse overdoses. The Works didn't send any staff outside to help with people overdosing. What we had heard, is that a chunk of staff had COVID.[4]

I didn't really know what COVID was in those early days, none of us did. One of the first days after I finished outreach, on my way home, I found a man outside ODing. As I administered Naloxone, I gave him mouth-to-mouth (rescue breaths) using the barrier provided in my overdose response kit. I was scared. He was grey. I wasn't scared of him or me getting COVID. I was terrified he was going to die right then and there. He survived.

Over those first few pandemic weeks, the Toronto Harm Reduction Alliance folks organized people to be out on the weekends, volunteering to be ready to respond to overdoses for people who were stuck using outdoors, as supervised consumption sites were forced to reduce capacity. I know you were also outside with people doing outreach trying to keep people alive. The normal places people could use indoors were closed to them – like the toilets in McDonald's, Tim Hortons, etc. There was so much public use because people couldn't be private. We hung Naloxone in trees and put up signs in the parks of what was open so people could run there for help if someone was overdosing. Staff would go running from the injection sites to respond. They were even doing outreach despite being short-staffed.

Addressing the housing crisis, the overdose crisis, and COVID. Real heroes, never talked about enough. I'm so proud of the workforce. It's been so intense and hard. Staff are barely hanging in there, and, distressingly, so many people have been leaving the work. Just like you, workers have died too – overdose and suicide. Even I had to leave front-line work after almost twenty years. How can we witness so much death and suffering over and over and lose our friends, family, and co-workers and keep going? How can we stay well? At some point, it breaks you.

The day I ended up in the CAMH emergency department was the day I heard that Slayer had died. You knew her for maybe as long as I did. I couldn't stop crying outside the emergency doors while I waited for a psychiatrist to see me. That's why I wasn't around as much, I had to go off work. In the emergency department, they kept asking "What was the event?" "What was it that brought you here that you feel like you aren't in this reality anymore?" It wasn't one event, I told them. I'm here and yet someone I have known since they were a teenager, a co-worker, has just died. I saw someone dead. I saw someone get hit by a car and die. I begged in a deputation at a Board of Health meeting last week for help while I cried – it made no difference. My chosen family are struggling. We have to fight at every turn for people to be treated with dignity. I have seen people near death more than I want to recall. So many friends have died. So many people I have supported have died. A community is being obliterated. I have had to watch funerals online …

IT'S NOT ONE EVENT.

NONE OF THIS IS NORMAL!!!!

I was told I have PTSD and got linked to a therapist and psychiatrist and went home. This isn't PTSD. It's an accumulation of trauma, it's state violence, it's bearing witness to mass death, it's compounded grief and loss. These are political deaths, as Vikki Reynolds, who came to Toronto from Vancouver to support harm-reduction workers, would call them. And it's fucked me up.

On outreach we had to carry emergency overdose prevention bags with us and be prepared to put on full PPE and gown up if someone OD'd outside. We sadly encountered this too often. Your co-workers were cool; they helped create a really good insert for the Naloxone kits in the time of COVID – it was practical and real. Verity illustrated it, Franky helped with it. In the inserts, we didn't take out rescue breathing. We encouraged people to do it if they were with someone they were in a "bubble" with. Oxygen is so vital in an opioid overdose. We encouraged people to stay in their groups together, and before masks really became a thing, we gave out masks to people – fabric ones mostly, because the safe injection sites and community health centres didn't have enough PPE. At first, we had one surgical mask for the whole day. I remember when we first started handing out masks to people. I would say to people, "The government doesn't care if we live or die, we're going to make sure we live." A tragic irony given how many people have died from overdose. At the time of writing you this letter, almost 5,000 people have died from opioid overdose in Ontario since January 2020. This doesn't include stimulant overdoses.

At the beginning of the pandemic, so many people who used the Moss Park injection site were staying on Power Street, where the ramp to get on and off the Gardiner is on Richmond. It was better known to people as the Field of Dreams. It was called that for as long as I can remember. This patch of grass, where there is now a dog park, was always a site where homeless people would set up homes. There was no washroom access, but people were there as a community, taking care of each other. Living in the cold, trying as best they could to survive. So many people we knew were down there, many of them Indigenous. Les created Indigenous harm-reduction kits. He brought sacred medicines to people in the encampments. They had sage, tobacco, masks, and cedar tea in them. I would go with him and we would all have a circle and pray for each other to survive. I have this beautiful memory of us smudging on the south side of Moss Park, among the trees, where it's currently fenced off. Les, you, me, Kristy was there, and a few others, Walking Wolf as well. People just kept joining us. We saw the red-tailed hawk that lives in the park. At first, it was over by

155 Sherbourne chasing pigeons but then made its way towards us, circling us as we prayed. We know the hawk is there for us, watching us. We weren't supposed to be gathering, but no one else was around on the streets besides those who had nowhere to live and those who came to support them. These circles happened daily in the Field of Dreams. I remember when Randy joined us for his first time, asking us what to do, people telling him to just speak from his heart. He died a couple months ago at the Bond Hotel. Can't believe he's gone too. I really loved Randy a lot. He was such a good man.

The day the City came to move everyone from the Field of Dreams was both hopeful and scary. People were promised apartments in Midtown, though no one really knew where that was. Les decided not to be there that day, but a few of us went to help pack people up to go. He didn't want to witness it; he kept saying "this isn't going to go well." He kept telling us that this is how white people have always acted and that they were going to displace people and it wasn't going to be good for everyone. That they make promises they have no intention of keeping. He was right.

We knew the City would just go after anyone left behind. The Parks Ambassadors were putting one-hour eviction notices in everyone's tents while people were packing up. Police had been raiding and harassing people, slashing their tents during those months. The pressure was on to either join people and go or be targeted. We were all really worried what would happen at the Broadway apartments in Midtown. Was it going to be OK? It was so far away from Moss Park and all the services people relied on for their survival, but the City was promising they would offer a range of services. But we know that in the first week, someone we know died there. People weren't allowed outside guests, but he snuck into a friend's apartment. The public health mantra "DON'T USE ALONE" suddenly meant nothing. When he OD'd, the person whose home he was in ran through the hall looking for Naloxone, but she couldn't find any. She was scared to tell staff, because of the no guest policy, that there was someone in her room that wasn't supposed to be on-site and that he was overdosing. He died before the ambulance came, and she was ejected back to the streets. She lost her friend and her home. Anyways, you know all of this, I'm just repeating myself.

They came with these City buses covered with plastic inside. People were ready to go; they had just survived outside for months in the cold and wanted somewhere to be indoors and felt hopeful that it might lead to permanent housing. When we all got off the bus, we walked in, but staff wouldn't let Sarah Grieg and me into the apartments to see where people were being housed. We asked to speak to a manager and explained how we had just supported sixty people to come there and that we planned to continue supporting them. It's like they really thought that they knew better than us. They didn't need us there, though we all know that building trusting relationships takes time. We were eventually allowed in, and we went to see the apartments. We left so many of your friends there. The City wasn't prepared at all for overdose response. Staff were all wearing Naloxone kits around their necks but there was none to be seen anywhere else. One staff who was newly deployed from another department at the City told us she actually had no idea how to use it. We learned that no one was allowed in each other's apartments. How were people going to keep each other safe? Everyone had been watching out for each other in the encampment and now they were going to be alone using during a toxic drug death crisis!

I felt like throwing up as soon as Sarah and I left and got on the subway home. Immediately as I walked through the door, I vomited on the floor of my bathroom, couldn't make it to the toilet. People were going to die in there. It was a death trap. I emailed City officials at Shelter Support and Housing Administration and Streets to Homes who were running the Broadway apartments and expressed the fears Sarah and I had. The next day, the policy was changed, and people could go into each other's rooms but not to the different sides of the building, and still no outside guests were allowed in.

The Broadway apartments didn't last long. People got kicked out for "breaking rules," ambulances and police were there all the time, the neighbours were rabid and held protests, filming people and saying really derogatory things about homeless people in general. I wasn't surprised – this was a more affluent area that didn't have shelters in it. The developers who "lent" the Broadway apartments to the City decided to pull out earlier than expected, leaving the City to scramble. At this time, hundreds of people were outside living in tents. Those connections to housing only happened for a handful of people. Some people went back outside, some people to other shelter-hotels, and then everyone else was shipped to the Bond Hotel. At least the Bond was downtown, and at least they wanted to operate an urgent public health needs site, which is just the government speak for an overdose prevention site. They wanted to be more prepared to accommodate people who use drugs. They're right across the street from The Works too, and in the Downtown Eastside, closer to services people used. Sadly, many people we know have died there too. Maybe better than the Roehampton where you died. Where its alleged security wouldn't let people into your room as you were overdosing. That's the word on the street. That they were blocking the door, not trying to physically save you, and people in the hallway couldn't get to you so they could. I can't even bear to think of you dying and no one helping you, while you helped so many. It's really fucked up.

The one time I went into the Roehampton and into their rooms was right after Kurtis died at the Edward shelter-hotel. You were at the Edward too when he died. You told me you found him. That must have been so hard. I negotiated for his girlfriend to get a transfer out of the hotel. She couldn't stay there anymore. How could she? But this is not a policy shelters have in place, and it's really hard to transfer people. I made them do it by calling higher-ups. I went with her by taxi to the Roehampton. The first thing I noticed was that there was no Naloxone right in the lobby. No signs to say where you could get it. We went up to her room. On the floor, there was a room with two staff in it. It was like this on every floor. They could have easily had something set up so people could call this room, or go by

*it and say, I am going to use, please check in on me in five or ten minutes;
they didn't.*

*I will always regret the day I watched Kurtis and his girlfriend get
on the bus from the Moss Park encampment and go to the Edward. I
showed them on my phone how far away it was, I described to them
how long it would take to get transit back downtown (almost an hour),
and I encouraged them to think about how far away from services it
was. These shelter-hotels were too far away for people who needed to access supervised consumption sites for their survival. But people wanted
somewhere to go, out of the parks. And so they went. He survived three
days there.*

*The grief I carry is like a river crashing into boulders, emptying into
an ocean. Its depths I barely recognize. Still unknown to me. I carry
this unreal burden of thinking we haven't done enough, and I know you
would tell me off for thinking this way. Writing this letter to you reminds
me of how much we have tried, collectively. I could probably write ten
more just like this one, filling the pages of what's happened over the past
two years, about people we know who have died and how the system and
those in charge are at fault and what needs to be done. We are up against
a brutal system that was built on the attempted decimation of human
life and continues its colonial capitalist agenda. The overdose deaths of
homeless people in the last two years could fill two shelters. Is this how
they manage occupancy levels? To let people die? It feels like it. They
scurry to evict the encampments, to get them out of the public eye, not
taking into account how they could be contributing to people's deaths. I
don't think they care.*

*I wish you were still here. It's hard to live through this tragedy that
never stops. I'm forever changed by this experience. You were a real one,
Cuz. A gem of this earth. A man with excellent swagger and charisma. A
kind soul. A friend. I will always remember you. I will always remember
how we all tried. How you tried. Sometimes I blast Mobb Deep "Shook*

Ones, Part II" in my living room and think of you and try to channel your energy to keep fighting. It's not easy to keep going.

I hope wherever you are, you're with Slim, Jenny, Bella, Jessica, Caleb, Kurtis, Randy, Mel, Frank, Steph, Johnny, Slayer, Shawn, Sketchy, Jonny, Damien … I hope you're all thinking of us too. I hope you're the DJ. I'm sure you are.

I love you, my friend.

ZOË DODD is a long-time harm-reduction worker and drug user advocate. She has spent nearly two decades working in the Downtown Eastside of Toronto on issues related to HIV, hepatitis C, overdose, harm reduction, drug policy, poverty, and homelessness.

 **CHAPTER 12**

Fighting Ableism (Disability Exists and So Do We)

Jennifer Jewell

I am a disabled queer woman in her fifties, a kitchen wych[1] and artist currently trying to survive homelessness in the shelter system.

Disabled people are often left out of the conversation when it comes to being unhoused or having our needs met. Homelessness is particularly hard on us.

Many of the resources available to those who are able-bodied (meal programs, showers, laundry, shelters) are not physically accessible for disabled people. We don't have the money (for transportation) or mobility to access them. Lack of access to services was exacerbated during the pandemic. Community centres and libraries (which are usually wheelchair-accessible and open to the homeless) were shut down. Churches were closing their doors.

During the pandemic, public washrooms were no longer available, and many of the porta-potties in parks were not wheelchair-accessible or not usable by people with various mobility and balance issues. Many parks today still don't have wheelchair-accessible washrooms or porta-potties, and that is an issue not just for the unhoused. It disproportion-ately affects people who are disabled.

I spent four months living in Dufferin Grove Park. At the time, the City of Toronto had only opened one pool with fully accessible shower facilities that was available to homeless people.[2] It was costing me $30 round trip to get to the pool and back, so I had to stop showering al-together. Another pool (at Wallace Emerson Community Centre) was right up the street from our camp, but it was closed to us (homeless people) due to COVID-19 – yet children's programs were operational.

Another community space (St. Stephen's) offered laundry services, but I was being denied access to the elevator. I had to carry my laundry down to the basement and back upstairs myself. During one of my visits, I had an allergic reaction. That, in addition to my pain and fatigue, made it impossible for me to leave via the stairs. I was stuck. I tried explaining and eventually had to insist. Without the elevator, I wasn't going any-where. They finally conceded and I never went back.

Ableism was systemic before the pandemic. It became much worse during.

There was no support in Dufferin Grove Park for the first two months we lived there. I was the only one with an income to buy us the food and supplies we needed, but I didn't have the mobility to do so. Rex,[3] one of the two men who lived in my camp, had a badly broken leg, and he wasn't mobile either. Our other friend was looking for work. It took time for people to start donating tents, blankets, and food. Time for the housing workers to find us. When the City of Toronto displaces people, they have to start again from scratch.

I didn't know about Streets to Homes (S2H) before my eviction. They came through the park two months after we started living there. When they finally visited the park, the only offer on the table was congregate shelter settings. I explained that aside from needing an accessible space (without stairs) and facilities, I was immunocompromised; I had a chronic respiratory illness and allergies that prevented me from going into shared settings. I told them what I needed to be housed. They left and did not return. Neither they nor the workers that followed informed me that shelter-hotels were an option.

From that point forward, the Parks Ambassadors started paying us weekly visits. If someone was away from their tent at the time, the Parks Ambassadors would illegally open their tent to check inside. They would take pictures of our tents, but no further visits from S2H happened once the weekly visits by Parks Ambassadors started. I met another disabled woman who had lived in the park the previous year. She gave me her S2H worker's card and advised me to send an email detailing all my needs around accessibility, which I did. I learned that the workers sent in response were the first ones to do an actual intake.

I received three offers of housing while living in the camp. All three were basement apartments and cost between $1,100 and $1,500 per month in rent. The workers were aware that the maximum rent allowance on the Ontario Disability Support Program (ODSP) was $497 and that I needed housing that supported a wheelchair. Almost thirty years of being disabled and I have never been able to afford a wheelchair-accessible apartment. Thank you, City of Toronto.

I was informed that I was taken off the housing wait list, where I had been for twenty years. S2H refused to tell me why. I tried contacting Housing Connections for my housing application number to investigate myself and was told that the office was closed because of COVID-19.

I eventually ended up in a shelter-hotel after a worker from Albion Neighbourhood Services started giving me those same "offers" of non-accessible basement apartments. I think I frustrated him by calling him out on his ignorance with each offer. The day he sent me to the shelter-hotel, he was standing in my camp calling landlord after landlord, asking, "How many stairs?" During one call, he said, "Only ten?" At one point he asked me why I couldn't just keep my motorized wheelchair outside year-round.

We live in an ableist society. It is often people who are physically able-bodied themselves, who have no experience of disability, that make the decisions for us and our lives. Our housing needs as disabled people are unique. Needs that are often overlooked or dismissed by housing workers.

My first night in Dufferin Grove Park, I was scared. I had not been homeless since 1988, when I fled my home at fourteen years of age to escape emotional, physical, and sexual violence. I was on the streets for three years and then in and out of rooming houses for another three. I had to use the furniture in my room to barricade the door to stop the men who would try and break in at night to hurt me. I was finally able to leave rooming houses and found stable housing. I spent the next twenty-nine years housed.

Becoming homeless again at the age of fifty had different challenges than when I had been a vulnerable teenage girl who was a target for sexual predators. I was stronger. I had a voice. But I didn't believe I could survive with my current chronic health issues and disabilities. I wasn't sure I wanted to. I knew that I couldn't go into congregate shelter settings without risking my health.[4] I was hoping at best to find a meal. So, I made the mistake of calling Central Intake – for the first and last time.

The worker who answered the phone believed that disability was a choice. She refuted my need for a wheelchair-accessible living space. I told her that I had little money and would need to take a taxi from the park to wherever she referred me. She refused to look for a place that I could get to. She explained that any space would require that I shower first. I told her that I was not physically able to shower that night, but that I probably could the next day. Her response was that all disabled people could shower themselves. She then told me that if I could not do something one night but could the next, I was not really disabled. The only space she would refer me to was in Scarborough, in a building with stairs with showers too small for a bath chair to fit. I never called back.

I have the same problems here at Bond Place shelter-hotel, which is run by Dixon Hall. There are several exits out of the building, but only one with a wheelchair ramp. Because I only had my cane, they refused me use of the ramp to come back into the building. I was unable to walk around the building without having to sit down on the ground every few steps. I'm still being denied my request for accessible shower equipment. The workers spent eight months denying me access to my home care agency and their laundry service, and it was not until a lawyer got involved that I received some concessions. There are basic accommodations being denied to disabled people in this space, even when it is illegal to do so. Even when such accommodations are mandated.

The City of Toronto mandates that all levels of shelter staff must get training on the Accessibility for Ontarians with Disability Act (AODA); on anti-racism and anti-oppression; on LGBTQ2S cultural competency, LGBTQ2S youth inclusion, and trans awareness; and on working with people who have disabilities within the first three to six months of starting their job as a shelter worker. Someone who has taken a course called "Working with People Who Have Disabilities" should not be routinely denying disabled people access to a wheelchair ramp.

By opening the shelter-hotels, the City of Toronto demonstrated that addressing homelessness could be done – if they had the will. But instead of listening to us – the homeless and disabled – and striving to do better, they remain steadfastly opposed to making changes. Systems cannot exist inside a vacuum; they need to grow and evolve.

A dialogue needs to be opened with the City of Toronto. They need to stop criminalizing us. They need to listen. Many of us have complex needs. Housing workers in shelters need to stop denying disabled people their personal autonomy. They need to listen to us and our doctors and respond with the appropriate supports or options.

Housing cannot be solely "adequate." We need housing that is safe, accessible, and affordable, with the needed wrap-around supports. We need to support people in their choice of location, where they may have

First morning in my Tiny Shelter, built and designed by Khaleel Seivwright.
Credit: Jennifer Jewell

their own existing support systems in place. People who are disabled and homeless cannot be separated from their supports, nor should the City try to do so. They need to do better.

As it stands right now, I am told there are still no options for me unless I give up those things I need to survive. It has been a constant battle, and it is killing me. I don't think I'm going to survive it.

JENNIFER JEWELL is an empath, artist, and outspoken advocate. Her politics lie at the intersection of disability, poverty, and homelessness. She champions the causes of equity and justice through positive change.

POEM: OUR WILDERNESS

Zachary Grant

We pray for all of us, God,
all who you see before you,
gathered together in your name
in your name we ask that you magnify who we are,
exactly as we are
we are your wild children, as wild as they come
we are the wild wilderness that your Child walked,
through our human landscape,
of dreams, of desires – of loves, and longings – memories and pastimes
and that's just the valleys, and peaks – the pastoral scenery of us
we too are the wilderness
of ravines of resentment,
of cliffs of things held over one another,
of the crumbling bluffs of internal screams,
gnarled trees that grew from angers not quite fully expressed
that formed a disorienting, maze-like landscape,
where from the sweetness of the top of the mountain
we still cannot find our bearings.
We pray, God, that you do not lose yourself in us
that you find your way through our wilderness
so we can follow you out.

Tents along the side of Church of the Holy Trinity at Trinity Square,
November 2021.
Credit: Zachary Grant

ZACHARY GRANT has been involved in prisoners' justice, drug user, and
HIV organizing for many years. They are Trans and continue to be Trans on
the territories of the Michi-Saagiig Nishnaabeg.

 **CHAPTER 13**

Living and Dying on the Streets: Providing Palliative Care during a Pandemic

Dr. Naheed Dosani and Dr. Trevor Morey

There she stood, on the corner of Church and King Streets in the downtown core of Toronto. Far from her social supports. Away from her shelter. Disconnected from her health care workers.

Why? Because of a new global pandemic called COVID-19. The World Health Organization had just declared the pandemic official, and government leaders were starting to normalize physical distancing and "staying at home."

But what did it all mean if you didn't have a home? What if you were also dealing with a serious, life-limiting illness at the same time? What if you were dying?

We met our unhoused client, forty-five-year-old Charlene,[1] on this cold morning in a park to support her difficult situation. She was confused, in a pain crisis, and feeling nauseous because of the new chemotherapy treatments she was undergoing. Charlene had lived on the streets for over a decade with a diagnosis of schizophrenia, and just the week before had been newly diagnosed with end-stage breast cancer.

We met Charlene as part of a palliative care outreach team we work on called the PEACH (Palliative Education and Care for the Homeless) program. Based out of the Inner City Health Associates (ICHA) in Toronto, Ontario, the PEACH program is a mobile, street-based, and shelter-based health care program that brings compassionate palliative care to people "where they are at" – physically, socially, emotionally, and spiritually. Formed in 2014, the PEACH team is an interdisciplinary health care and social care team that includes a nurse coordinator, health navigator, home care coordinator, five palliative care physicians, a psychiatrist, and a dedicated roster of allied health care professionals who provide home care in non-traditional home spaces (e.g., respites, rooming houses, shelters, drop-ins, parks, and the street). The team aims to provide palliative care, an approach to care that emphasizes quality of life and dignity for people who experience homelessness and serious, life-limiting illness. Within the palliative care approach is a backbone of support to help the PEACH clients we see through their complex disease journeys, but also, for many, through their end-of-life journeys as well. The overall goal is to make sure that everyone has access to palliative care, so no person falls through the cracks of our convoluted systems. So no person suffers while they die.

But why is the PEACH program even necessary? People experiencing homelessness are some of the sickest in Canada. This population is twenty-eight times more likely to have the hepatitis C virus, five times more likely to have heart disease, and four times more likely to have cancer than the average housed Canadian.[2] While it is noted that the average housed Canadian has a lifespan that is typically between seventy-seven and eighty-two years, people experiencing homelessness have an average lifespan that is typically between thirty-four and forty-seven years.[3] When all of the social and health factors are taken into account, homelessness causes a person's lifespan to be cut in half. At the PEACH program, we recognize that homelessness is a terminal diagnosis of the social determinants of health (i.e., the social factors that impact how we live, learn, work, and play).[4] On top of this, many people who experience homelessness also have to deal with serious medical diagnoses, for example, heart disease, cancer, or liver disease, which makes palliative care even more important for this population.

What we have learned over the last several years in providing PEACH care is that the social ailments that people face (e.g., homelessness, food insecurity, poverty, social isolation, and many more) are wreaking havoc on people's physical health, accelerating illness, and in many cases quickening death. The need for the PEACH program reflects how the structures around people – including social policies, such as a lack of affordable housing, poor social assistance rates, over-policing, stigma, and a lack of coordination between health and social services – are creating significant barriers for people to access the care they need. We call this *structural vulnerability*, a term that aims to take away the blame from individuals and forces us to look at the societal structures around them that cause them to be vulnerable in the first place. The problem of structural vulnerability and the need for palliative care is not specific to Toronto. In fact, this issue is so pervasive that the PEACH model of care has been replicated in cities across Canada, including Victoria, Edmonton, and Calgary, and even around the world in places such as the US and Australia.

When COVID-19 hit our communities and the streets, it meant the PEACH team had to think differently and adapt quickly so that we could better serve the needs of people like Charlene, and better respond to the humanitarian crisis that was about to impact thousands of people experiencing homelessness in Toronto.

From Encampments to Shelter-Hotels: Living and Dying on the Streets during a Pandemic

Alexandra was diagnosed with incurable colon cancer just as the news was starting to pick up that the virus now known to be SARS-CoV-2 (i.e., COVID-19) had been detected in Canada. She had presented to hospital with severe abdominal pain, and doctors found that her cancer had obstructed her bowels. She was offered chemotherapy to help keep her disease stabilized and to relieve some of the symptoms, but the doctors expected that her cancer would progress and that she may only have up to a year to live. On top of her medical issues, Alexandra had just removed herself from an abusive relationship and had packed up her life into just two bags. She managed to get a bed at one of the respite shelters in Toronto. As she was going back and forth from the shelter to the hospital to get her chemotherapy, she would hear on the news that the number of COVID-19 cases was steadily increasing in the shelter system. She would tell us about how her and her friends at the shelter had to make a difficult decision. Should they stay at the congregate setting in the shelter or grab their things and try to sleep outside in encampments to protect themselves from the virus? Alexandra was also hearing on the news that people with weak immune systems, like her, were at increased risk of complications and death from COVID-19. She couldn't imagine how she would manage to get to and from her appointments living in an encampment, but she was also extremely worried about contracting COVID-19 herself.

In response to the experiences of people like Alexandra, the City of Toronto opened shelter-hotels to help people follow public health guidelines on physical distancing and to further prevent the spread of COVID-19. Alexandra's shelter unfortunately did have an outbreak of COVID-19, and, as a result, she was moved to one of the City-run shelter-hotels. All of a sudden, she was in a new area of the city and had lost contact with many of her friends who had chosen to stay in the encampments. Worse, she was disconnected from her social and health care supports.

Fortunately, Alexandra did not contract COVID-19, but she did end up having another complication of her cancer that required an emergency procedure to drain fluid from her abdomen. This required the insertion of a permanent drain, which would require daily nursing visits for the foreseeable future. She initially declined this treatment as she was not sure how she was going to be able to manage this at her shelter. When she was offered assistance to find housing, she worried that if she had to pay rent, she wouldn't have enough money left over from her funding through the Ontario Disability Support Program (ODSP) to buy food and other necessities of life. These very practical concerns are often not factored into the medical decisions that are made in the hospital and can often lead to people being labelled as "difficult" or "not compliant" when in reality they are simply advocating for themselves. We were able to work with the hospital team and Alexandra to apply for a private unit in a transitional housing program, where she would have enough income to pay for groceries, and where we could arrange for a nurse to come visit her daily. Once Alexandra felt comfortable that she would have enough support in the community, she agreed to go ahead with the procedure.

When people have the resources they need to live well, they feel empowered to make their own choices around their health.

Today, Alexandra continues to live in her transitional housing unit and our team visits her there to ensure that her pain and other symptoms from her cancer are managed. She is able to go to hospital for her ongoing chemotherapy treatments and has a nurse that visits throughout the week to check on her. It is hard enough to live well with a terminal cancer diagnosis, but Alexandra's resiliency shows the strength one needs to be able to deal not only with a life limiting illness but also precarious housing and income insecurity.

Harm Reduction and Advanced Care Planning in a Pandemic

With the arrival of COVID-19, public health officials were announcing more and more deaths from the virus at their press conferences every day. We would constantly be hearing about people who were "at increased risk" of having serious complications and dying of COVID-19. For example, people who were elderly, living with diabetes, heart disease, or lung disease. One of those people was Connor, a gentleman who had been moving in and out of various shelters within the city and who was cared for by our PEACH team as they followed his progressive heart failure. Connor also used street fentanyl, which often would lead to overdose and ultimately cause him to be hospitalized for extended periods of time, with no one knowing if any one of these events would result in his death.

Throughout the pandemic, many shelter and social service workers were left wondering what would happen to many of their vulnerable clients if they were to develop COVID-19. As a palliative care team, we are used to helping with advanced care planning and recognize how important it is for people living with a life-limiting illness to have their wishes respected and to understand their illness and treatment options. We also recognize that for people experiencing homelessness, there is often a history of trauma, substance use, and problematic interactions within the medical system that make having these conversations with health care professionals even more difficult. The importance of having people you trust who can provide trauma-informed care – an approach to care that goes from asking "What's wrong with you?" to "What matters to you?" – is crucial. As soon as the pandemic hit, our team worked to develop an advanced care planning tool that case managers, shelter workers, and social service providers could use to start some of these conversations.

The COVID-19 public health emergency has intersected with and exacerbated the already existing housing and opioid overdose death emergencies. During the pandemic, overdose deaths continued to increase, and people who use drugs were further isolated. This was the case with Connor, who had difficulty maintaining regular appointments and, when he was hospitalized, had difficulty staying in hospital due to withdrawal symptoms from his fentanyl use. He required care that took a harm-reduction approach; that is, an approach that recognized that substance use was a part of his life and that helped empower him to live the life he wanted while ensuring he received the care he deserved. Our team helped to ensure that he received care with dignity and met him where he was at; not just geographically in the place he considered home but emotionally, meeting him on his own terms. People who use drugs often are stigmatized for their drug use, even when nearing the end of life. Many hospices and palliative care units will not allow people to use drugs, which often leads to many deciding not to go to these places when they are dying.

We need to ensure that everyone has access to comfort and dignity at the end of life, and that our palliative care system recognizes that for people who use drugs, a harm-reduction approach is essential.

Grief amid the Homelessness and COVID-19 Crises

Many are surprised to learn that social and health care workers receive little to no support or training in how to process their grief. This is especially surprising given how much suffering front-line workers who support unhoused people witness on a day-to-day basis. From the failures of our systems to serve people, to the opioid overdose death crisis, to unmet social and health care needs, there is a lot of moral distress that goes unaddressed. Because of the dire lack of resources, the culture in many spaces of the homelessness sector is to just "carry on," which leaves no opportunity to grieve when we lose the people for whom we care.

We recognized the importance of addressing grief when we first launched the PEACH program in 2014, noticing that many of the care workers, both in social services and in health care, who were working to support our clients were experiencing moral injury and compassion fatigue. We noted that in spaces where the number of deaths were especially high, like harm-reduction shelters or shelters where many people had palliative care needs, there was an especially high rate of turnover among staff. Don't get us wrong – the staff really did care about the clients, but they didn't always have the support and tools they needed to deal with the suffering they were witnessing and the grief they were experiencing. This is why we created the concept of the Grief Circle to better support the workers who are caring for our clients.

Grief Circles are our response to the grief crisis that front-line workers are experiencing. How do they work? After a site (e.g., a shelter) experiences a death, we gather with every member of the care circle (i.e., every person who was a part of caring for the client), regardless of their role or skill set. We light a candle, hold a minute of silence, and we … grieve. We cry. We laugh. We remember what it was like to care for the person who died. We reflect on what it was like to care for them. We think of ways to renew ourselves to be able to support people in these situations. We commit to reinvesting in each other so we can build a stronger community for the future. We call it the 4 Rs (Remember, Reflect, Renew, Reinvest), and we end our Grief Circles by putting out the candle and holding a final minute of silence before we invariably have to do it all again. Trust us when we say that we always have to do it again.

During COVID-19, we held more Grief Circles than ever before – not because we wanted to, but because more people were dying of both acute and non-acute causes than we had ever witnessed before. It got to the point where the City of Toronto tapped the PEACH team on the shoulder to be one of the official interventions to support front-line workers in the city's COVID-19 shelter-hotels. As the pandemic went from just a few weeks to many months, and then into the next year, the PEACH team continued to conduct Grief Circles, often several times a week, to support workers who needed structured spaces for healing, a virtual shoulder to cry on, and to know they didn't have to be resilient all on their own. Many reported feeling relieved, supported, and happier, and sometimes people even reported having more strength to take on the next day, no matter how challenging it might be.

While our clients undoubtedly experienced unthinkable suffering due to the pandemic, they needed a workforce that was as healthy and well as possible to support them every step of the way. And just maybe our Grief Circles helped in that. In fact, amidst all the ongoing tears, sharing, caring, and mutual solidarity, we continue to hear that our Grief Circles became a beacon of hope for many front-line homeless sector workers during a time when hope was hard to find. While we know that Grief Circles address just a small drop in the ocean that is grief, they are a reminder that in times like these, we must address the psychological and emotional well-being of front-line workers.

We won't end the homelessness crisis if we don't care for our front-line workers.

How a Pandemic Led a Team of Street-Based Palliative Care Health Workers to Think Outside the Box

When the COVID-19 pandemic started, many health care providers were forced to provide care over video chat or by phone. People were forced to have discussions virtually about whether their cancer was getting better or worse rather than in-person in an office with their cancer specialists.

But what happens if you don't have a phone? What happens if an office tries to mail you an appointment notice, but you've moved from one shelter to another?

During the pandemic, the PEACH caseload doubled, and as a result our outreach palliative care team brought on a new member: a health navigator. The clients that we see are both structurally vulnerable, because of systems set up against them in our society, and also living with a life-limiting illness – this leads to them becoming "doubly vulnerable."[5] In order to receive dignified care, a vulnerable person needs a team that is adaptable and can meet them wherever they happen to be when care is needed.

The team needs to be able to think outside the box, and that means recognizing that access to housing, income, and food … is health care.

Within the PEACH team, we recognize how important this type of care is, which is why we created this unique health navigator role. When a client is referred to our team, we will discuss their current living situation and strategize ways we can help improve it and bring this care to them. Our health navigator will begin the process of applying for housing and income supports. Even with maximal supports through social assistance programs, however, there often isn't enough money left after paying for rent and food to purchase the other basic necessities that one needs. Our team has thus helped to develop a program called the Good Wishes Project, where we have a set of funds that help us grant a "wish" for each of our clients. Our clients' wishes have fallen into one of five groups: practical necessities, end-of-life preparations, personal connections, paying-it-forward, and leisure. Ultimately, the goal of these wishes is to empower truly person-centred care that helps provide dignity for people facing life-limiting illness. Often our nurse coordinator and health navigator will collaborate and truly "make magic" to be able to grant these wishes, which can include covering transportation costs to help clients reconnect with their loved ones or finally be able to see the Toronto Maple Leafs at their home arena.

Our health navigator also plays an essential role in helping our clients navigate their way through the health care system to ensure that they receive the same level of care as anyone else in the community. Sometimes this takes the form of joining our clients for medical appointments, whether in-person at a clinic or virtually using the health navigator's phone.

As a health care system, we can't just accept the status quo, we need to constantly be thinking of ways we can improve the way we deliver care. For example, we need services that are low barrier so that someone's friend or a shelter worker can reach out for help and be able to secure access to care on their behalf. We've learned that an effective way to do this is to provide resources to teams so that they are able to meet clients wherever they are – whether it's in an encampment, in a shelter, or in supportive housing – to deliver the care that people need at every stage of their illness.

By Understanding the Experiences of People Downstream at the End of Life, We Can Better Fix Health Inequities Upstream during Life

Even before the pandemic, people experiencing homelessness were hanging on by a thread to survive. When COVID-19 happened, that thread snapped.

Through the lens of providing palliative care, we see on a day-to-day basis what the cumulative effects of inequity do to people over a lifetime. For example, people who live poor typically die poorer. People who live hungry, die hungrier. And people who live socially isolated typically die more socially isolated. This is why so much of what we do as members of the PEACH team is about more than providing front-line social support and health care. We advocate, too.

Why?

Because we have a moral obligation to care for people downstream while we inspire social change upstream.

How can we do this? By telling the stories of the people we care for, by empowering voices of lived experience to share their stories, and by learning from the communities we aim to serve. We can't stop there, though. We must train the next generation of health workers to do better, we must conduct research on how to improve care, and we must use innovative solutions to do more with the resources we have – all while advocating for more. But ultimately, we must dig deep and remind Canadians that the reason people are dying earlier and faster is because of inequities in the social determinants of health.

But do we really care?

If we do, we will adopt harm-reduction approaches and safe supply to support people who use drugs. We will better resource outreach-based health care to meet those who aren't able to come see us in clinics and hospitals. We will practise trauma-informed care to better connect with people who have experienced trauma, often at the hands of health care. We will create social housing, ensure people have a liveable income, stop over-policing those living in poverty, and direct resources towards healing our communities.

It's clear that we live in a world where people live differently, but should we really die differently?

If we really do care, we'll do better.

Dr. Trevor Morey and Dr. Naheed Dosani.
Credit: Chris Young

DR. NAHEED DOSANI is a Toronto-based palliative care physician and health justice activist. He serves as an assistant professor with the University of Toronto Department of Family and Community Medicine's Division of Palliative Care.

DR. TREVOR MOREY (he/him) is a family medicine and community-based palliative care physician for people experiencing homelessness in Toronto, Ontario. He is the communications lead for Health Providers Against Poverty, a community-based advocacy organization. Trevor is passionate about providing equitable access to health care, housing, and food and income security.

 **CHAPTER 14**

Building Tiny Homeless Shelters

The Canadian Human Rights Commission

For most of 2020, Canadians were told to stay safe at home. It was sound public health advice in the context of a global pandemic. But for the hundreds of thousands of Canadians currently experiencing homelessness, it presented a major problem.

Khaleel Seivwright wasn't homeless when the pandemic struck his hometown of Toronto, Ontario, but he didn't really have a fixed address. He was drifting. It's a state of being he's chosen to live in for much of his adult life. It affords him freedom but also a deep appreciation of the need to have a place to call home.

As the city went into lockdown and Khaleel's work in construction dried up, the twenty-eight-year-old carpenter and musician decided to head north to Manitoulin Island to spend some time in an "intentional community." The concept wasn't new to him. In his mid-twenties, he spent three years living in another such community in northern British Columbia. He found it enlightening. "I became a lot more involved

Homeless individuals in
Ontario are over

five
times

more likely to die from COVID
compared to other people.

27.3%
of people experiencing
homelessness
are women, and

18.7%
are youth.

34%
of First Nations women
and girls and 21% of
racialized women and girls,
are living in poverty.

At least

35,000
Canadians are homeless
on a given night.

1 in 5
Indigenous people live
in a dwelling that is in need
of major repairs.

Canadian Observatory on Homelessness, Canadian Alliance to End Homelessness;
Lawson Research Institute and the Institute for Clinical Evaluative Sciences;
Canadian Women's Foundation;
Statistics Canada;

Credit: Graphic by Gontran Blais Design

in what I needed to live," he says, contrasting the life of growing food, collecting water, and creating shelter to his upbringing in the Toronto suburb of Scarborough.

When Khaleel returned to Toronto at the end of [the] summer, he was struck by the number of tents scattered around city parks. While the City's shelter system scrambled to adopt physical distancing rules and increase its capacity to serve Toronto's roughly 10,000 homeless people, many opted for a different solution: provisional encampments in parks.

Khaleel felt for them. Having spent a winter sleeping in the rough in Vancouver, he knew what that life was like. "You're constantly fighting against nature, against reality," he said. So one September night in 2020, he loaded some building materials onto his truck and drove into the Don Valley, the wild ravine that snakes its way through Toronto's east end. He found a clear spot in the undergrowth, cranked up his generator

Khaleel Seivwright in his workshop.
Credit: CP Images

to create some light and got to work, building a giant, habitable box. Modelled after the one he made for himself in British Columbia, it was complete with fibreglass insulation, a double-glazed casement window, and a lockable door.

Over the next few days, he kept going back to work on it. On day three, he discovered a pile of possessions inside and a name painted on its wall.

The "Tiny Shelter" had cost Khaleel roughly $1,000 in materials and eight hours of his time. If that's all it took to get a person through the winter, he felt it was more than worthwhile. He started a campaign on GoFundMe. After his project was featured on the CBC nightly news, donations went from a trickle to a flow. Within weeks, he was able to rent a warehouse in downtown Toronto, order materials in bulk, and focus exclusively on building Tiny Shelters – with the help of some thirty-five volunteers.

The shelters [were then] distributed to tent dwellers across the city. "I've met every person that took one," Khaleel says. "And they're really happy."

But in November, Khaleel received a letter from the City of Toronto's general manager of the Parks, Forestry and Recreation division prohibiting the shelters' placement on City property; it claimed the dwellings contributed to "dangerous and unhealthy" living conditions and interfered with the City's objective of clearing the encampments.

Khaleel didn't buy it. How could the City claim to be concerned about these people's well-being, while depriving them of a safe, warm place to spend the winter? He knew from conversations with encampment dwellers that many would not enter a shelter even if it did have space.

According to street nurse Cathy Crowe, who has been working with Toronto's homeless for thirty-three years, the City's already overburdened shelter system presents very real health risks. In October [2020], the Ontario Superior Court ruled that the City's shelters had failed to follow physical distancing guidelines.

By that time, some 659 shelter residents had tested positive for COVID-19 and at least five had died.

Khaleel knows that his Tiny Shelters won't begin to fix the problem of homelessness in Toronto. But he's pragmatic, focussed squarely on a problem that many would prefer to look away from – and that is getting worse. Recently a young man called Khaleel to "reserve" a Tiny Shelter; he and his father had been served an eviction notice and had nowhere else to go.

"This isn't a permanent solution," Khaleel acknowledges. "This is just to make sure that people – some people – don't die in the cold this winter."

The City Cruelly Uses the Court System to Deny Homeless People Tiny Shelters

On 12 February 2021, the City of Toronto filed an injunction application against Khaleel Seivwright. The City wanted a court order that would permanently stop Seivwright from placing or relocating structures on City-owned land.

Despite broad community support for Seivwright's Tiny Shelter project, the City won its demand.

On 27 August 2021, an agreement was reached between the City of Toronto and Seivwright. In the agreement, the City agreed to withdraw its court application, and Khaleel Seivwright agreed not to install any new Tiny Shelters on City land without the City's permission, nor to maintain or relocate any existing Tiny Shelters on City land without permission.

Seivwright issued the following statement on social media:

> I have settled with the City and agreed not to build and place structures in parks.
>
> The City's practices of violently removing people living in encampments is a demonstration of its fundamental mentality towards homeless people. The future of our city doesn't depend on ruthlessly enforcing policies that have no regard for the human beings who live here. It does not depend on squeezing out anyone who finds themselves unable to afford rent. The future of our city depends on cohesive, sustainable solutions that address the real issues: poverty, lack of affordable housing, and a broken shelter system. Leading up to this agreement I have been in conversation with the City in an attempt to secure permanent housing for encampment residents that want and need it. But it has been obvious that putting this problem out of sight has been the City's main concern instead. With this settlement finalized, Toronto Tiny Shelters will no longer exist in the same way.
>
> Last September, I decided to build small shelters for people living outside in the winter. Thousands of people donated money, and many volun-

teers came to help build. I want to thank everyone for their support. It's late August now, and cold weather is only a few months away. Although the City decided to file an injunction against me, there is only one name on this application. I hope that others continue to do what they are inspired to do to support people living outside, until the day comes when the people who run this City step up and do their job.[1]

Over the next few months, despite the ongoing shelter crisis in Toronto, the City removed and destroyed the majority of the Tiny Shelters.

Cathy Crowe

Chapter content reprinted with permission from the Canadian Human Rights Commission and Khaleel Seivwright.

CATHY CROWE is a recipient of the Order of Canada and a pioneer of street nursing. She is currently a public affiliate in the Department of Politics and Public Administration at Toronto Metropolitan University. She has fostered numerous coalitions and advocacy initiatives that have achieved significant public policy victories, including the 1998 Disaster Declaration. She is the author of *A Knapsack Full of Dreams* and *Dying for a Home* and producer of the Home Safe documentary series. Her work is the subject of the documentary *Street Nurse*, by filmmaker Shelley Saywell. With the Toronto Disaster Relief Committee, she delivered prefabricated houses for shelter to Tent City, a homeless encampment on Toronto's waterfront from 1999 to 2002.

POEM: LORD, WE PRAY

Zachary Grant

For those who cannot enter the towers
the green hued, glass-enshrined lobbies of the buildings
to sit for a while in the black vinyl chairs
with deep seats you could just disappear into
Lord, we pray

For those who can't use the bathrooms
in the restaurants on the main drag
to feel the comfort of the silence of a toilet throne
and some peace and quiet to scroll endlessly through their phones
Lord, we pray

For those who must take the subway to the end of the line
and then back again. and again. and again.
they must know each of the stations by heart,
and how many people get on and get off and get on and get off
before the service stops for the night
Lord, we pray

For those who do not have clean water
who gather up from the puddles, the dust from the job site,
the dirt from the sneakers, the burned rubber of tires,
the spit and piss and grime of humanity
who gather that water to put drugs in their veins
Lord, we pray

For the security guard, or guards, or guardas
guarding our fortress walls, the plywood 12 by 5s lining the sidewalk
as a moat around the construction site
who drive around and around in their sedan all night
to keep us from falling into the hole we have dug
Lord, we pray

PART III

HOUSING IS A HUMAN RIGHT

 **CHAPTER 15**

In the Parks and in the Courts: The Legal Fight against Encampment Evictions

A.J. Withers and Derrick Black

In March 2021, the City of Toronto tweeted a photo of Derrick Black, who had been housed the month before. Derrick is a fifty-eight-year-old Black man with a short salt and pepper beard and matching hair with black thick-framed glasses. He is holding his tabby cat, Munchkin. They are sitting on the couch of his new apartment. Derrick's left arm is holding Munchkin under her front legs, their faces touching. Munchkin's back legs are propped up on Derrick's right arm, her belly exposed.

The tweet says:

> Derrick found himself homeless in early 2020. He didn't feel safe accessing the shelter system & so like many, set-up in Moss Park encampment ... He believed it was his right to remain in the park until he was able to secure safe & adequate housing. With support of City's S2H [Streets to Homes] & encampment teams, he secured 1-bdrm in

Moss Park area … He's thankful to City for support to help him find appropriate housing …[1]

This story, like so much City of Toronto spin, purposely leaves out key information to make the City appear much more compassionate and competent than it is.[2]

Derrick lived with his parents when the COVID-19 pandemic hit. His mom was eighty years old at the time. They were worried about her health and the possibility of contracting the deadly disease. Together, they decided it was best for Derrick to move out. But, living on welfare in a city with a housing crisis meant that there was nowhere for Derrick to go. Even before the pandemic, the shelter system had high rates of violence, bedbugs, and theft. Diseases like tuberculosis (TB), strep A, norovirus, and influenza spread rapidly and were difficult to get rid of. For years, advocates had been warning that the cramped conditions would lead to a deadly disease outbreak. Lives had been lost in the TB outbreak of 2001–2 and the flu outbreak of 2018. Derrick didn't think the shelters were safe given the situation with COVID-19.

Michelle Plourd, Derrick's partner, lived in the Fred Victor housing complex just around the way from Moss Park. The Fred Victor took some measures for COVID-19, like not allowing guests, including Derrick whom Michelle was bubbled with. But it also had COVID-19 in the building. Michelle had also endured significant threats to her physical safety and had been robbed many times.

So, with nowhere else to go, Derrick and Michelle got a tent and moved into Moss Park. It was March 2020, and, at that point, there was one other person living in a tent there. When the encampment eviction moratorium was inexplicably lifted by the City less than two months later, the now much larger Moss Park encampment was at risk of eviction.

Homelessness in winter: a Toronto park encampment.
Credit: Jeff Bierk

Community organizing, including direct action, hadn't been successful in stopping the evictions or getting the moratorium back. By June of 2020, it seemed like a tactical shift was needed. There had been several court victories in British Columbia that allowed unhoused people to sleep in tents in public parks. This case law was not ideal because it only gave people the right to camp overnight. According to the law, each morning, people had to pack up their stuff.[3]

This permanent transience jeopardizes people's safety and means they can't create the kinds of communities that existed in many of Toronto's parks by then. It was possible that the COVID-19 pandemic could be used to get better case law in Toronto. Many encampment residents and some community groups wanted the "no camping" bylaw declared unconstitutional so folks couldn't be evicted. In July 2020, we filed suit against the City of Toronto.

In a capitalist, settler colonial state like Canada, every courthouse is built on a foundation of injustice. The courts uphold the oppressive social relations that produce and proliferate homelessness. This does not mean it is not possible for unhoused people to win in the courts, but the story Canada tells about fairness and equality in the courts is part of a national mythology and doesn't match the lived experience of many unhoused people. Those of us working on the encampment lawsuit didn't believe in the mythology of the justice system. We believed we might have a chance at winning but if not, this court case would be used as a tactical organizing tool to generate publicity and support and pressure the City not to evict.

There had recently been a settlement won by a coalition that took the City to court because the City wasn't implementing sufficient COVID-19 safety measures. Though this action was likely life-saving, several community organizers had two main critiques of this lawsuit that they did not want to be replicated in the encampment lawsuit: it wasn't resident led and it (largely) didn't make information available for organizing. A precondition of the encampment lawsuit was that residents be named applicants and they lead the case to the extent that they want. Two community groups were also signed on. This ensured the whole City was covered by the suit, not just the four parks that were the named applicants. The applicants in the shelter lawsuit were "a coalition of public interest organizations and legal aid clinics"[4] because, as they told the court, "there [were] no reasonable alternative means available."[5] That is legal speak for "shelter residents can't reasonably be applicants in a lawsuit." This reinforced problematic stereotypes about unhoused people. It is also paternalistic to bring forward a case on behalf of a group without having them be part of it. One of the problems with how people in encampments and shelters have been treated is that the City thinks it knows what is best for people. One person who represented one of the applicant organizations in the shelter case told some of the encampment legal team that he was against encampments and a positive aspect of the shelter suit was it would make the shelters safe so the encampments could be eliminated.[6]

Because there were no unhoused people as named applicants, the legal coalition made a settlement agreement with the City that is secret. One of the conditions of the settlement is that it was not to be made public. A summary of the agreement is public,[7] but the whole agreement is not available and never will be. Non-shelter residents decided what is best for shelter residents and no shelter resident is allowed to know exactly what "best" means. Was this group that excluded shelter residents acting in the best interests of the people impacted or simply replicating the dynamic of "we know better"? Many of the people in the shelter lawsuit are tremendous advocates, all of them had good intentions and the case resulted in important changes. Do these ends justify these means? This is not a rhetorical question – we are honestly unsure because we don't know what would have been possible if shelter users were involved.

The other key critique of the shelter lawsuit is that lawsuits create access to information that the community doesn't normally have access to. In the shelter lawsuit, only the City's progress reports on physical distancing and the settlement summary were made public. Research conducted for the lawsuit about the shelter system was then kept secret from the public. The shelter lawsuit even got a lot of people to participate in conducting and filling out surveys about the shelter system that were kept secret from the community. The encampment lawsuit was committed to generating *and sharing* knowledge. It was through this lawsuit that community advocates finally had the proof that the City "identified opportunities to have dedicated staffing and infrastructure within encampment sites," which included COVID-19 protection measures, sanitation, meals, and on-site supports. However, staff believed that the City elected to enact a policy of deprivation instead because "building infrastructure in encampments would require spending scarce resources in parks and risk encouraging larger encampments."[8] This suit also allowed FactCheck Toronto, a group that exposes the City's lies and misleading statements about homelessness and housing, to demonstrate that the City was exaggerating the number of fires in encampments: the sworn statement said there were far fewer fires than was publicly claimed.[9] Using the lawsuit as a way to gather information was a tactically useful way the case supported ongoing community organizing.

A.J. Withers, the activist who initiated and was a key organizer in the lawsuit, and Brendan Jowett, the lawyer who took on the case, started going to Moss Park to talk to the residents to see what they thought of the lawsuit. They found residents overwhelmingly supportive.

The work on the case was unexpectedly expedited when Moss Park was served with a twenty-four-hour eviction notice on Wednesday, 15 July 2020. There were sixty-four individual encampments in the park at the time.[10] The City's own laws required seventy-two-hours' notice. Was the City breaking its own law? Of course it was! This is a regular occurrence for unhoused people. Jowett sent the City a letter saying the eviction was illegal; the City extended the notice to the proper length to Saturday, 18 July 2020.

Starting that Wednesday, Brendan Jowett, A.J. Withers, and Selwyn Pieters, a lawyer who had joined the legal team that day, wrote the court application that signed on fourteen encampment residents, the Toronto Overdose Prevention Society (TOPS), and the Ontario Coalition Against Poverty (OCAP) and had it ready to file Friday evening. Derrick and Michelle were two of the first people to sign on as Applicants in the suit.

On Saturday morning, the Moss Park residents were at the ready and many community members were gathered to support them. The residents' resolve, community support, and lawsuit worked together to make the City back off from its threat to evict.

Rather than a full trial, there was an injunction hearing first. The injunction hearing heard a small part of the case and gave an interim decision. The trial itself could take years to happen. The hearing was 1 October 2020. By that time, Toronto was well into the second wave of COVID-19, but we were working with facts from the summer of 2020, when cases were much lower.

Derrick, Michelle, and supporters watching the court proceedings from
Moss Park.
Credit: Zoë Dodd

Derrick, like many Moss Park residents, watched the hearing from
a large screen in Moss Park. The judge suggested only having two encampments and forcing everyone into those controlled spaces: a ter-
rible and violent proposition. He gave the applicants the lunch hour
to propose what he would consider a more reasonable proposal than
eliminating the no-camping bylaw. So, Brendan hopped on his bike
to race to Moss Park to meet Derrick, other residents, and the TOPS
spokesperson. A.J., sick at home, and representing OCAP, was on the
phone. It was decided that any proposal we put forward would result
in the forced eviction of some encampment residents, which we were
trying to prevent with the lawsuit. We could not compromise when it
came to basic human dignity. The lawyers told the judge that our position remained the same.

The verdict came down about a month later. We lost. The judge said the City, like always, had the choice not to act. So while we legally lost, we actually won: the City chose not to act. It left Moss Park and the other encampments alone for a long time. The lawsuit did what we set out for it to do – it stopped the evictions and it helped give encampment organizing a strategic shift.

Derrick remained steadfast in his encampment. He said he would remain there until he was housed and the attention the lawsuit brought to him as the lead applicant made the City work harder to find him something. Michelle was so sure that Derrick would get housing that she would spend a hundred or more dollars on stuff for the new house each month. She would keep it in Moss Park because she had been robbed so often at Fred Victor. Derrick amassed sheets, dishes, pots and pans, towels, and so on. He had nearly everything he needed to establish his new place "and good quality, too, not that cheap stuff," Michelle says.

It took until February 2021 for Derrick to get housing.

On moving day, he left by foot with a cart. He had to move his stuff: tent, tarps, generator, coolers, a love seat, and clothes, as well as all of the new stuff for his home. Derrick loaded his cart to make the block-long walk in the snow to his new apartment. Before he left, he told the City workers, who were there to throw out anything he didn't take and erase any sign of the "Mayor of Moss Park," that he was coming back to get the rest. When Derrick came back the next day to move the rest of his belongings, they had been thrown in the garbage. Almost everything he owned was gone. Derrick complained to City staff about it and was told "bring in the receipts and we will reimburse you." Clearly, this was an outrageous request! Amazingly, Derrick had many of the receipts for the things Michelle had bought for the new place. The City threw out many other receipts along with the things Michelle had bought too.

Derrick fought for housing and won. But there are thousands of unhoused people in Toronto that need housing. Rather than meet people living in parks with police boots, the government should meet them with house keys.

Derrick and Michelle.
Credit: Jeff Bierk

DERRICK BLACK was the "Mayor of Moss Park" as a long-time resident of the encampment there. He fought for and won housing for himself and continues to support encampment residents.

A.J. WITHERS is a long-time housing and homelessness activist. They are the author of *Fight to Win: Inside Poor Peoples' Organizing* (Fernwood Publishing, 2021) and *Disability Politics and Theory* (Fernwood Publishing, 2012), and co-author with Chris Chapman of *A Violent History of Benevolence: Interlocking Oppression in the Moral Economies of Social Working* (University of Toronto Press, 2019).

CHAPTER 16

COVID Life

Sarah White

Pre-COVID-19, a store clerk would never allow me to set foot in the establishment with a bandana covering my face, hiding my identity.

Nowadays, they won't let me in without some sort of face covering.

What a strange world we live in …

Ironically, in many ways, this pandemic has enhanced my quality of life.

I'm generally a pretty socially distant person as it is and, thanks to COVID-19, the number of people invading my personal space is at an all-time low.

On the subway, on the sidewalk, in elevators et cetera … let out a little cough and anyone in earshot starts tripping over themselves to get out of range.

Sorry! Next time keep your distance!

Thanks to COVID-19 I am now living in a 4.3-star hotel that I could hardly afford to stay at for a whole weekend back before I became homeless.

And here's the real kicker … it's entirely free. I have a California king-size bed, a 60-inch smart TV, unlimited Wi-Fi, three meals per day.

They come in to change my sheets once a week.

I even have the option to have them do my laundry once a week. I opt to do it in my sink instead.

It's almost sickening. When I was working two jobs, I couldn't afford to stay here three nights in a row.

I'm thankful that the City was able to pull all this together, to get the homeless off the streets during the pandemic … It's just sad that this [pandemic] had to happen for that to happen.

There is still so much more that the City could be doing.

Toronto is experiencing a housing crisis while there are more than 65,000 unoccupied condo units.[1]

There are hard-working people, people with families, people with little kids, struggling to keep up with their rent, their hydro, their car payments … struggling to afford groceries. Their struggling has been going on long before COVID-19.

One thing I can say is that this pandemic has caused the general population to be a little more compassionate towards people experiencing homelessness. When we were all in the encampments, the number of donations we received was astounding. You expect that sort of thing from the social justice organizations, but it was truly incredible to witness so many individuals from the community reaching out to us!

For us living on the streets, never having quite enough is just something that you get used to.

For those who have never experienced poverty, it has been extremely difficult to adapt to.

So many businesses have foreclosed. Countless individuals have lost their jobs. People have had to take so much time off work either because their place of employment had to close or because they came in contact with someone who has had a COVID-19 positive test.

The government implemented CERB (the Canada Emergency Response Benefit) but for those who truly needed it, it wasn't nearly enough. So many people have lost everything they spent their whole lives building and are now on the street while people who have never had much are suddenly being housed.

It's nice being in the Novotel. I grew up on the Esplanade and recently I've run into a few of my childhood friends.

Last year they put me in the Roehampton shelter-hotel and I honestly felt safer being in my tent.

The staff were not properly trained to work with marginalized demographics, and the long-term members of the Midtown community weren't too fond of us.

It felt like the program was not designed to help any of us succeed.

But they provided three meals a day and a washroom. With a shower!

If you've never been homeless, you probably don't know the impact such a menial thing can have on a person. We all take so much for granted …

Sarah White.
Credit: Sarah White

For each bedroom light
Switched off each night
Out of mind
Out of sight
Another friend has lost the fight

For each stuttering bulb
In each desolate Hall
Once so bright
Now feeble and dull
Another Soldier about to fall

For each star that falls from the skies
For each bulb that burns out and dies
I light a candle
And close my eyes
Another gone with no goodbye

This perfect city skyline
Particularly at night time
Is the perfect backdrop
For Nightmares of the worst kind
Each Light lost is a loss of mine

Sarah White

SARAH WHITE is a poet, a painter, and a candlestick maker. She is an advocate for marginalized communities. She spends her free time offering therapy to squirrels in inner-city parks.

 **CHAPTER 17**

Two Metres: The Legal Challenge

Noa Mendelsohn Aviv, Doug Johnson Hatlem, and Geetha Philipupillai

Governments in Canada should have done everything possible to protect people, including some of the most vulnerable members of society, during the COVID-19 pandemic. When they failed to do so in Toronto, where Canada's largest homeless population lives, advocates, front-line workers, and organizations came together to fight. This chapter tells the story of our legal battle – how it came to be, and what we achieved.

The housing and homelessness crisis in Toronto was already decades old by March 2020. Government supports were inadequate for far too many people, especially those who faced intersecting forms of marginalization. For decades, governments had failed to provide appropriate supports for young people aging out of child welfare, for refugees and immigrants, and for people leaving mental health, correctional, and other institutions. Governments had also failed to ensure adequate and affordable housing.

Noa Mendelsohn Aviv speaking at what is possibly the first physically distanced protest in Canada at Toronto City Hall, April 2020.
Credit: Cathy Crowe

Health care professionals, front-line workers, advocates, and many others have long known, since before the pandemic, that people experiencing homelessness have worse health outcomes and higher morbidity rates for a variety of reasons, including poverty and barriers to accessing health care. Further, inadequate shelter conditions such as poor ventilation and crowding lead to the spread of infectious illnesses.

Government officials who were authorized to create emergency plans in the years prior to 2020 should have understood that people experiencing homelessness would be far more vulnerable to many kinds of emergencies – including a pandemic – than the general population.

City Inaction

And yet, when COVID-19 hit Canada in the middle of March 2020, City of Toronto officials had very little to say about what they were doing to protect people experiencing homelessness.

Activists, front-line workers, and journalists started demanding answers. They were concerned that the City was not doing what it should to find solutions. Even Toronto's recommendation of 2 metres of physical distancing for the general public was not adopted to protect the people seeking refuge in Toronto's crowded shelters.

Around this time, hundreds of Toronto residents actively left or avoided the shelter system because of the increased risk of exposure to the virus in shelters. Instead, they set up tents and encampments in the cold outdoors. Young and old faced extreme deprivations as the COVID-related closures of many social services, businesses, and community facilities seriously limited access to adequate sanitation, shelter, food, and health care services.

These individuals' fears were justified: several thousand people in the shelter system contracted COVID-19. Shelter users were already at higher risk of serious health implications from the virus due to pre-existing respiratory conditions and other illnesses.

A study published in January 2021 showed that people with a recent history of homelessness were twenty times more likely to be admitted to hospital for COVID-19, over ten times more likely to require intensive care, and over five times more likely to die within twenty-one days of their first positive test result.[1]

First Letter

The situation was dire. We had to act. On 29 March 2020, the Canadian Civil Liberties Association (CCLA) sent a letter to Mayor John Tory.[2] The letter demanded the implementation of extraordinary measures to deal with the crisis, including reducing overcrowding in homeless facilities consistent with the distancing standards everywhere else; procuring facilities that allowed for real distancing and safety, with one person or family in each unit; maintaining transparency through the proactive disclosure of the City's plan and related statistics; and providing adequate personal protective equipment (PPE) to homeless people and facility staff. The letter pointed out how a number of cities in Canada and around the world had taken just such measures. A proper emergency plan should have made the necessary funding and logistics possible.

The City, meanwhile, announced that it had secured 1,200 hotel rooms for the purpose of physical distancing. Unfortunately, many of these rooms remained empty for weeks, and the other problems raised in the letter were not resolved.

The crisis worsened. The need for shelters was growing, as was the size of the encampments. Crowding in shelters and the use of bunk beds had not been fixed, and most concerning, there were more and more COVID-19 cases in the shelter system. People were frightened and fighting for their lives.

The First Physically Distanced Protest

On 15 April 2020, what may have been the first physically distanced protest in Canada's history took place in Nathan Phillips Square, organized by the Ontario Coalition Against Poverty. Its goal was to get Toronto to speed up protections for the homeless population. Afterwards, two of the speakers, Cathy Crowe and CCLA's Noa Mendelsohn Aviv, joined forces in a legal action against the City of Toronto.

Participating in the protest was risky and frankly uncomfortable. Despite the organizers' great care to limit the number of protestors to twenty, and to draw physically distanced "standing squares" for everyone present, there were a great many unknowns about what was or was not legal, how police might react, and about the risk of getting COVID-19 at this early stage of the first wave. Ontario was in a state of emergency, and emergency orders prohibited gatherings of more than five people, including organized public events. Attending the protest as a participant or speaker meant risking a one-year jail sentence or a fine of up to $100,000 – and even this seemed less concerning than the danger of arrest. Criminal lawyers had volunteered to assist if charges were laid but being held in a crowded detention or police cell meant risking exposure to a new and dangerous virus for oneself and one's family. Even still, the protest was well attended.

Coalition Letter

A few days later, participants from the protest, activists, organizations, and allies came together determined to support people experiencing homelessness and to make change. This new legal Coalition was made up of six public interest organizations and legal aid clinics, each one dedicated to the protection of human rights for historically marginalized people and groups: Sanctuary Toronto, Aboriginal Legal Services (ALS), the Advocacy Centre for Tenants Ontario (ACTO), the Black Legal Action Centre (BLAC), the Canadian Civil Liberties Association (CCLA), and the HIV & AIDS Legal Clinic Ontario (HALCO). These groups' commitment to equity – and to fighting for critical protections in the pandemic – is evident in their reasons for joining the Coalition:

"Since the pandemic began, we have been worried about our community members who use shelters and sleep on the streets." – ALS

"Sadly, Ontario's long-standing housing crisis has meant that ACTO has extended its mandate to include homeless and precariously housed people and the conditions of shelters generally and more specifically during the pandemic became a matter of great concern to us." – ACTO

"[BLAC participated in this litigation out of a] recognition that poverty is racialized and a desire to protect the health and safety of those members of the Black community who access the shelter system, particularly during COVID-19." – BLAC

"We got involved in this matter to ensure people staying at shelters are able to do so safely and with dignity." – HALCO

"[CCLA] believes that every person has the right to equality, to liberty, to security, and to life – and we felt compelled to step up and support the demand that these rights be provided to people using the shelter system." – CCLA

Cathy Crowe, longtime street nurse and distinguished visiting professor at Toronto Metropolitan University (formerly Ryerson University), helped to bring the Coalition together and acted as a consultant. The Coalition also had an amazing pro bono litigation team of lawyers including Jessica Orkin, Louis Century, and Geetha Philipupillai from Goldblatt Partners LLP; Andrew Porter and Sahar Talebi from Lenczner Slaght LLP; and Emily Hill and Christa Big Canoe from Aboriginal Legal Services. Our Coalition was fortunate as well to receive support from Legal Aid Ontario's test case program.

Meet the Coalition

Sanctuary Toronto is a church community organization that has drop-in programming, a medical clinic, offers outreach services, and comes together regularly at memorials to grieve for friends and at social and other events to celebrate life.

Aboriginal Legal Services' mission is to strengthen the capacity of the Aboriginal community and its citizens to deal with justice issues and provide Aboriginal controlled and culturally based justice alternatives.

The Advocacy Centre for Tenants Ontario is the only legal clinic in Canada wholly devoted to systemic advocacy on housing issues.

The Black Legal Action Centre is an independent not-for-profit community legal clinic whose mandate is to combat anti-Black racism in the province of Ontario.

The Canadian Civil Liberties Association is an independent, national, non-governmental organization that fights for the civil liberties, human rights, and democratic freedoms of all people across Canada.

HIV & AIDS Legal Clinic Ontario is a charitable not-for-profit community-based legal clinic that provides free legal assistance to people living with HIV/AIDS in Ontario.

The Role of Sanctuary Toronto

Sanctuary Toronto played an important role in the legal Coalition. Their connection to people with lived experience kept all the legal proceedings grounded in the lives of their community and provided important information about the many risks for unhoused people during the COVID-19 crisis.

To ensure that the City of Toronto did not target individuals, Sanctuary agreed to be included in the lawsuit. Sanctuary staff regularly updated people who attended their meal services and people they encountered in encampments about the progress of the suit and what Sanctuary hoped to gain for the people they served.[3]

Coalition Letter

On 20 April 2020, the legal team wrote on behalf of the Coalition to notify the City of Toronto that if it did not take action to address the deepening crisis in the shelter system, the Coalition would initiate a legal proceeding against the City. The letter called on the City to comply with federal and provincial health guidelines, to require a minimum separation of 2 metres between beds, to cease the use of bunk beds, and to fill to capacity the 1,200 hotel rooms leased by the City for the crisis – the majority of which were still empty.

On 23 April 2020, the City of Toronto replied, insisting that "imposing a mandatory standard requiring 2 metres of physical distancing between beds in all shelters was not workable given the space restrictions and number of residents that are served in Toronto shelters." Rather, where physical distancing guidelines could not be met, the City's focus "has been on reducing the site's capacity and relocating people to other sites."[4] To this end, the letter indicated that the City had moved 770 people into shelter-hotel rooms and 492 people into community spaces.

We were concerned this posturing and foot-dragging would cost lives. On 24 April, the Coalition issued a Charter application in the Ontario Superior Court. The Coalition alleged that the failure to make sure that there were 2 metres of space between shelter beds and the failure to stop the use of bunk beds increased the risks of COVID-19 transmission and was contrary to the constitutional rights of people experiencing homelessness. In particular, the Coalition alleged these conditions in shelters were discriminatory and risked the health and safety of people experiencing homelessness, contrary to the guarantees of sections 7 and 15 of the Charter.

Given the rising number of COVID-19 cases in the City's shelter system, the Coalition moved for a temporary and immediate order requiring the City to enforce 2 metres of separation between beds and to prohibit the use of bunk beds.

In mid-May 2020, the Coalition and the City entered into a binding and written settlement agreement. Based on the terms of the settlement, the Coalition's urgent motion for a temporary and immediate order did not proceed and was not heard by the Court.

However, the terms of the settlement brought a measure of accountability and public transparency to the City's approach to dealing with COVID-19 within the shelter system. Pursuant to the settlement, the City was required to provide regular, detailed reports about its efforts and progress in achieving and sustaining physical distancing standards.

The relevant terms of the settlement were as follows:

- The City was required to use best efforts to "achieve without delay and thereafter sustain" 2 metres between beds and end the use of bunk beds across the City's shelters, respites, and overnight drop-ins.
- The City was required to use best efforts to provide shelter to all shelter system clients by making available the number of beds necessary to achieve physical distancing standards across the shelter system.
- All individuals who received any support services from the City's shelter system since 11 March 2020, including those in encampments who left the shelter system because of fears of COVID-19, were included within the scope of the City's obligations under the settlement.
- The City was required to report regularly on its progress until it reached and sustained compliance for two months.

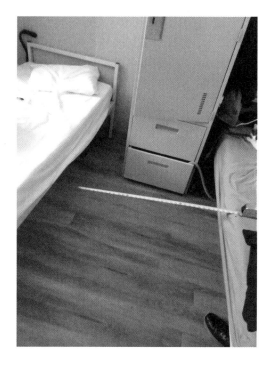

Measuring the distance between beds in a Toronto shelter on 16 May 2020, the day after the Coalition and the City entered into a settlement requiring that all beds be at least 2 metres apart. It appears here that the distance between the two beds is just over 1 metre. It definitely is not 2 metres. Credit: Brian Cleary

- In exchange for the City's commitments as contained in the agreement, the Coalition agreed to adjourn its injunction motion.[5]

Inside the Shelter-Hotels

Many front-line workers believed that unhoused people, many older and with vulnerable health, could simply be given keys to a shelter-hotel and most would be able to care for themselves safely and responsibly, perhaps with meal or grocery help. The City had other ideas, rejecting the wisdom of front-line workers and instead setting up "wrap-around supports," including frequent invasive room checks for all shelter-hotel residents. These checks were and are resented by the vast majority of shelter-hotel users. These invasive room checks also did very little to stem a burgeoning tide of opioid-related overdose deaths; periodic surveillance of people in their rooms simply won't ensure people don't die from a poisoned drug supply.[6] Room checks reinforce distrust and a sense of institutionalization and don't actually address the risk of an overdose death.

Issues facing the homeless community exploded into public attention on 15 May 2020, when advocates showed up en masse and mostly stopped the City's planned clearing of all tents under the Gardiner Expressway, west of Yonge Street. School teacher Anna Jessup stood in front of a bulldozer that had begun making its way towards a tent near the corner of Lakeshore Boulevard and Bay Street. Major media covered the event and lawyers for the City dropped their final remaining objections to the terms that we had proposed for the interim settlement.

Non-compliance

Despite the legal agreement, the City did not provide the safety that shelter users needed. On top of this, it attempted to distract us. On 15 June 2020, the City asserted that it had achieved compliance with the physical distancing standards in the settlement and, as such, the settlement agreement would terminate within two months if the City sustained its compliance.

We weren't convinced. We had reason to believe that the City's Central Intake line was continuing to turn away individuals who were entitled to a shelter bed under the agreement. Hundreds of people remained in encampments or were sleeping rough due to difficulty finding shelter spaces and well-grounded concerns about the continuing spread of COVID-19 in the shelter system.

The Coalition also had serious concerns about the City's lack of transparency. In the settlement agreement, the City had agreed to report on its progress and to respond to the Coalition's questions, yet after signing the agreement, the City refused to provide basic information about physical distancing in shelters, respites, and drop-ins. For example, the City refused to provide requested information about room dimensions and its plans to demonstrate how it arrived at its target capacity numbers for shelters, while at the same time relying on these very numbers to assert that it had achieved physical distancing at these sites.

As we were concerned that the City was not following through on its commitment to shelter users, we were forced to return to court. The Coalition brought a motion to enforce the settlement. Specifically, the Coalition sought declarations that

- the interim settlement agreement continued in effect;
- the City had not achieved 2 metres of separation between beds across the shelter system;
- the City had failed to maintain the capacity of the shelter system; and
- the City had failed to disclose relevant and proportionate information including physical plans and dimensions for shelter sites to the Coalition.

Following cross-examinations of City managers and having obtained documents and data, the Coalition uncovered evidence that the City asserted it had achieved compliance with physical distancing standards on 15 June 2020, despite knowledge by multiple City managers that it had not in fact done so. The Coalition also obtained documents that demonstrated that the City filed affidavit material on the enforcement motion containing false and misleading claims regarding the nature and extent of the City's quality assurance process, which the City relied on for its assertion of compliance.[7] This evidence demonstrated the insufficiency of the City's verification and implementation efforts, as well as the City's possession of this information on 15 June, the very day the City asserted compliance with physical distancing standards.

By early August 2020, efforts, including the lawsuit, were showing great promise for many of Toronto's poorest residents, but all was still far from well. Jason Greig, for instance, told the Canadian Press that COVID-19 "made my life better," describing that pre-pandemic there were countless hoops to jump through to secure housing, but that in the wake of the pandemic, the red tape seemed to disappear. However, the looming closure of the Broadway temporary apartments had raised his anxiety level enormously.[8] Jason was right to be worried. While the lawsuit may well have ensured that he was owed a shelter-hotel room or other accommodation when the Broadway apartments abruptly closed, he has since bounced through multiple shelter-hotel spaces and spent significant time sleeping outdoors. The City's reluctance to provide safe shelter is part of a bigger pattern of not investing in lasting solutions for people without housing.

A Breached Agreement

On 15 October 2020, Justice Lorne Sossin of the Ontario Superior Court ruled in favour of the Coalition's key arguments, finding that the City failed to comply with its commitment to ensure physical distancing in Toronto homeless shelters during the ongoing COVID-19 crisis. Justice Sossin agreed with the Coalition that the City's obligations under the settlement remained in force and highlighted the importance of ongoing vigilance and monitoring of the City's adherence to its legal commitments.[9]

Justice Sossin found that the City had breached its obligations under the agreement that it signed with the Coalition when it asserted on 15 June that it had complied with physical distancing standards between all beds in the shelter system, having not, in fact, reached that milestone nor made its best efforts to do so.

Justice Sossin was critical of the City's interpretation of physical distancing requirements as solely applying to the distance between the longest sides of beds and not applying to the distance between the head and foot of a bed, noting that this interpretation was decided upon "without the benefit of public health guidance."[10] Justice Sossin held that future decisions about the configuration and distancing of beds in shelters must be rooted in specific and transparent public health expertise and guidance. Justice Sossin ordered the City to obtain such guidance and to share the results with the Coalition that started the legal challenge. The decision also required the City to resume its regular reporting to the Coalition about its progress in achieving physical distancing in shelters.

Justice Sossin confirmed in his judgment that "any failure by the City to take all reasonable steps to meet physical distancing standard in congregate shelter settings heightens an already significant risk of the spread of COVID-19 to some of the most vulnerable members of our society."[11]

The Coalition was pleased with the decision, which confirmed its position that the City had not done enough to reduce the risks of COVID transmission within Toronto's shelter system, and that the City's assertion of compliance with physical distancing standards was premature. Justice Sossin's judgment also ensured that going forward, decisions about physical distancing within the shelter system should come from evidence-based guidance from independent public health experts.

Over time, there was a steady increase in the number of shelter-hotel rooms available from 1,200 in March 2020 to 2,500 by early fall 2020. Around 300 more rooms became available in February 2021.

However, the City has still not fully spaced shelter residents at 2 metres in all directions. By early 2021, it was also not following what we would consider best practices in terms of testing, ventilation, and the use of PPE. A major outbreak had already begun in early February 2021. At times, there were more than a dozen shelter, respite, or shelter-hotel sites in outbreak and hundreds of cases related to those outbreaks.

In April 2021, we learned of the deaths of two women who had been staying at Shelter Support and Housing Administration's Women's Residence shelter and who had tested positive for COVID-19. Only one of the deaths was reported in the City's public data because the other woman died of a drug overdose while staying at the Recovery Hotel site, far from her usual harm-reduction scene. The main Women's Residence shelter where the outbreak occurred would have been sleeping a maximum of fifty-two women per night if the beds had been spaced 2 metres in all directions. In fact, it was sleeping between sixty-seven and seventy-five women. Despite inquiries, front-line workers were not able to ascertain whether the two deceased women had been sleeping in rooms that would have had fewer beds if the City had complied with the Coalition's understanding of the interim agreement.[12]

Another COVID-related death connected to the Fleet Street respite was never reported publicly.[13] This respite was also overcrowded and further evidence of the City's lack of compliance with its agreement with the Coalition.

As of November 2021, the number of people shelter-hotels could accommodate had shrunk slightly to 2,600. Multiple waves of outbreaks in the shelter system seem to have subsided, and leases on shelter-hotels are being extended, per the most recent report from the City, until April or in some cases June 2022.

While the Court ruled in favour of the Coalition's enforcement motion, the Coalition and the City continued to litigate the issue of whether the City had obtained the necessary public health guidance to meet the requirements set out in Justice Sossin's judgment to terminate the interim settlement agreement. At the time of writing, the Coalition and the City continue to litigate the issue of whether the City has obtained the necessary public-health guidance to meet the requirements set out in Justice Sossin's judgment to terminate the interim settlement agreement.

While we cannot make an exact assessment of the impact of the individualized shelter-hotel rooms and the litigation, things certainly have shifted dramatically since the City's initial lack of attention to this issue in March 2020. It is concerning to think what the result might have been – how many more shelter spaces would have closed and individualized shelter spaces never opened, how many more people would have been on the streets, how many more outbreaks and illnesses there would have been and how many more lives lost – had it not been for legal, media, and front-line advocate intervention. As it was, too many people were exposed to COVID-19, and even one death is a death too many.

NOA MENDELSOHN AVIV is the executive director and general counsel of the Canadian Civil Liberties Association (CCLA). Since 2002, Noa has stewarded CCLA's litigation on such issues as racial profiling, refugee protection, 2SLGBTQI+ rights, reproductive justice, freedom of expression and religion, socio-economic rights, and intersectionality. Noa also advocates before public bodies, makes public appearances and commentary, and engages in public education on human rights.

DOUG JOHNSON HATLEM started as a street pastor at Sanctuary Toronto in 2005 after completing his Master of Theological Studies and one year of law school at Duke University. In 2014, Doug produced *What World Do You Live In?*, a feature-length documentary film directed by Rebecca Garrett that focused primarily on the Sanctuary community and resistance to police violence. From 2016 to 2019, Doug co-pastored a Mennonite church in Waterloo alongside Jodie Boyer Hatlem, with whom he has three children.

GEETHA PHILIPUPILLAI (she/her) is a lawyer at Goldblatt Partners LLP practising civil litigation, constitutional law, and public law. She is counsel in *Sanctuary et al. v. Toronto (City)*, an application regarding physical distancing in Toronto shelters during the COVID-19 pandemic.

 **CHAPTER 18**

Homelessness, Housing, and Human Rights Accountability

Leilani Farha

Introduction

Canada has an acute housing crisis that is protracted in nature and baked into its economic and social fabric. More than 235,000 people live in homelessness in any given year in Canada. Consider what living in homelessness means: it is the ultimate threat to one's physical and mental health; it is a near complete deprivation of dignity, equality, and respect; and if it doesn't threaten life itself, it substantially undermines life expectancy. More than 1.5 million households are in core housing need, either spending too much of their income on housing or living in substandard conditions. Social housing wait lists are many years long in cities across the country. Evictions and the threat of eviction are standard business practice, regardless of the consequences for tenants. These are not just social policy issues; they are an assault on human dignity and security, equality, health, and, at times, life itself. As such, they must be understood and regarded as significant human rights concerns requiring human rights responses by all orders of government.

The Value of Human Rights

Deploying human rights to both understand and address a housing crisis can be transformative. While most governments regard human rights as a stick used to periodically thrash governments for poor performance, human rights can, in fact, be a carrot. In the case of Canada, a human rights approach to housing could set the country on a more sustainable path, resulting in greater equality between people, better overall socio-economic outcomes, and greater human well-being.

A commitment to implementing human rights compels a paradigm shift and introduces new priorities in several ways. Human rights help governments set priorities. They affirm that deprivations of the right to housing such as homelessness and grossly inadequate housing are not just program failures or policy challenges but human rights violations of the highest order, depriving those affected of the most basic human rights to dignity, security, and to life itself. As such, human rights compel recognition that the needs of people living in parks, or shelters, or in grossly unaffordable or inadequate housing be addressed as a priority. It ensures human rights problems are identified and addressed as such.

A rights-based approach also clarifies who is accountable to whom: all levels of government are accountable to people, particularly marginalized and vulnerable groups. While access to adequate housing for all involves many actors, it is the legal obligation of states to be a key actor and a regulator of private actors.

Human rights change the way governments interact with people who are homeless and inadequately housed, recognizing them not as beneficiaries of charity but rather as rights holders and active subjects, empowered to engage and be involved in decisions affecting their lives.

By recognizing the expertise of rights holders, a human rights framework can be corrective, using the experiences of those living in homelessness or inadequate housing to assess the efficacy of government programs and policies and to identify any shortcomings and problems and address them to ensure progress continues to be achieved.

Human rights apply to a broad range of policies and programs and incorporate universal norms that bring coherence and coordination to multiple areas of law and policy through a common purpose and shared set of values.[1]

Canada's Human Rights Obligations

Canada's housing crisis has been unfolding, government decision after government decision, with relative impunity, despite the fact that long-ago Canada made a legal commitment to implement the human right to housing when it ratified the International Covenant on Economic, Social and Cultural Rights (ICESCR) in 1976. Article 11 of the ICESCR states that parties to the Covenant "recognize the right of everyone to an adequate standard of living, including adequate food, clothing and housing."[2] Governments in Canada continue to make international human rights commitments related to housing – for example, ratifying the Convention on the Rights of Persons with Disabilities (2010), committing to implement the United Nations Declaration on the Rights of Indigenous Peoples (2007), and committing to the 2030 Agenda and the Sustainable Development Goals – all of which require Canada to effectively implement the right to housing.

These international human rights instruments require governments to ensure the most disadvantaged and marginalized populations live in adequate housing that allows for a life of dignity and security. Housing is only adequate if it provides legal security of tenure, is affordable, habitable, has access to services, is in a location proximate to health care, education and other essential services and employment, and if it is culturally adequate.³ Affordability and security of tenure are cornerstones of adequacy. Affordability is defined as commensurate with household income, not what can be fetched through the private market. Security of tenure means that tenants should not be fearful that they may be evicted, including as a result of increases in rent that they cannot afford.

To uphold the human right to housing, governments must (a) refrain from actions that would violate the right to housing; (b) protect individuals, groups, and communities from violations of the right to housing by third parties (e.g., landlords and financial actors); and (c) take steps to progressively realize the right to housing using the maximum available resources and through all appropriate means, including legislative measures.⁴

Upon ratifying the ICESCR, governments are required to take steps towards achieving the full realization of the rights contained in the Covenant. This is known as the obligation to "progressively realize" the right to housing. Some of the most egregious violations of the right to housing occur as a result of governments' failures to take action to address situations of homelessness, housing need, and other housing injustices.⁵ The progressive realization of the right to housing requires that states take positive measures to "fulfil the right to housing as swiftly and efficiently as possible," and the "measures taken must be deliberate, concrete" and undertaken "within a reasonable time frame."⁶ This requires that States implement and adopt strategies to realize the right to housing in collaboration with relevant stakeholders and actors. Such strategies must "clarify the responsibilities and roles of all levels of government, institutions and private actors, with goals, timelines, accountability mechanisms, appropriate budgetary allocations and measures to ensure access to justice."⁷ Further, if a state adopts a retrogressive measure – that is, one that weakens the protection of the right to adequate housing – it will have to demonstrate that it carefully weighed all the options, considered the overall impact on all human rights of the measure, and used all of the resources available to it.[8]

While progressive realization of the right to housing is the general obligation, there are circumstances that impose immediate obligations on states. Under the ICESCR, any state that allows a significant number of people to experience homelessness is, prima facie, failing to uphold its obligations.[9] As such, parties to the ICESCR "are required to demonstrate that every effort has been made to use all resources that are at their disposition in an effort to satisfy, as a matter of priority, those minimum obligations."[10]

It is clear that under international human rights law, people living in homelessness – in parks, under bridges, or on the streets, for example – are not to be treated as criminals, encroachers, or trespassers. They are rights holders. Thus, pitching a tent in a park or under a bridge, or rolling out a sleeping bag on the pavement is a human rights claim – a claim to the right to life and the right to a home. States are accountable to rights holders and must respond appropriately and on an urgent and priority basis.[11]

Under international human rights law, forced eviction – that is, the involuntary removal of people from their homes – is also a prima facie violation of the right to housing and is prohibited. As such, strict guidelines must be met before people can be removed from their homes including (a) an exploration of all viable alternatives to the eviction; (b) significant and meaningful consultation with those affected such that they can influence any decision taken that will affect their lives; and (c) the offer of long-term adequate, affordable, and secure housing in a location agreed to by those being evicted.[12] Eviction into homelessness is also a violation of the right to housing.

Those who may have suffered a violation of their right to housing must have a mechanism they can use to seek a remedy.[13] This does not necessarily have to be a court of law, though often recourse to courts will be required to allow for the review or enforcement of any non-judicial remedy.

Human Rights Denied

It is beyond the scope and purpose of this chapter to do a full assessment of Canada's compliance with its international human rights obligations with respect to the right to housing. However, an overview of the prominent housing conditions across the country sheds light on some of the ways in which governments across Canada are failing to meet their international human rights obligations and the consequences.

HOMELESSNESS

To say that Canada is failing to meet its international human rights obligations with respect to housing is an understatement. One is hard pressed to find a city in the country that doesn't have substantial numbers of people living in homelessness – that is, living on the streets, in parks, in overfilled shelters, in their cars, in motels, or in such decrepit and overcrowded housing that it is tantamount to homelessness.

A snapshot of numbers across the country in cities big and small is bleak and in many cases only growing. Toronto, Canada's largest city, saw a 26 per cent increase in city shelter use between 2018 and 2021, reaching close to 6,000 people, and reports estimate that approximately 9,000 people are living in homelessness in any given year. Ottawa, with a population of just 1 million people, saw more than 8,000 of its residents using homeless shelters in 2019.[14] Montreal, Edmonton, and Halifax saw their homeless populations double in recent years, reaching 4,000,[15] 2,800,[16] and 477[17] people respectively. PEI's homeless population increased by 70 per cent between 2018 and 2021,[18] Winnipeg's most recent count found over 1,100 people living in homelessness,[19] and Victoria's point-in-time count in March 2020 revealed over 1,500 people living in homelessness.[20] Of course, these numbers only account for homelessness that is easily measured – where people are living in shelters, motels, or public spaces. Women, especially women with children, and youth who are homeless tend to stay with family or friends to avoid living on the streets or in shelters. Hidden homelessness such as this is rarely measured.

Indigenous people are disproportionately represented amongst Canada's homeless population, which is also comprised of persons with disabilities, racialized and migrant communities, and gender-diverse people. Women have very particular experiences of homelessness, often suffering gender-based violence.

Since the onset of the COVID-19 pandemic, many cities across the country have also seen an increase in the number of people living specifically in parks, referred to as "homeless encampments." For example, in a one-month period at the beginning of the pandemic, Victoria saw an increase in tents in parks from approximately 25 to more than 400. At one point in 2020, Toronto reported more than 500 tent homes across the city in parks big and small. The rise in tent encampments is attributed in part to the downsizing of many emergency shelters to accommodate social distancing health requirements imposed at the beginning of the pandemic. Choosing a park over a shelter has also been a decision taken by some on the basis that congregate settings are unsafe in the COVID-19 context as compared to encampments, which are outdoors and allow for social distancing. Those who have used shelters and advocates also note that shelters are often violent places where substance use and overdoses are common, where theft is rampant, and where rules are in place that are difficult for some to navigate, including no pets and no alcohol rules, daytime closures, curfews, restricted access to social spaces, and constant surveillance and monitoring.

The treatment of people living in homeless encampments in city parks by local governments has been shocking, particularly during the pandemic, and completely inconsistent with international human rights law. Rather than being treated as rights holders, encampment residents are often treated as trespassers and criminals and live under nearly constant police surveillance. Moreover, they are often denied basic services and necessities including toilets, showers, electricity, garbage collection, food, and water. When homeless people living in parks erect structures for privacy, security, and to prevent frostbite and hypothermia, their structures are torn down as a potential fire hazard. A number of Canada's big cities, including Halifax, Toronto, and Calgary, have resorted to forced evictions, often deploying large numbers of armed police officers (including those on horseback) and private security forces to dismantle and disperse encampment residents. Sometimes encampment residents are offered alternative places to sleep, such as shelters and hotel beds, but often they are not. Only on the rarest of occasions are they offered long-term housing. These forced evictions simply disperse the homeless population and break up the social support networks they have created, driving many of them to live in less public areas and making it harder for them to access the supports and services they may need.

This treatment of people living in parks is completely inconsistent with governments' international human rights obligations, including those outlined by the UN Special Rapporteur on the right to adequate housing in a Canadian-specific protocol.[21] Rather than being treated as rights holders who have been denied the right to housing, people living in homeless encampments in Canada are penalized for their homelessness. Only in the rarest of circumstances are they meaningfully engaged in discussions regarding their housing. Though the removal of people from their homes must only be used as a last resort under international human rights law, alternatives to eviction are rarely pursued. Relocation rarely results in viable long-term housing options, and those who have been evicted from homeless encampments have few options to seek justice for a violation of their human rights outside of what can be intimidating and costly legal proceedings. Despite the disproportionate number of Indigenous people living in homeless encampments located mostly on unceded territory, Indigenous rights to self-determination and free, prior, and informed consent are never mentioned or implemented. This is contrary to the UN Declaration on the Rights of Indigenous Peoples.

INADEQUATE AND UNAFFORDABLE HOUSING

The picture doesn't brighten much when we look at those who are housed across the country. Approximately 1.6 million households are living in "core housing need"[22] – in other words, housing that is unaffordable, in disrepair, or overcrowded. The unaffordability of housing and evictions of tenants due to rental arrears have become an acute problem. The Canadian Centre for Policy Alternatives has mapped the affordability of rental housing – representing one-third of all households in Canada – and has concluded that there are no neighbourhoods in the Greater Toronto Area (GTA) or Metro Vancouver where a full-time worker earning minimum wage could afford either a modest one- or two-bedroom apartment without spending more than 30 per cent of their earnings. In Vancouver and the GTA, for example, a minimum-wage worker would have to work 112 or 96 hours a week, respectively, to afford a two-bedroom apartment, and 84 or 79 hours a week, respectively, for an average one-bedroom apartment. In fact, "of the 36 metro areas in Canada, 23 have no neighbourhoods where the average-priced one-bedroom is affordable to a minimum-wage worker, and 31 have no neighbourhoods where a two-bedroom apartment is affordable."[23] In light of these figures, it is not surprising that at the onset of the pandemic, when many lost their jobs or became precariously employed, tenants feared that they would be unable to pay their rent and be displaced into homelessness.

Governments across Canada have done little to ensure they are meeting their obligations with respect to affordability of housing to ensure that low-income households can find adequate housing that fits within their household budget.

THE FINANCIALIZATION OF HOUSING

Homelessness, unaffordable rental housing, and housing precarity are manifestations of the gross inequality that characterizes most cities in Canada, which is increasingly tied to the role of housing and real estate in Canada's economy. Those with few resources who have no choice but to rent in the private market – Canada has some of the lowest rates of social housing among OECD (Organisation for Economic Co-operation and Development) countries – find themselves living in an ever more expensive housing market, often displaced from what is affordable as rents escalate or the properties where they are living are repurposed into more expensive accommodation. Renters can never get ahead, putting increasing proportions of their income towards rent. For this cohort, it is difficult to accrue any personal savings. Meanwhile, individual and institutional investors who have the means to invest in housing or residential real estate see their wealth growing exponentially, often thanks to the rents being paid by tenants. As a result, wealth inequality grows, with housing at its core and homelessness, unaffordability, and precarity the outcomes.

Wealth inequality created through real estate has become pronounced in recent years, including throughout the pandemic. Canada's housing market is now dominated by investors – those with capital or access to it. For example, 20 per cent of all residential real estate purchases in Canada are made by investors, a figure that is higher by a few percentage points in centres like the GTA and Hamilton.[24]

While much of this investment is by individuals with wealth, apartment buildings and multi-family housing have also become targeted for purchase by institutional investors, such as pension funds and insurance companies, who use these properties to grow capital and as a financial tool to amass more capital for other investments. While housing has commonly been used as an investment, what makes this different is the unprecedented amount of capital now being poured into residential real estate and the drive for quick, high double-digit returns on investment. This is called the financialization of housing.

In Canada, individual landlords with small- to medium-sized holdings are increasingly being rivalled and squeezed out of acquisitions by real estate investment trusts (REITs), which raise rents and file evictions at disproportionately higher rates. Martine August has been tracking this phenomenon, and her research shows that over the last thirty years financial landlords have become increasingly dominant owners of multifamily apartment homes: "REITs alone have grown from owning zero suites (units in apartment buildings) in 1996 to nearly 200,000 by 2020. In total, the largest 25 financial landlords (REITs and other types of firms) held about 330,000 suites last year – nearly 20 per cent of the country's private, purpose-built stock of rental apartments."[25] The names of these landlords will be familiar to many: Starlight Investments, King-Sett Capital, CAPREIT, Boardwalk REIT, and Hazelview Investments, to name a few.

Institutional investment in rental accommodation may not be inherently problematic, but under existing models, where buildings are owned by REITs that trade publicly on stock markets or other institutional investors, the drive for profits to satisfy investor-clients comes at the expense of tenants through ever-increasing rents and the threat of eviction (and homelessness) for rent arrears or minor infractions. Tenants also report that financialized landlords use renovations to displace them, ultimately raising rents when the upgrades are completed. In a 2021 report, RenovictionsTO found that from 2012 to 2019, financialized and corporate landlords were responsible for 64 per cent of all above guideline rent increase (AGI) applications filed in Toronto, and for 84 per cent of all units impacted by AGIs.[26]

Landlord–tenant legislation in place in provinces and territories across the country does not provide sufficient tenant protections to ensure security of tenure and affordability of rental accommodation for tenants.[27] Governments are allowing financialized landlords to implement their business practices without sufficient human rights oversight and are thus failing to protect the rights of tenants.

Towards an Accountability Framework

Advocates, front-line workers, academics, health practitioners, and others have been raising alarm bells for more than twenty years and continue to do so. Moreover, since 1993, numerous review bodies at the United Nations have considered Canada's record, have expressed considerable outrage, particularly with respect to homelessness, and have provided concrete recommendations for improvement and rights compliance.

It is now well understood that successive governments in Canada created the current realities of widespread homelessness and core housing need witnessed in every part of the country. They accomplished this through their fiscal decisions, the ineffective housing policies and programs they devised, and through their failure to act. In short, governments in Canada embraced neo-liberalism, removed themselves from social housing provision, failed to regulate and oversee the private housing market to ensure the implementation of the right to housing, and failed to adopt human rights–based housing strategies, despite being told to do so by the United Nations review bodies.

Over the years, the Government of Canada's response to domestic and international critique has been mixed. To state the obvious, no order of government in Canada has taken seriously enough the urgency with which homelessness must be addressed and eliminated. Equally, no order of government has taken the necessary steps to dismantle some of the obvious structural causes of the housing crisis – measures such as ensuring social benefit schemes and the minimum wage are set at liveable and realistic levels; investing in the construction of social housing or non-profit housing to accommodate low-income households that may not be able to afford market rates; and maintaining strict oversight of the private housing market and reviewing all housing related laws (including tax laws), policies, and programs to ensure consistency with and promotion of the right to housing.

Despite this neglect, in recent years the Government of Canada has started to erect foundational pieces that, over time and if implemented, should lead to improvements in Canada's housing situation. In 2017, the Government of Canada introduced the National Housing Strategy, which purports to adopt a rights-based approach to addressing a number of housing issues confronting the country. Without supporting legislation and system-wide capacity building regarding the implementation of the right to housing, however, it may have been premature for the government to introduce this approach.

Two years later, in 2019, the National Housing Strategy Act came into force. This is an historic piece of legislation, which articulates for the first time in Canada that the federal government's housing policy is one that recognizes housing as a fundamental human right affirmed in international law, and that housing is essential to the inherent dignity and well-being of the person and to building sustainable and inclusive communities. The legislation also commits the Government of Canada to further the progressive realization of the right to housing as recognized in the ICESCR. The legislation includes a commitment to improving housing outcomes for persons in greatest need, which would have to include Indigenous peoples, persons with disabilities, migrants, refugees and racialized communities, and women and gender-diverse people.

Perhaps most importantly, the Act establishes for the first time a Federal Housing Advocate, who will be responsible for holding the Government of Canada accountable to the right to housing through the National Housing Strategy and other measures. The Advocate[28] was appointed in early 2022 and will be receiving and reviewing systemic complaints regarding barriers to the right to housing experienced by people across the country.

The COVID-19 pandemic floodlit Canada's housing crisis, and the federal government has responded by ramping up some of its commitments, including those concerned with homelessness. In late 2020, the Government of Canada announced a new commitment to ending chronic homelessness by 2030 – an improvement over the National Housing Strategy, which had only committed to halving it. They have also rolled out – and in Budget 2022 renewed – the Rapid Housing Initiative, a multi-billion-dollar fund to assist local governments in securing assets that can be used for affordable housing for those in need. It is anticipated that this will result in the creation of more than 12,000 new housing units over time.[29] Budget 2022 also doubled over the next four years the funding for Reaching Home, the federal government's flagship program to address homelessness.

Mariana Mazzucato, one of the world's leading economists, has said that solving the world's "wicked problems" – the biggest crises confronting humanity – requires that we think bigger and mobilize resources in a way that is as bold and inspirational as the moon landing.[30] In its current form, the National Housing Strategy and its accompanying Act will not solve Canada's housing crisis. Not only are the allocated resources still too limited, but these measures lack the ambition and creativity required to address one of the most significant social crises of our times. For example, the Strategy fails to contemplate new mechanisms to enhance inter-governmental cooperation and collaboration, despite this being necessary to solve Canada's housing crisis, especially in light of Canada's thorny constitutional division of powers between different orders of government. The Strategy also relies too heavily on the private sector for housing supply without the requirement of stakeholder engagement or any direct human rights oversight or conditionality. Moreover, the Strategy reinforces people living in homelessness as beneficiaries of charity or unproven social programs rather than rights holders requiring human rights responses to their living conditions.

That being said, the National Housing Strategy and Act signal the government's interest in a human rights framework through which to achieve better outcomes. The Strategy has been presented as a living document that can be responsive to housing and homelessness conditions as they evolve. This suggests that as government officials become better acquainted with what it means to implement the right to housing, and as they receive recommendations from the Federal Housing Advocate, as required by the National Housing Strategy Act, the strategy itself could be adapted and strengthened.

* * *

The future for those living in homelessness and inadequate housing in Canada is not particularly bright.[31] In the face of a once-in-a-century pandemic, governments in Canada have underperformed. Rather than coming together to use the pandemic as an opportunity to develop new relationships, new methods of work, and new resources, governments have tended towards the same old. Homeless people have been displaced from spaces and places in which they felt safe, and governments have largely denied renters any significant support while wringing their hands about the best way to assist first-time home buyers and support developers. If governments are truly committed to solving the housing crisis, they cannot take a road well travelled; they are going to have to shoot for the moon.

HOMELESS ENCAMPMENTS & YOUR HUMAN RIGHTS

If you are living in an encampment, you have human rights. Governments must respect your human rights, including your right to housing.

You have the right to housing under Canadian legislation and international human rights law. These rights are found in:

/ Canada's National Housing Strategy Act - S.C. 2019, c. 29, s. 313
/ The International Covenant on Economic, Social, and Cultural Rights, Article 11.1
/ The United Nations Committee on Economic, Social, and Cultural Rights, General Comments No. 4 and No. 7

In April 2020, experts at United Nations developed *A National Protocol for Homeless Encampments in Canada: A Human Rights Approach* (Leilani Farha & Kaitlin Schwan). The Protocol is a guide to make sure Canadian governments protect and respect the rights of people living in encampments based on the law. This booklet is a summary of the Protocol.

Homeless encampments will never fulfil the right to housing – only adequate housing can do that. But since they exist, governments must respect the human rights of people who live in them.

DOWNLOAD RESOURCES & LEARN MORE

https://www.make-the-shift.org/homeless-encampments/

Want to know more about the right to housing?

THE SH/FT

E-mail us here: info@maketheshift.org
Visit us here: www.maketheshift.org
Twitter: @Make_TheShift

Farha, L. & Schwan, K. (2020). A National Protocol on Homeless Encampments in Canada: A Human Rights Approach. Geneva, Switzerland: Office of the United Nations Special Rapporteur on the Right to Adequate Housing
https://www.make-the-shift.org/wp-content/uploads/2020/04/A-National-Protocol-for-Homeless-Encampments-in-Canada.pdf

The Shift.
Credit: The Shift, www.maketheshift.org

Leilani Farha, then UN Special Rapporteur on the right to adequate housing, speaking at a panel discussion to commemorate the seventieth anniversary of the Universal Declaration of Human Rights in 2018.
Credit: Jean-Marc Ferré

LEILANI FARHA is the global director of The Shift and former United Nations Special Rapporteur on the right to adequate housing (2014–20). Her work is animated by the principle that housing is a social good, not an asset or commodity. Leilani helped establish global human rights standards on the right to housing now used by governments and advocates around the world. She is the subject of the highly acclaimed documentary PUSH, which is about the financialization of housing, and she is the co-host of PUSHBACK Talks, a podcast about cities, finance, housing, and human rights.

POEM: THERE IS A DEVELOPMENT PROPOSED FOR THIS SITE

Zachary Grant

There is a development proposed for this site
it's right around the corner from where you are
a new marvel to feast your eyes on
is planned for this dreary scene
a monumental success
will ascend to its greatest heights by crane.

There is a development proposed for this site
we call you to see the plans we have drawn
they are BEYOND your imagination
or, at least, what you imagined
a marked difference from what was there before.

There is a development proposed for this site
that place that you've walked, or biked, or drove by
or that you sat, or met your friends, or held a hand, or snuck a drink in
or smoked and stared at obliquely, committing each corner to memory
that are recanted only upon the next smoke later.

There is a development proposed for this site
and that is just the way it's going to be
that holding on tight isn't going to be of any help
as the handrails that you've been bracing against,
they are on the slate too,
for shinier plexi-brass milled and carved handrails
from a designer that understands these things
and that will do a very good job
of tying this whole space together.

Photo taken during March 2020.
Credit: Zachary Grant

Afterword

Shawn Micallef

What kind of a city is Toronto?

A city that is one of the richest places on earth, where supercars roll through the streets, cranes keep putting up skyscrapers, and money keeps being made. It's possible to walk for an entire afternoon or ride a bike for a few hours through neighbourhood after neighbourhood of incredible wealth, of multi-million-dollar homes, many of them once considered working-class dwellings. Where does all the money come from? How can there be so much of it? Even with some familiarity of the economic foundations of Toronto, it still doesn't feel like the physical size of wealth here, the sprawl of it, is possible. It seems vast and never-ending, and then, of course, it ends.

The starkness of the "end" of wealth here was magnified by the pandemic, with tent encampments appearing in parks and ravines, built by people trying to escape a shelter system made inadequate and dangerous by both the pandemic and systemic issues. This end of Toronto was, to be sure, always here. The "Toronto the Good" or "New York run by the Swiss" narratives were convenient myths that always obscured the inequity here, even if it was in plain view. Toronto was never without those who didn't get to share in the prosperity of this place that has, through its history, had more boom times than not.

There was The Ward neighbourhood, one of those inconvenient inequalities that existed right next to prosperity in the form of Old City Hall, a Victorian trophy of sorts for a proud mercantile city. It was no wonder then that The Ward and its shacks and privies, its burlesque halls and immigrant enclaves, were bulldozed to get it all out of sight but also to create a clean slate for a new symbol of postwar boom times. New City Hall rose as Toronto coasted into the last half of the twentieth century as a magnet for immigration across Canada and around the world, but it erased something too. Toronto doesn't much care for seeing the poor.

The prosperous story of Toronto in the last decades was slowed down by the recession of the early 1990s and then the doldrums created by the amalgamation of Metro Toronto in 1998, but it soon boomed again and has never really stopped booming since: the city kept building and growing even as the United States went into a deep recession in 2008. When would, or will, the Toronto bubble pop? That particular question hasn't had an answer yet, but perhaps a better question is when will we collectively recognize the partial deflation of the Toronto bubble?

Despite these decades of growth and of the kind of success that make most North American cities envious, the divides that were always here grew as the most basic necessity of life, housing, has become a crisis of access, affordability, and livability. The city is a real estate money-making machine for some, but Toronto is increasingly a desperate and hard-to-live-in place for many others. The question "is it even possible to live in Toronto?" is being raised often, and many people have already made their exit. Indeed, if it wasn't for immigration, Toronto's population would actually decrease with this steady stream of outward migration, another fact contrary to the city's popular mythology.

Left behind are the hundreds of thousands of people without much of an option to move away, the people who keep this place running, the ones who used to be able to afford the shacks that sell for millions of dollars now. Their place in the city has been pinched and squeezed and made more uncomfortable. Even middle-class people, once the foundation of the city, wonder if they, or their kids, will be able to live here. It wasn't always this way though.

On those long walks or bike rides through the city there's something else to notice: the incredible amount of affordable housing that was built in the few decades after the Second World War. A lot of this housing was stand-alone or semi-detached housing, an incredible building boom that grew as the boomer generation exploded, encouraged by the Canadian Mortgage and Housing Corporation and various government policies. The idea behind it all was that Canadians needed secure housing if this country was to prosper. It was nation-building, not just home-building.

More importantly, actual affordable housing was built. Out of the city centre into what were once the suburbs but now are as much "the city" as downtown, social housing of various kinds was constructed in the form of low- and high-rise apartments, townhouses, courts, and other sometimes unique configurations. The ubiquitous slab apartment building is a Toronto architectural look if there ever was one, built in the style of the day with gusto.

By the 1980s, the slabs and brutalist apartment blocks had evolved into a postmodern style, with quirky references to older styles of architecture and a pastel palette of pinks, greens, and oranges, with some darker accent colours here and there, like the series of co-ops on Lake Shore Boulevard in New Toronto, built on the site of the former Goodyear factory, or the Hugh Garner co-op in Cabbagetown. On a long wander, these sorts of buildings will often turn up in slivers of land next to transportation or utility corridors, as the choicest land was most often scooped up by the stand-alone homes earlier, though there are some stunning ravine-edge locations that give the impression of a space-age utopia, buildings rising out of a green canopy.

The postmodern buildings are particularly striking, not just because the style fell out of favour quickly by the mid-1990s, but because they represent the last great era of affordable housing in Toronto and Canada. In 1993 the federal government got out of the business of funding housing with Finance Minister Paul Martin's austerity budgets, followed by Ontario leaving the game when Premier Mike Harris was elected in 1995, and then the maintenance budgets of the existing stock were starved and those buildings began to decay and affect the quality of life of the people in them. We, as a civilization, decided something as essential as housing should be left entirely to the market, and thirty years later the effects are evident.

Another factor is just how few places it's possible to build in Toronto. Though it appears there's a lot of new construction – and there is, but not enough – it's limited to relatively few places, as much of the city is off limits to even the gentlest additions of density due to exclusionary zoning. This is why so much of the dense housing, truly affordable or not, is relegated to the corridors with the most pollution. Think of Liberty Village, a place scorned for its density by people with backyards, wedged in between the Gardiner Expressway and two rail corridors, all of them linear carbon bonfires, spewing pollution. What messages does Toronto send to its current and potential residents by pushing density, and humans, to busy streets and worse?

All of this, the intentional limiting of where housing can be built and the absence of housing programs on a scale that would make even the slightest difference, makes the violence of encampment evictions even more egregious. The profound meanness of Toronto has been in full view these past three years, as has its long tradition of wanting to get what makes it uncomfortable out of view. What we have witnessed is a profound failure of empathy.

Is this the kind of city Toronto is?

SHAWN MICALLEF is the author of *Frontier City: Toronto on the Verge of Greatness* (McClelland & Steward, 2016), *Stroll: Psychogeographic Walking Tours of Toronto* (Coach House, 2010), and *The Trouble with Brunch: Work, Class and the Pursuit of Leisure* (Coach House, 2014). He is a weekly columnist at the *Toronto Star*, and a senior editor and co-owner of the independent, Jane Jacobs Prize–winning magazine *Spacing*. Shawn teaches at the University of Toronto and was a 2011–12 Canadian Journalism Fellow at Massey College. In 2002, while a resident at the Canadian Film Centre's Media Lab, he co-founded [murmur], the location-based mobile phone documentary project that spread to over twenty-five cities globally.

Above: National Housing Day media conference on 23 November 2020 at 214–230 Sherbourne St., a site where advocates have demanded expropriation of the vacant lot for social housing. Pictured are (left to right) Zoë Dodd, Toronto Overdose Prevention Society; Les Harper, Indigenous health promoter at South Riverdale Community Health Centre; Melody Alderton-Ballik, nurse at Street Health; Kayla Sutherland; Bob Rose, SHJN; and Greg Cook, SHJN and outreach worker at Sanctuary.

On left: Lorraine Lam speaking at the National Housing Day rally at 214–230 Sherbourne St. on 22 November 2021. Advocates continue to demand the expropriation of this site for social housing.
Credit: *Above*: Tommy Taylor; *on left*: Cathy Crowe

Acknowledgments

This book was written on land: soil, plants, water, rocks, and non-human creatures. As white settlers, we were not the first people on this land, and we are culpable in the oppression of Indigenous peoples here. We name this to work towards truth and reconciliation with original peoples and with the land itself.

This book came to be because Natalie Fingerhut at University of Toronto Press saw on the streets of our city the immediate impact of COVID-19 on people who were unhoused. She and an amazing team at University of Toronto Press brought this book to fruition with incredible commitment and passion. We'd like to especially thank Janice Evans, Beth McAuley, Samantha Rohrig, Chris Reed, and Anna Del Col.

We wish to thank the funders of this project, Maytree Foundation and Atkinson Foundation. Their support enabled us to provide honorariums for people without secure income.

Special thanks to Anna Willats and Shawn Micallef for their early feedback on the manuscript.

We also have deep appreciation for Sanctuary Toronto for their work on the ground and for their administrative support for this project.

Greg would especially like to thank his co-workers at Sanctuary for allowing him to take some time away from his outreach role to work on this book. In addition, he'd like to thank the community of people that call Sanctuary home. There are too many to name. Each person has taught him so much about himself and this city we live in. He also would like to thank his partner Shannon Blake for her stellar editing advice and invaluable feedback throughout this project.

Cathy would like to acknowledge the numerous ways Toronto Metropolitan University has supported her nursing work – where the community truly is the campus.

Many wonderful artists contributed to this project. We especially want to acknowledge Michael DeForge, who translated his activism at encampments into art for *Displacement City*'s book cover and graphics. In addition, as long-time admirers of photographer Chris Young, we appreciate his contribution of profile pics of several of the authors.

We thank the community of activists and colleagues we have worked alongside over the years. Your efforts, bravery, and ingenuity make this a gentler, more just city. We especially thank the people who contributed chapters to this book. We know their offerings will shed light on the immense violations of human rights that have taken place, and will fuel the fight for housing for all.

Notes

Foreword

1 "26 Arrested at Toronto's Lamport Stadium Park as City, Police Clear Encampment," CBC News, 21 July 2021, https://www.cbc.ca/news/canada/toronto/lamport-stadium-encampment-homelessness-toronto-1.6110697.

2 Correspondence from Sima Atri, co-director of the Community Justice Collective, on 20 July 2022, regarding the arrests connected to the Lamport clearing. The full statement is as follows: "Forty people total were arrested or detained by Toronto Police for events that day. Thirsty-one people were arrested or detained at Lamport Stadium Park on July 21st, with most receiving $65 trespassing tickets on release from 11 Division. Four people were arrested on criminal charges, three of whom are still fighting in Court, during jail support at 14 Division for the individuals who were arrested and not released from Lamport Stadium arrests. An additional five people were later arrested and criminally charged for incidents at Lamport and 14 Division after a press conference protesting the police violence at encampment clearings. Seven of the criminal charges have already been withdrawn, with nine remaining outstanding. Most remaining defendants are fighting their charges collectively and challenging the city-police operation constitutionally."

3 Dionne Brand, "Dionne Brand: On Narrative, Reckoning and the Calculus of Living and Dying," *Toronto Star*, 4 July 2020, https://www.thestar.com/entertainment/books/2020/07/04/dionne-brand-on-narrative-reckoning-and-the-calculus-of-living-and-dying.html.

4 Ruth Wilson Gilmore, "Organized Abandonment and Organized Violence: Devolution and the Police," video, from the Humanities Institute at the University of California, Santa Cruz, 9 November 2015, https://vimeo.com/146450686?embedded=true&source=video_title&owner=3965169.

Introduction

1 Cathy Crowe, *A Knapsack Full of Dreams: Memoirs of a Street Nurse* (Victoria, BC: Friesen Press, 2019).

2 Alessandro Busà, *The Creative Destruction of New York City: Engineering the City for the Elite* (New York: Oxford University Press, 2017), 54.

2. The Housing Crisis and the Indian Residential School Legacy

1 Jesse Thistle, "Definition of Indigenous Homelessness in Canada," Canadian Observatory on Homelessness, 2021, https://www.homelesshub.ca/IndigenousHomelessness.

2 Gidigaa Migizi (Doug Williams), *Michi Saagiig Nishnaabeg: This Is Our Territory* (Winnipeg: ARP Books, 2018).

3 The Sixties Scoop is a term used to describe a series of policies enacted by provincial child welfare authorities, starting in the 1950s, which saw thousands of Indigenous children taken from their homes and families and placed in the foster home system, and eventually adopted out to non-Indigenous families across Canada and the world. The state-sponsored destruction of families is an act of genocide. As discussed in this chapter, the forced apprehension of Indigenous children is ongoing. This contemporary crisis is often referred to as the Millennial Scoop.

4 Murray Sinclair, "Reconciliation Reality Check with Murray Sinclair," Unreserved with Rosanna Deerchild (podcast), CBC Radio, 25 September 2021, https://www.cbc.ca/listen/live-radio/1-105-unreserved/clip/15868493-reconciliation-reality-check-murray-sinclair.

5 Sinclair, "Reconciliation Reality Check." In his interview, Truth and Reconciliation Commissioner the Honourable Murray Sinclair states that "150,000 kids went to 138 schools in the Residential School Settlement Agreement, if there's an additional 1,000 schools, then there is probably an additional 1,000,000 kids that went to those schools. And if we figure 10–15 per cent of kids who went to residential schools died then you do the math, we are talking about hundreds of thousands of kids dying in residential schools."

6 The Three Sisters Soup recipe is a traditional recipe from the Haudenosaunee Confederacy. The "Teachings of the Three Sisters" would take multiple days to recount, but they refer to the interdependence of the crops corn, beans, and squash.

7   Mayor John Tory, "Proclamation," City of Toronto, 21 June 2021, https://www
    .toronto.ca/wp-content/uploads/2021/06/8f86-National-Indigenous-Peoples-Day
    -Proclamation.pdf.

3. Inconvenient Bodies and Toronto's History of Displacement

1   Name changed for privacy.
2   The term "City Table" refers to City-led webinars/meetings on COVID-19 with
    various combinations of community organizations.
3   Shelter and Housing Justice Network, "Mayor Tory: Declare Homelessness an
    Emergency to Prevent More Death and Suffering," accessed 8 April 2022, https://
    www.change.org/p/mayor-john-tory-mayor-tory-declare-homelessness-an
    -emergency-to-prevent-more-deaths-and-suffering.
4   Araundhati Roy, "The Pandemic Is a Portal," *Financial Times*, 3 April 2020, https://
    www.ft.com/content/10d8f5e8-74eb-11ea-95fe-fcd274e920ca.
5   Canadian Human Rights Commission, "Building Tiny Homeless Shelters," accessed
    8 April 2022, http://2020.chrcreport.ca/building-tiny-homeless-shelters.html.
6   Margaret Sault, "A Story about the Toronto Purchase," in *Indigenous Toronto: Stories
    That Carry This Place*, ed. Denise Bolduc, Mnawaate Grodon-Corbiere, Rebeka
    Tabobondung, and Brian Wright-Mcleod (Toronto: Coach House Books, 2021), 37–43.
7   Wanda Nanibush, "Williams Treaties," in *Indigenous Toronto: Stories That Carry
    This Place*, ed. Denise Bolduc, Mnawaate Grodon-Corbiere, Rebeka Tabobondung,
    and Brian Wright-Mcleod (Toronto: Coach House Books, 2021), 29.
8   Nanibush, "Williams Treaties," 32.
9   Dara Culhane, *The Pleasure of the Crown: Anthropology, Law and First Nations*
    (Burnaby, BC: Talonbooks, 1998), 48.
10 Gaetan Heroux, "The Stone Yard," in *The Ward: The Life and Loss of Toronto's First
    Immigrant Neighbourhood*, ed. John Lorinc, Michael McClelland, Ellen Scheinberg,
    and Tatum Taylor (Toronto: Coach House Books, 2015), 117.
11 Heroux, "Stone Yard," 120.
12 Brian D. Palmer and Gaetan Heroux, *Toronto's Poor: A Rebellious History* (Toronto:
    Between the Lines, 2016), 141.
13 Palmer and Heroux, *Toronto's Poor*, 175.
14 Julia Mastroianni, "There's No Such Thing as Affordable Housing in Toronto," *Now
    Toronto*, 5 November 2020.
15 Alessandro Busà, *The Creative Destruction of New York City: Engineering the City
    for the Elite* (New York: Oxford University Press, 2017), 51.
16 Jonathan Greene, "Urban Restructuring, Homelessness, and Collective Action in
    Toronto, 1980–2003," *Urban History Review* 43, no. 1 (2014): 21–37, https://www
    .erudit.org/en/journals/uhr/1900-v1-n1-uhr01893/1030805ar/.
17 Greene, "Urban Restructuring," 30.

18 Greene, "Urban Restructuring," 32.

19 Greene, "Urban Restructuring," 32.

20 Desmond Cole, "NO Vacancy," *Cole's Notes* (blog), 2 January 2018, https://thatsatruestory.wordpress.com/2018/01/02/no-vacancy/.

21 Cole, "NO Vacancy."

22 CBC News, "City Considering Use of Moss Park Armoury as New Winter Respite Centre, Mayor Says," 3 January 2018, https://www.cbc.ca/news/canada/toronto/tory-shelter-update-1.4471040.

23 CBC News, "City Considering."

24 The Canadian Press, "Toronto Opens Armoury Ahead of Schedule to Shelter Homeless," iPolitics, 6 January 2018, https://ipolitics.ca/2018/01/06/toronto-opens-armoury-ahead-schedule-shelter-homeless/.

25 Name changed for privacy.

26 Jennifer Pagliaro, "As the City Scrambles to Head Off a COVID-19 Outbreak at Homeless Shelters, Frontline Workers Worry It Won't Be Enough," *Toronto Star*, 27 March 2020, https://www.thestar.com/news/city_hall/2020/03/27/as-the-city-scrambles-to-head-off-a-covid-19-outbreak-at-homeless-shelters-frontline-workers-worry-that-it-wont-be-enough.html.

27 City of Toronto, "Shelter System Flow Data," accessed 12 April 2022, https://www.toronto.ca/city-government/data-research-maps/research-reports/housing-and-homelessness-research-and-reports/shelter-system-flow-data/.

28 Victoria Gibson, "More than 81,000 Households Are Waiting for Subsidized Housing in Toronto," *Toronto Star*, 19 January 2021, https://www.thestar.com/news/gta/2021/01/19/more-than-81000-households-are-waiting-for-subsidized-housing-in-toronto-the-city-hopes-a-new-waitlist-system-will-help-fill-its-units-faster.html.

29 City of Toronto, "Rent Geared-to-Income Subsidy," accessed 12 April 2022, https://www.toronto.ca/community-people/employment-social-support/housing-support/rent-geared-to-income-subsidy/#:~:text=There%20is%20currently%20a%20long,for%20a%20one%2Dbedroom%20unit.

4. Displaced There, Displaced Here

1 From the poem "Home" by Warsan Shire.

2 While the number of refugee claimants accessing Toronto's emergency shelter system has fluctuated significantly over the years, even in periods when refugee claimants have had their highest representation, they have still only constituted somewhere between 30 and 40 per cent of total shelter residents. Moreover, in recent years, the City has received funds from the federal government to develop temporary "refugee response" programs to provide emergency shelter to refugee claimants, which do not impact the capacity of other emergency shelter programs in the city. And when the pandemic all but ended the arrival of new refugee claimants to Toronto due to travel restrictions, resulting in very few refugee claimants in the shelter system, we still

experienced some of the greatest strains the shelter system has ever faced. Recognizing this, it's clear that refugees are not the cause of this crisis.

6. Responsibility Downloaded: How Drop-In Centres Stepped Up and Pushed Back during the Pandemic

1 Diana Chan McNally, *Meeting the Meal Gap: How Drop-Ins Addressed Food Insecurity during the Pandemic* (Toronto, ON: Toronto Drop-In Network, 2020), 7, https://tdin.ca/res_documents/TDIN_MeetingTheMealGap_Report2020.pdf.
2 Community centres and pools were closed on 25 March 2020 and did not reopen until the city moved into Stage 2 of the province's reopening strategy on 24 June. Showers remained inaccessible until 2 May at several locations.
3 McNally, *Meeting the Meal Gap*, 15.
4 Diana Chan McNally, *Demands for Immediate Action to Address COVID-Related Risks and Harms for People Experiencing Homelessness*, Toronto Drop-In Network, 9 March 2021, https://www.tdin.ca/announcement.php?id=2301.
5 TDIN and SHJN, *Joint Statement Re: COVID-19 Response Update: Protecting People Experiencing Homelessness and Ensuring the Safety of the Shelter System*, 4 June 2021, http://www.shjn.ca/tdin-shjn-joint-statement-re-covid-19-response-update-protecting-people-experiencing-homelessness-and-ensuring-the-safety-of-the-shelter-system/.
6 Kaitlin Schwan and Leilani Farha, *A National Protocol for Homeless Encampments in Canada*, UN Special Rapporteur on the Right to Adequate Housing, 30 April 2021, https://www.make-the-shift.org/wp-content/uploads/2020/04/A-National-Protocol-for-Homeless-Encampments-in-Canada.pdf.
7 The noun *kettle* refers to the area in which a crowd is confined. It has been suggested that the term is a metaphor for a boiling kettle about to spill over. Another theory posits a connection to the German noun *kessel*, which, apart from literally meaning "cauldron or boiler," has been used in military contexts for an armed force that is about to be overtaken by a superior one. Kettling has been sharply criticized for keeping both protestors and bystanders unjustly (and sometimes hazardously) confined. Some police departments, including the Toronto Police Service, have sworn off the practice. On the history of the term, see "Fire Burn and Cauldron Bubble: On 'Kettling,'" Merriam-Webster, accessed 6 April 2022, https://www.merriam-webster.com/words-at-play/kettling-police-tactic-history-meaning-usage.
8 Diana Chan McNally, *A Path Forward*, Toronto Drop-In Network, 9 July 2021, https://tdin.ca/announcement.php?id=2355.
9 City of Toronto, "City of Toronto Update on Lamport Stadium Park," news release, 21 July 2021, https://www.toronto.ca/news/city-of-toronto-update-on-lamport-stadium-park/. All city media releases from these dates include speaking points that councillors and the mayor used.
10 Canadian Association of Journalists (CAJ), "CAJ Calls on Toronto to Stop Restricting

Journalists from Covering Evictions of Homeless People in Alexandra Park," *CAJ* (blog), 20 July 2021, https://caj.ca/blog/CAJ_calls_on_Toronto_to_stop_restricting _journalists_from_covering_evictions_of_homeless_people_in_Alexandra_Park.

11 Diana Chan McNally and Naheed Dosani, "Violent, Militarized Park Encampment Clearings Won't End Homelessness in Toronto. Here's a Human Rights Approach," *Toronto Star*, 26 July 2021, https://www.thestar.com/opinion/contributors/2021/07/26 /working-with-the-unhoused-we-know-violent-militarized-encampment-clearings -wont-end-homelessness-in-toronto-heres-a-human-rights-approach.html.

12 Ombudsman Toronto, "Toronto's Ombudsman to Investigate City's Clearing of Encampments," news release, 28 September 2021, https://www.ombudsmantoronto .ca/Publications/News-Releases/News-Folder/Toronto-s-Ombudsman-to-Investigate -City-s-Clearin.

13 Chris Murray, "Re: Administrative Inquiry Regarding the Clearing of Encamp-ments," City of Toronto, 30 September 2021, https://www.toronto.ca/legdocs /mmis/2021/ia/bgrd/backgroundfile-171485.pdf.

14 Murray, "Re: Administrative Inquiry."

7. Surviving COVID-19 in the Shelter System

1 "Being formed" means a person is detained, usually by the police, and taken to hospital to allow a psychiatric assessment of their mental state. This can only occur when a physician reasonably believes the person is at risk of self-harm, harm to others, or is unable to care for self. In Ontario, the most common use of this is a Form 1, "Application by Physician for Psychiatric Assessment."

2 St. Felix Centre is near Kensington Market. It operates two twenty-four-hour respite programs, one at its main location, and another in Liberty Village in Toronto's west end.

3 Seaton House has a notorious history of poor conditions, overcrowding, poor infrastructure and staffing, and is colloquially dubbed "Satan House." It saw at least eight separate COVID-19 outbreaks during the first two years of the pandemic. CBC News, "City Admits Seaton House 'Inadequate' after Guest Shares Photos Taken inside Facility," 11 January 2019, https://www.cbc.ca/news/canada/toronto /seaton-house-city-repsonse-1.4974659.

4 The Rapid Rehousing Initiative is a relatively recent housing program meant to facilitate finding housing for people the City considers to be "experiencing chronic homelessness." For more information, see https://www.toronto.ca/community-people /employment-social-support/housing-support/rent-geared-to-income-subsidy /rapid-rehousing-initiative/.

8. Social Murder: We Need More Than Band-Aids

1 "Social murder" is a phrase used by Friedrich Engels in his 1845 work *The Condition of the Working Class in England*, wherein he describes how the class that

holds social and political control places hundreds of proletarians in such a position that they inevitably meet a too early and unnatural death. The phrase is increasingly used today to reflect the results of conservative economic policies.

2 Francine Kopun, "How a Haven for Refugees Became Home to the Worst COVID-19 Outbreak in Toronto's Shelter System," *Toronto Star*, 24 May 2020, https://www.thestar.com/news/gta/2020/05/24/how-a-haven-for-refugees-became -home-to-the-worst-covid-19-outbreak-in-torontos-shelter-system.html?rf.

3 Roxie Danielson, "I watched as people's homes were being destroyed," Facebook, 23 June 2021, https://www.facebook.com/roxie.ducharme/posts /10165201834115408.

4 In March 2022, the Ontario government ended special funding that allowed for expanded nursing care for people who were homeless. As a result, Inner City Health Associates terminated forty-four nursing positions.

9. Slipped through the Fingertips of the System

1 Randy Padmore Park and Alexandra Park are both located near Kensington Market in downtown Toronto.

2 See chapter 14 in this volume.

3 It is currently almost impossible to get a transfer from one TCH unit to another due to the lack of TCH units when compared to the demand. See Kate McGillivray, "TCH Tenants Waiting Years to Leave Apartments That Endanger Their Health and Safety, City Ombudsman Says," CBC News, 26 January 2018, https://www.cbc .ca/news/canada/toronto/tch-ombudsman-report-1.4505581.

10. Report on Toronto: The Encampment Support Network

1 In 2005, under Mayor David Miller, the City banned City-funded agencies from giving out survival supplies. The practice was widely understood to be part and parcel of American-style Housing First approaches to homelessness, which focus on removing visible people from the streets, especially if they have addictions or mental health issues.

2 Centre for Urban Health Solutions, "Respite and Warming Centres: Locations & Capacity: Winter 2019/20 & Winter 2020/21," accessed 11 April 2022, https:// maphealth.ca/wp-content/uploads/Respite-Warming-Centres-Fact-Sheet-Maps -Winter-2019-21.pdf.

3 Plastic sharps containers are what people use to dispose of sharps (i.e., needles) safely. They can be found in most public washrooms.

4 Toronto City Council, "Economic and Community Development Committee – December 7, 2020," YouTube video, 11:02:50, 7 December 2020, https://www.youtube .com/watch?v=pTwEKfrLnys&t=31006s.

5 Melissa Goldstein and A.J. Withers created FactCheck Toronto to challenge misinformation put forth by the City of Toronto. See https://factchecktoronto.ca/blog/.

6   Chris Fox, "Toronto Mayor Calls Charter Challenge over Shelters amid COVID-19 'Disappointing,'" CTV News, 26 April 2020, https://toronto.ctvnews.ca/toronto -mayor-calls-charter-challenge-over-shelters-amid-covid-19-disappointing -1.4912365.

7   FactCheck Toronto, "Claim: In 2020, Toronto Fire Services Responded to 253 Fires in Encampments," *FactCheck Toronto* (blog), 7 June 2021, https://factchecktoronto .ca/2021/06/07/encampment-fires/

8   Office of the Chief Coroner, "Verdict of Coroner's Jury into the Death of Grant Faulkner," 20 June 2018, https://www.toronto.ca/legdocs/mmis/2019/ec/bgrd /backgroundfile-136738.pdf.

9   Doug Johnson Hatlem, "Is It Arson? Seven Suspicious Fires in Seven Days Rock Toronto's Homeless Encampments," *CounterPunch*, 15 December 2020, https:// www.counterpunch.org/2020/12/15/is-it-arson-seven-suspicious-fires-in-seven -days-rock-torontos-homeless-encampments/.

10 City of Toronto, "City of Toronto Supporting People Living in Encampments with Safe, Supportive Indoor Space," news release, 16 March 2021, https://www.toronto .ca/news/city-of-toronto-supporting-people-living-in-encampments-with-safe -supportive-indoor-space/.

11 Scadding Court NC, "Report on the Violent Evictions at Alexandra Park from ESN's Scadding Neighbourhood Committee," accessed 8 April 2022, https://drive .google.com/file/d/1Nzakoy-oeA105_NRBiQg2fQ7x4CpWVZW/view.

12 See chapter 6 in this volume.

11. Wish You Were Still Here

1   Toronto Shelter-Hotel Overdose Action Task Force, "Toronto Shelter-Hotel Overdose Preparedness Assessment Project: Final Report and Recommendations," 19 May 2021, https://sherbourne.on.ca/wp-content/uploads/2021/06/TSHOPAP -Report-Final-May-19-2021.pdf.

2   T. Gomes et al., *Changing Circumstances Surrounding Opioid-related Deaths in Ontario during the COVID-19 Pandemic* (Toronto, ON: Ontario Drug Policy Research Network, 2021), https://odprn.ca/wp-content/uploads/2021/05 /Changing-Circumstances-Surrounding-Opioid-Related-Deaths.pdf.

3   Jennifer Pagliaro, "City's Busiest Supervised Injection Site to Reopen after Month-long Closure over COVID-19," *Toronto Star*, 16 April 2020, https://www .thestar.com/news/city_hall/2020/04/16/citys-busiest-supervised-injection-site-to -reopen-after-month-long-closure-over-covid-19.html.

4   Kevin Donovan, "Loblaws up the Street Had Better Sanitary Precautions Than We Did at Toronto Public Health," *Toronto Star*, 6 April 2020, https://www.thestar.com /news/gta/2020/04/06/loblaws-up-the-street-had-better-sanitary-precautions -than-we-did-at-toronto-public-health.html.

12. Fighting Ableism (Disability Exists and So Do We)

1 My magick is based on hearth and home – intentional healing through nourishment of body and spirit.
2 Many City of Toronto pools are fully accessible. We were denied entry at those pools, when housed people were not. In addition, barriers were put into place, including having to book ahead, having to keep your appointment, and having to bring valid ID.
3 This person's name has been changed for privacy.
4 Most shelters in Toronto are not wheelchair accessible and do not have accessible facilities or access to home care, and they are not necessarily located near any of my medical supports. Moreover, I'm allergic to perfume, soaps, shampoos, moisturizers, lotions, sprays, and detergents. Most personal care products and chemicals make me very sick, and I would be subjected to all these things in a congregate shelter setting. My mental health would also never survive in that space as a queer woman and political activist.

13. Living and Dying on the Streets: Providing Palliative Care during a Pandemic

1 Individuals' names have been changed for privacy.
2 Stephen Hwang et al., *Palliative Care Services for People Experiencing Homelessness in Toronto: A Preliminary Needs Assessment* (Toronto: Centre for Urban Health Solutions, St. Michael's Hospital, 2017).
3 Tina Podymow, Jeffrey Turnbull, and Doug Coyle, "Shelter-Based Palliative Care for the Homeless Terminally Ill," *Palliative Medicine* 20, no. 2 (March 2006): 81–86, https://doi.org/10.1191/0269216306pm1103oa.
4 Social determinants of health refer to a specific group of social and economic factors within the broader determinants of health. These relate to an individual's place in society, such as income, education, or employment. Experiences of discrimination, racism, and historical trauma are important social determinants of health for certain groups, such as Indigenous peoples, LGBTQ people, and Black Canadians. See Health Canada, "Social Determinants of Health and Health Inequalities," last modified 7 October 2020, https://www.canada.ca/en/public -health/services/health-promotion/population-health/what-determines-health .html.
5 Sheryl Reimer-Lorlham et al., "Death Is a Social Justice Issue," *Advances in Nursing Science* 39, no. 4 (October/December 2016): 293–307, https://doi.org/10.1097 /ANS.0000000000000146.

14. Building Tiny Homeless Shelters

1 Reprinted with permission from the author.

15. In the Parks and in the Courts: The Legal Fight against Encampment Evictions

1 City of Toronto (@cityoftoronto), "Derrick found himself homeless in early 2020," Twitter, 9 March 2021, 3:48 p.m., https://twitter.com/cityoftoronto/status /1369389641401524228.

2 FactCheck Toronto, "Claim: People Experiencing Homelessness in Toronto Have Access to Safe, High Quality Emergency Shelter," 7 June 2021, https://factchecktoronto .ca/2021/06/07/shelter-violence/.

3 See *Abbotsford (City) v. Shantz*, 2015 BCSC 1909, and *Victoria (City) v. Adams*, 2009 BCCA 563.

4 *Sanctuary et al. v. Toronto (City) et al.*, Notice of Application (29 April 2020), para. 2(e).

5 *Sanctuary et al. v. Toronto (City) et al.*, Notice of Application, para. 2(f).

6 Some of the other people involved in this suit, however, are among the most dedicated and respected encampment support organizers in Toronto.

7 *Sanctuary et al. v. Toronto (City) et al.*, "Schedule A," Interim Settlement Agreement, Public Summary (19 May 2020), https://ccla.org/wp-content/uploads /2021/09/Interim-Settlement-Agreement-.pdf.

8 Affidavit of Scott McKean, "Motion Record of the Respondent City of Toronto," *Black et al. v. Toronto*, 2020 ONSC 6398, para. 18.

9 FactCheck Toronto, "Claim: To Date This Year, Toronto Fire Services Has Responded to 216 Fires in Encampments. That Is a 218% Increase over the Same Period in 2019. Sadly, One Person Has Died as a Result of an Encampment Fire This Year. Seven People Have Lost Their Lives as a Result of Encampment Fires in Toronto since 2010," 22 December 2020, https://factchecktoronto.ca/2020/12/22/claim-to-date-this-year -toronto-fire-services-has-responded-to-216-fires-in-encampments-that-is-a-218 -increase-over-the-same-period-in-2019-sadly-one-person-has-died-as-a-result-of-an -encampment-2/.

10 According to City of Toronto court filings, "on July 15, 2020, there were 64 encampments at Moss Park." The City's count is not always entirely accurate, however. Also, "tents" does not necessarily equal people as there can be multiple people per encampment. Affidavit of Troy Ford, "Motion Record of the Respondent City of Toronto," *Black et al. v. Toronto*, 2020 ONSC 6398, para. 4.

16. COVID Life

1 May Warren and Gilbert Ngabo, "How Many Condos Are Sitting Empty in Toronto? One Man Investigated and What He Found Out Surprised Him," *Toronto Star*, 24 November 2019, https://www.thestar.com/news/gta/2019/11/10/how -many-condos-are-sitting-empty-in-toronto-one-man-investigated-and-what-he -found-surprised-him.html.

17. Two Metres: The Legal Challenge

1 ICES, "People Experiencing Homelessness Are More Likely to Be Infected with and Die of COVID-19 Than the General Ontario Population," news release, 12 January 2021, https://www.ices.on.ca/Newsroom/News-Releases/2021/People -experiencing-homelessness-are-more-likely-to-be-infected-with-and-die-of -COVID-19.

2 Noa Mendelsohn Aviv, "CCLA's Urgent COVID Response for Toronto Homeless Population," letter to Mayor John Tory, 29 March 2020, https://ccla.org/major -cases-reports/safe-shelters/cclas-urgent-covid-response-for-toronto-homeless -population-our-submission-to-mayor-of-toronto/.

3 During outreach, Sanctuary staff members regularly spoke with community members, including those in encampments, about the lawsuit. We asked people what they wanted to see come out of it. Housing or a shelter-hotel room were the most frequent answers. Sanctuary staff often noted that it was the intention of our lawsuit to compel the City to open up more shelter-hotel rooms, which community members enthusiastically supported.

4 Chris Murray to Goldblatt Partners LLB, 23 April 2020, 2, https://ccla.org/wp -content/uploads/2021/09/2020-04-23-Letter-from-Chris-Murray-re-response -to-Apr.-21-letter-01476036x7A7FA.pdf.

5 City of Toronto, Interim Settlement Agreement, Schedule "A," https://ccla.org /wp-content/uploads/2021/09/Interim-Settlement-Agreement-.pdf.

6 Toronto Public Health's data for 2018 shows that there were ninety-four deaths of those with no fixed address. The City reported the exact same number – ninety-four – for just the first six months of 2021. "Drug toxicity" accounted for 53 per cent of the 143 such deaths in all of 2020 and for 49 per cent of those ninety-four deaths in the first half of 2021. See City of Toronto, "Deaths of People Experiencing Homelessness," accessed 13 April 2022, https://www.toronto.ca /community-people/health-wellness-care/health-inspections-monitoring /monitoring-deaths-of-homeless-people/.

7 See "Factum of the Moving Parties," Ontario Superior Court of Justice, Court File No. CV-20-640061, 24 September 2020, https://ccla.org/wp-content/uploads /2021/09/2020-09-24-Applicants-factum-on-enforcement-motion-FINAL1.pdf.

8 Jake Kivanç, "Toronto's COVID-19 Housing Project Winds Down, but Residents Hope for Change," CBC News, 4 August 2020, https://www.cbc.ca/news /canada/toronto/covid-toronto-housing-homeless-1.5673373.

9 Sanctuary et al. v. Toronto (City) et al. [hereafter Sanctuary v. Toronto], 2020 ONSC 6207 (CanLII), https://canlii.ca/t/jb46b.

10 Sanctuary v. Toronto, para. 124.

11 Sanctuary v. Toronto, para. 74.

12 City of Toronto, "Daily Shelter & Overnight Service Occupancy & Capacity," Open

Data Portal, accessed 13 April 2022, https://open.toronto.ca/dataset/daily
-shelter-overnight-service-occupancy-capacity/.

13 See Doug Johnson Hatlem (@djjohnso), "News Per 4 sources (incl email below) – 701
Fleet/1A Strachan respite in serious outbreak (19 cases) but @cityoftoronto & @
TOPublicHealth have not incl in public reporting," Twitter, 31 March 2021, https://
twitter.com/djjohnso/status/1377388436047327232?s=21, and Doug Johnson Hatlem
(@djjohnso), "My info on the 701 Fleet/1A Strachan outbreak is solid. I've posted
email from the Fred Victor CEO confirming it was known outbreak since Mar 21,"
Twitter, 4 April 2021, https://twitter.com/djjohnso/status/1379614685935378432?s=21.

18. Homelessness, Housing, and Human Rights Accountability

1 UN Human Rights Council (UNHRC), "Report of the Special Rapporteur on
Adequate Housing as a Component of the Right to an Adequate Standard of
Living, and on the Right to Non-Discrimination in This Context," A/HRC/37/53,
15 January 2018, paras. 9–15, https://sdgs.un.org/documents/ahrc3753-report
-special-rapporteur-23896.

2 See https://www.ohchr.org/en/instruments-mechanisms/instruments/international
-covenant-economic-social-and-cultural-rights.

3 UN Committee on Economic, Social and Cultural Rights (CESCR), "General
Comment No. 4: The Right to Adequate Housing (Art. 11 (1) of the Covenant),"
E/1992/23, 13 December 1991, https://www.refworld.org/docid/47a7079a1.html.

4 UN Office of the High Commissioner for Human Rights (OHCHR), "Fact
Sheet No. 21: The Right to Adequate Housing," Fact Sheet No. 21/Rev.1, November
2009, https://www.refworld.org/docid/479477400.html.

5 UNHRC, "Report of the Special Rapporteur on Adequate Housing as a
Component of the Right to an Adequate Standard of Living, and on the Right to
Non-Discrimination in This Context," A/69/274, 2 August 2014, para. 19, https://
documents-dds-ny.un.org/doc/UNDOC/GEN/N14/498/19/PDF/N1449819
.pdf?OpenElement.

6 UNHRC, "Guidelines for the Implementation of the Right to Adequate Housing,"
A/HRC/43/43, 26 December 2019, para. 19, https://documents-dds-ny
.un.org/doc/UNDOC/GEN/G19/353/90/PDF/G1935390.pdf?OpenElement.

7 UNHRC, "Report of the Special Rapporteur on Adequate Housing as a
Component of the Right to an Adequate Standard of Living, and on the Right to
Non-Discrimination in This Context," A/HRC/34/51, 18 January 2017, para. 13,
https://documents-dds-ny.un.org/doc/UNDOC/GEN/G17/009/56/PDF
/G1700956.pdf?OpenElement.

8 OHCHR, "Fact Sheet No. 21: The Right to Adequate Housing."

9 See CESCR, "General Comment No. 3: The Nature of States Parties' Obligations
(Art. 2. Para. 1, of the Covenant)," E/1991/23, 14 December 1990, para. 10, https://
www.refworld.org/docid/4538838e10.html.

10 CESCR, "General Comment No. 3," para. 10.

11 UNHRC, "Report of the Special Rapporteur on Adequate Housing as a Component of the Right to an Adequate Standard of Living, and on the Right to Non-Discrimination in This Context," A/HRC/31/54, 26 February 2016, https://documents-dds-ny.un.org/doc/UNDOC/GEN/G15/294/52/PDF/G1529452.pdf?OpenElement.

12 See UNHRC, A/HRC/43/43.

13 UNHRC, "Access to Justice for the Right to Housing" Report of the Special Rapporteur on Adequate Housing as a Component of the Right to an Adequate Standard of Living, and on the Right to Non-Discrimination in This Context," A/HRC/40/61, 1 March 2019, para 2, https://documents-dds-ny.un.org/doc/UNDOC/GEN/G19/007/29/PDF/G1900729.pdf?OpenElement.

14 Ottawa shelter-use numbers are from the Ottawa Mission, https://ottawamission.com/homelessness-in-ottawa/.

15 Matt Gilmour, "Number of Homeless Montrealers Doubled in Pandemic; Plante Floats New Approach on Campaign Trail," CTV News, 22 October 2021, https://montreal.ctvnews.ca/number-of-homeless-montrealers-doubled-in-pandemic-plante-floats-new-approach-on-campaign-trail-1.5619434.

16 Emily Mertz, "Number of Homeless Edmontonians Has Doubled; City Facing Lack of Shelter Space This Winter," Global News, 16 November 2021, https://globalnews.ca/news/8377760/homeless-winter-pandemic-shelter-alberta-edmonton/#:~:text=A%2B,since%20the%20end%20of%202019.

17 Emma Smith, "Number of Chronically Homeless More Than Doubles in Halifax," CBC News, 17 November 2020, https://www.cbc.ca/news/canada/nova-scotia/homeless-report-2020-covid-19-affordable-housing-association-of-nova-scotia-1.5805458.

18 Numbers provided by the John Howard Society through email correspondence, 5 December 2021, on file with author.

19 Kayla Rosen, "New Data Sheds Light on Homelessness in Winnipeg," CTV News, 2 November 2021, https://winnipeg.ctvnews.ca/new-data-sheds-light-on-homelessness-in-winnipeg-1.5649031.

20 Greater Victoria Coalition to End Homelessness, *Hope for Tomorrow: 2019/20 Annual Report* (Victoria, BC: Greater Victoria Coalition to End Homelessness Society, 2020), https://victoriahomelessness.ca/wp-content/uploads/2020/09/Annual-Report_2019_20_GVCEH.pdf.

21 See Leilani Farha and Kaitlin Schwan, "A National Protocol for Homeless Encampments in Canada," UN Special Rapporteur on the Right to Housing, 30 April 2020, https://www.make-the-shift.org/wp-content/uploads/2020/08/A-National-Protocol-for-Homeless-Encampments-in-Canada.pdf.

22 In 2018, Statistics Canada reported more than 1.6 million, or one in every ten, households in Canada are in core housing need (see https://www150.statcan.gc.ca/n1/daily-quotidien/201002/dq201002a-eng.htm). A household is said to be in

"core housing need" if its housing falls below at least one of the adequacy, afford-ability, or suitability standards and it would have to spend 30 per cent or more of its total before-tax income to pay the median rent of alternative local housing that is acceptable (meets all three housing standards). Housing standards are defined by Statistics Canada as follows: (1) Adequate housing is reported by their residents as not requiring any major repairs; (2) Affordable housing has shelter costs equal to less than 30 per cent of total before-tax household income; (3) Suitable housing has enough bedrooms for the size and composition of resident households according to National Occupancy Standard (NOS) requirements. See https://www12.statcan.gc .ca/census-recensement/2016/ref/dict/households-menage037-eng.cfm.

23 David Macdonald, "Canada's Rental Market Is, to Say the Least, Unaccommodat-ing," *The Monitor*, 18 July 2019, https://monitormag.ca/articles/canadas-rental -market-is-to-say-the-least-unaccommodating.

24 Rachelle Younglai, "Real Estate Investing Frenzy Rips through Canadian Housing Market," *Globe and Mail*, 19 February 2022, https://www.theglobeandmail.com /business/article-real-estate-investing-is-off-the-charts-ramping-up-demand/.

25 Martine August, "The Rise of Financial Landlords Has Turned Rental Apartments into a Vehicle for Profit," *Policy Options*, 11 June 2021, https://policyoptions.irpp .org/magazines/june-2021/the-rise-of-financial-landlords-has-turned-rental -apartments-into-a-vehicle-for-profit/.

26 Philip Zigman and Martine August, "Above Guideline Rent Increases in the Age of Financialization," RenovictionsTO, February 2021, https://renovictionsto.com /agi-report/RenovictionsTO-AGIReport-Final.pdf.

27 The province of New Brunswick recently reviewed and updated its landlord tenant legislation to better protect tenants, but advocates say the measures are not strong enough. See Laura Lyall, "New N.B. Legislation Aimed at Helping Renters Falls Short, Advocates Say," CTV News, 4 November 2021, https://atlantic.ctvnews.ca /new-n-b-legislation-aimed-at-helping-renters-falls-short-advocates-say -1.5651334.

28 Federal Housing Advocate: 344 Slater Street, 8th Floor, Ottawa, Ontario, K1A 1E1; phone: 613-995-1151; email: Info.Com@chrc-ccdp.gc.ca; website: www.housingchrc.ca.

29 See Canada Mortgage and Housing Corporation, "Rapid Housing Initiative (RHI)," accessed 18 April 2022, https://www.cmhc-schl.gc.ca/en/professionals/project -funding-and-mortgage-financing/funding-programs/all-funding-programs /rapid-housing.

30 See Mariana Mazzucato, *Mission Economy: A Moonshot Guide to Changing Capitalism* (London: Allen Lane, 2021).

31 To learn more, go to https://www.make-the-shift.org; for local organizing, see www.shjn.ca.